ONLY CONNECT…

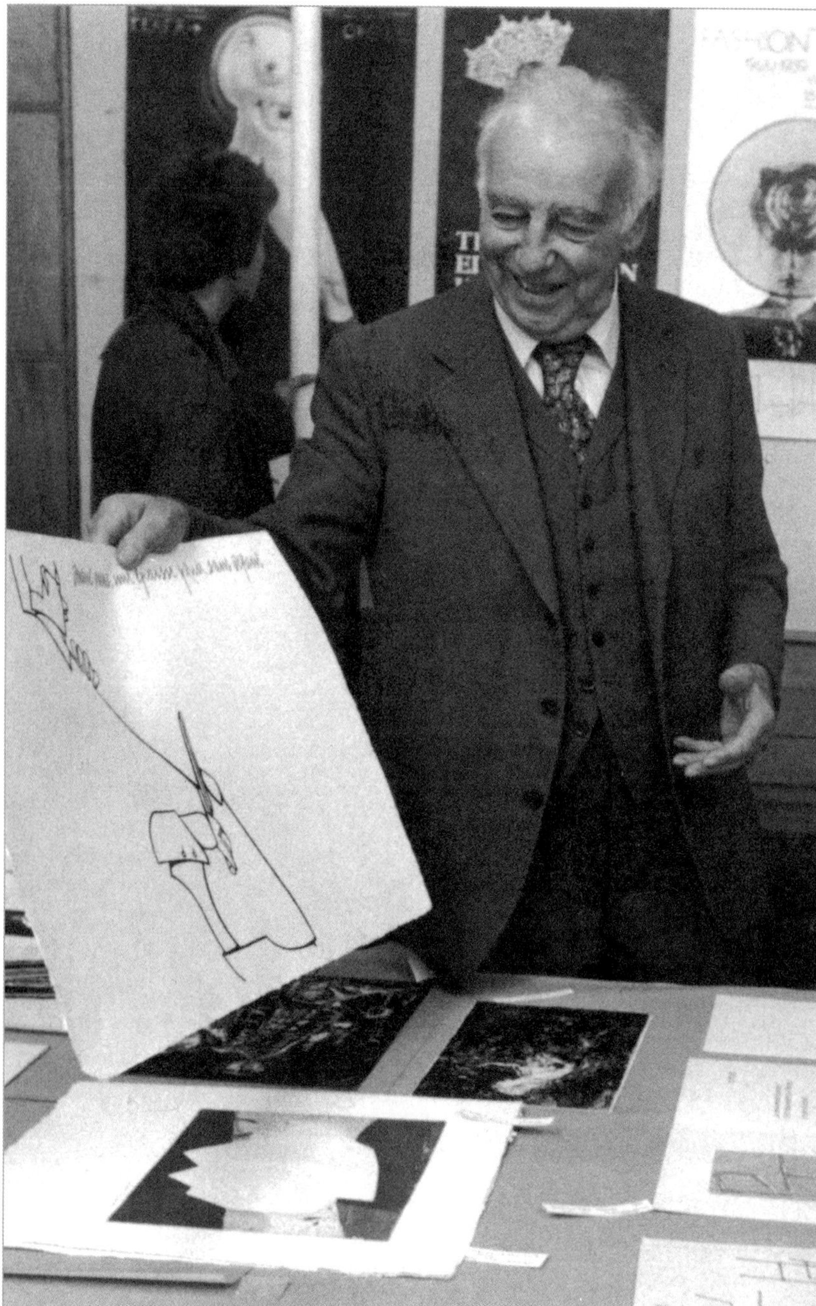

Walter Strachan

ONLY CONNECT...

POETS, PAINTERS, SCULPTORS:
FRIENDSHIPS AND
SHARED PASSIONS
1924–1994

*Edited, with an introduction
and notes by*

Geoffrey Strachan

JON CARPENTER *for*
THE WALTER STRACHAN ARCHIVE

The image on the front of the cover is taken from the lithograph by Jean Lurçat: 'La chouette de bonne espérance'.

The image on the back of the cover is taken from the portrait engraving by Abram Krol, included in *Masks and other poems*.

Published in 2005 by Jon Carpenter Publishing
Alder House, Market Street, Charlbury OX7 3PH
in collaboration with The Walter Strachan Archive,
Audley House, The Slade, Charlbury, Oxfordshire, OX7 3SJ

ISBN 1-897766-95-5 hardback
ISBN 1-897766-94-7 paperback

Designed by Sarah Tyzack

Printed in England by Antony Rowe Ltd, Chippenham

Acknowledgments

The compilation and publication of this book would have been impossible without the assistance, understanding and generosity of many people, to whom its publishers are most grateful.

Thanks, in particular, are due to the following: the Archive of Percy Horton for providing copies of Walter Strachan's letters to Percy Horton, for permission to reproduce the portrait drawing of Margaret Strachan by Percy Horton and an image of a plate decorated by him; George Jason Wood for providing a copy of a letter to Tom Jason Wood; Susanna Pinney for permission to quote from Sylvia Townsend Warner's letters; Cecily Mackworth for permission to quote from her writings and letters; the Estate of James MacGibbon for permission to quote from Stevie Smith's letters and to reproduce her drawing for the poem 'Wretched Woman'; Anthony Hobson for permission to quote from Nancy Cunard's letters; the Taylor Institution Library for permission to include an edited version of the text 'The Genesis and Growth of the Collection' from *Le Livre d'Artiste;* the Henry Moore Foundation for permission to quote from Henry Moore's letters and to reproduce an etching by Henry Moore and also book illustrations and covers featuring lithographs, drawings and sculpture by Henry Moore; Pierre Lecuire for generously donating Walter Strachan's letters to him to the Walter Strachan Archive, for permission to quote from a letter written to the Editor in 1994 and for permission to reproduce the dedication page from the copy of *Bestiare* he presented to Walter Strachan; Wendy Taylor for generously providing copies of Walter Strachan's letters to her and for permission to reproduce an etching 'Tortoise Walking' and a photograph by John Donat of 'Timepiece'. Paul Thompson, David Wright and Peter Murray for permission to quote from their letters written to the Editor in 1994; also to William Hughes for permission to quote from his father's letter and to Colin Clark for permission to quote from his contribution to the last Taranman catalogue.

Thanks are also due to the following in respect of other illustrations in the text: Peter Rhoades for permission to reproduce the portrait drawing of Walter Strachan by Geoffrey Rhoades and the flyleaf drawing by him; Catherine Prassinos for permission to reproduce the etching 'Le Hibou' by Mario Prassinos and the jacket for *The Artist and the Book in France* incorporating a wood engraving for *The Raven* by Mario Prassinos; André Krol for permission to reproduce a woodcut ('P'), a colour etching and a portrait engraving of Walter Strachan by Abram Krol, also a letter written by him to Walter Strachan on the invitation to Krol's Dijon exhibition; Mario Avati for permission to reproduce his mezzotint 'Chouettes' and his new year card for 1991 with a written message to Walter Strachan; Catherine Ballestero and les Amis d'Albert Flocon for permission to reproduce a pen and wash drawing by Albert Flocon and for generously donating copies of Walter Strachan's letters to him to the Walter Strachan Archive; Vincent Guiro for permission to reproduce his hand drawn dedication in the copy of *Huit Psaumes Messianiques* he presented to Walter Strachan; Madame Simone Lurçat for permission to reproduce a hand coloured lithograph by Jean Lurçat within the text and on the cover of this book, also his handwritten dedication within the book *Tapisseries de Jean Lurçat 1939-1957*, presented to Walter Strachan; Paul Croft for permission to reproduce his 1968 rhyme sheet and Patrick Cullen for permission to reproduce his calligraphic owl.

Every effort has been made to identify the owners of copyright in materials quoted or reproduced in this volume and to seek their permission. For any inadvertent omissions the publishers offer their apologies.

Particular tribute should be paid to the family of Christopher Hewett, who enabled the volume *The Living Curve* to be published in 1984, as well as the last Taranman catalogue, which included Walter Strachan's text 'The Formative Years', quoted here, together with some of Hewett's letters and drawings sent to Strachan over the years.

Thanks are also due to the then Director of the Victoria and Albert Museum, Elizabeth Esteve-Coll, whose prefatory appreciation to the March 1994 exhibition catalogue, quoted here, appeared with such poignant timing,

A special tribute should also be paid to Timothy Rogers who greatly assisted Walter Strachan with the typing and editing of a number of chapters in this volume.

I am personally grateful, as the volume's editor, for the support of Jean Clissold, Ali Holloway and Simon Strachan. A great many people have helped me with encouragement, advice and often immensely practical detailed work in its preparation, most notably and heroically Jane Bacon, Barbara Bader, Barry Cole, June Elks, Roger Peers, Michael Schmidt, Susan Strachan, Sarah Tyzack and my co-publisher, Jon Carpenter. To them and to all the countless others who over the past four years have helped me to solve problems, given me ideas and smoothed paths for me, I offer my thanks.

G. S. August 2004.

Contents

List of Illustrations

MOMENTS OF TIME

Menacing clouds tear by;
A few bistre leaves
Catch fitful gleams of sunshine
As they dangle precariously
Against the greyness;
The structure of the branches
Breaks through the ever-thinning foliage
And in this landscape
Where nothing seems permanent,
Least of all the clouds,
Suddenly for a pin point of time
They are orchestrated to the scene
Like a crescendo

And I think how Constable would have fixed the moment
As he fixed gloriously so many;
How Poussin,
Calculating classic,
Not without emotion
Must have quit the studio-drawing
And the posed figure
In search for the noble bank of cloud
Needed for some legendary subject;
How El Greco, inward and tense,
Chose the frenzied second of cloud-rift
For his *Agony in the Garden*...
All three knowing in their different ways
How unreal could be the solid, everyday,
Until caught at a heightened moment.

And I think how our hearts, too,
Are caught and cradled in such moments
Of intensity;
And the most fleeting, evanescent-seeming,
Become the fixed and finite points
By which we steer
Our strange but not unmeaning course,
Hearing, while we are faithful to them,
Above the monotonous ocean sounds
The hidden music that those moments held.

Introduction

To many of the people who encountered him during his long life, whether they were students or creative artists, my father, Walter Strachan, poet, translator, teacher, propagandist, romantic, offered a beacon of light in a sometimes grey world. He was a standard-bearer, a white knight of arts and letters. During the course of seven decades of teaching, writing, lecturing and translating he championed and interpreted the work of countless writers, painters, graphic artists and sculptors, both British and European. Born in 1903, himself a poet and a translator of French poetry, he translated novels from French, German and Italian (Julien Gracq, Hermann Hesse, Cesare Pavese among others.) He was the author of pioneering books on graphic art and sculpture, a translator of art books, a teacher of modern languages and an informed enthusiast in many fields, including architecture, calligraphy and typography. This is a book about his friendships and shared passions, compiled from his reminiscence, letters and poems.

Strachan's love of France and his awareness of the challenging work done by some of her most creative spirits, even under the German occupation, lay behind the publication in 1948 of *Apollinaire to Aragon*, a volume of the translations he had made of a wide range of modern French poetry, encouraged by francophile writers such as Nancy Cunard, Cecily Mackworth and Sylvia Townsend Warner. This love also informed his writings on the *livre d'artiste* — the artist's book — limited editions of texts ancient and modern, illustrated by an astonishing range of twentieth-century French painters, print-makers and sculptors, in which each illustration is an 'original' — an etching, engraving, lithograph, woodcut, mezzotint or other autographic print. He wrote countless articles about these books — then scarcely known in England — over four decades, from the nineteen-fifties to the early nineties, lectured on them and arranged exhibitions of them from his growing collection. His authoritative study, *The Artist and the Book in France,* was published in 1969, the year in which the French government made him a *Chevalier des arts et des lettres.*

Throughout the same period he also developed a keen interest in and an almost encyclopedic knowledge of the work of a wide range of modern European sculptors from Rodin onwards, which partly grew out of his friendship with his near neighbour in Hertfordshire, Henry Moore. He wrote and lectured on sculpture and published three important books: *Towards Sculpture: Drawings and Maquettes from Rodin to Oldenburg* (1976); *Henry Moore: Animals* (1983), and, a seminal work, *Open Air Sculpture in Britain* (1984).

The depth of Strachan's responses both to poetry and art and the articulate infectiousness of his enthusiasms had led him to become a charismatic and influential schoolmaster for over forty years, and in later years an equally captivating lecturer on modern art. His evolving sensitivity to nature as well as to words, colour and form, also made him a delightful amateur painter and an eloquent poet in his own right in *Moments of Time* (1947), *The Season's Pause* (1950) and *Poems* (1970). Strachan's passionate interest in the work of living artists and writers both grew out of and blossomed into many friendships, some sustained through regular meetings, some mainly by correspondence, throughout his adult life. During the last ten years or so of his life he wrote a number of draft chapters of reminiscence about some of the writers and artists he had met and known, often quoting from their letters to him, which he envisaged gathering together and publishing under the tentative title *Encounters and Relationships*. This sequence of chapters was never quite completed, although brief versions of some of them did appear in a few periodicals during his lifetime.

My purpose in preparing this somewhat wider-ranging volume for publication, has been to present these chapters in book form, arranging them in a more or less chronological sequence, edited for publication, as he knew they needed. But it seemed to me, as I read, that in composing his accounts of meetings with some of the writers and artists he liked and admired and quoting from their correspondence, Strachan was sometimes unduly reticent in recording his own responses, his own vivid contribution to a friendship, an encounter, a correspondence, a shared passion. I have therefore sought to enhance the resonance of these chapters by including alongside them a number of his own poems, many of which take inspiration from or comment on works of art or literature. These are sometimes placed where the theme suggests it, but more generally at the rough chronological moment when they were written.

In two places I have also included, again more or less chronologically, some extracts from Strachan's letters to friends written during the main period covered by the book, from the nineteen-thirties to the nineteen-eighties, so that, as in the poems, the reader may savour something of the writer's off-the-cuff reaction to events experienced, people met, works read and seen during the course of his life, alongside the recollections written in the (relative) tranquillity of old age. In the process of writing about people and events that made a mark on him he was, of course, also charting the development of his own interests and passions.

Strachan's voice, in his lifetime, whether he was teaching, as he did for over forty years at Bishop's Stortford College, lecturing, or conversing with friends (not to mention the surprised strangers he sometimes buttonholed on railway trains), was inimitable. Sometimes these writings capture a trace of that voice's heady impact, though they cannot capture the gleaming eye, the eager smile, the resonant timbre and tumbling concatenations of provocative asides. (The extracts from letters come closest to this.)

Like most of us, Strachan was a man of his time. The social and political background to his life; the writings, works of art and individuals that appealed to him; the causes that he championed; the interaction between poets and graphic artists that he shared in; all are part of the cultural history of England and Europe in the mid-twentieth century. His perceptions of these people, this work, these experiences, are shared with the reader sometimes in expected, sometimes in unexpected ways: but often in a manner, whether consciously or innocently, that brings us face to face across the decades with the period he lived through.

After his death Pierre Lecuire, the poet and creator of monumental *livres d'artiste,* wrote: *'Il aimait enseigner, mais cet enseignement bousculait la routine et ouvrait une voie vers le Beau... La figure anglaise de Walter fut grande comme la nature anglaise, comme l'arbre anglais aux vastes dimensions, jamais taillé, développant librement, largement, sa majesté de bois et de feuilles à travers les saisons.'**

* 'He loved teaching, but his teaching turned routine on its head, opening up a path towards Beauty... Walter was a figure on a grand scale, like English nature, like a vast English tree, never pruned, whose majestic timber and foliage grow freely, broadly, through all the seasons.'

A book offers written words, not spoken ones. Its dynamic is ultimately in the reader's hands, not the writer's. But I hope that the wide variety of the causes Strachan championed and the people and topics he chose to write about in his memoirs, poems and letters, may enable readers of this volume either to explore the development of his interests and friendships chronologically or to dive in at random, selecting those themes that have the greatest resonance for them personally. I hope, too, that the juxtapositions, parallels and contradictions within these pages may set up reverberations which bring to life the writer, the friends he wrote about and the age they lived through.

Walter was a great lover of echoes and connections. Among many quotations he cherished (including Edward Bond's 'Was anything done?' and Théophile Gautier's *'Je suis un homme pour qui le monde visible existe'**), it was E.M. Forster's 'Only connect...' that was surely his favourite. In selecting and placing these texts I have attempted to arrange them so that echoes and connections within them may be discovered and enjoyed. Although I do not think he himself would have envisaged compiling a volume of his own writings with quite such a title, or quite such an arrangement, I venture to hope he would not have been too displeased with this one.

Geoffrey Strachan
Charlbury July 2004

* 'I am a man for whom the visible world exists.'

PRELUDE

1903–1924

MASKS

How should our children guess
We once were the same
Who have so grotesquely outgrown that name

A frog-prince wins credence,
But what son or daughter delves
Into our lost, unimaginable selves.

In vain we advance proof;
Story or photograph
Evoke silence or the incredulous laugh.

No more than a mirror
Can they see within,
Know the continuity under the skin

That past or present are one,
And there persists still,
Under time's accretions, the original.

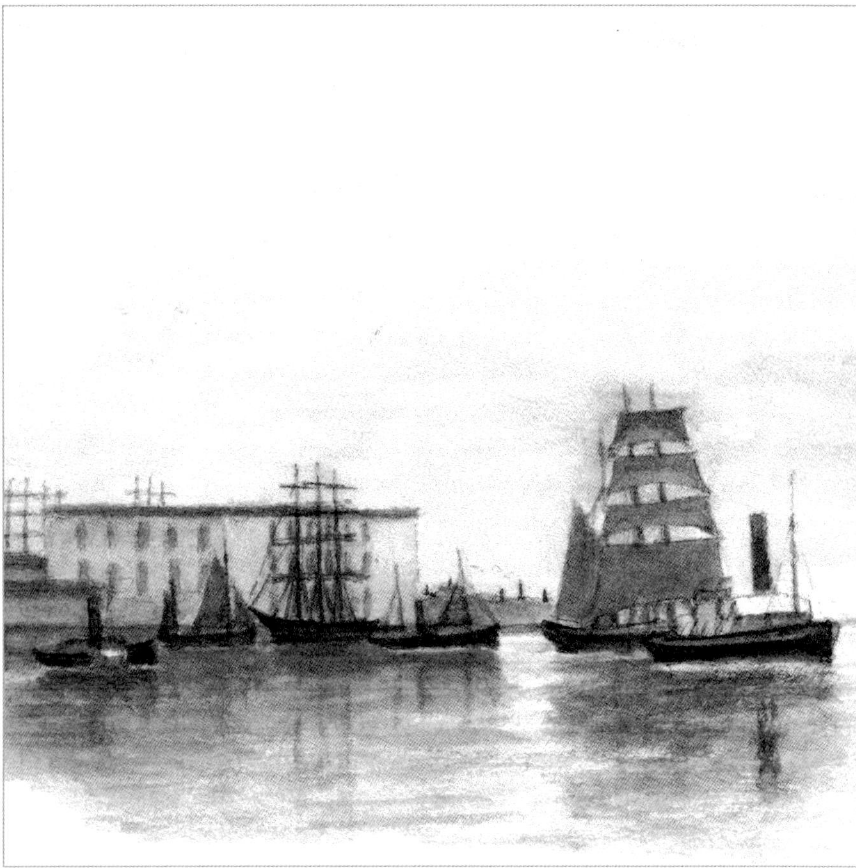

PRELUDE

Walter Strachan begins his reminiscences with an account of his great-grandfather and grand-parents and some tantalizingly brief glimpses of his own boyhood and schooldays. He was born in Hull in 1903, attended Hymers College there and was the first in the family to go to University. His father, Bertram Lionel, had left school at thirteen, worked for Reckitts, one of the most prominent firms in Hull in the nineteenth and early twentieth century, and rose to become a manager. He had a love of books which he came to share with his son. Both were eager readers in the twenties of the novels of Conrad, Lawrence and Hardy.

Walter's Mother, Edith, was musical and had a beautiful singing voice. Their home at Hull Garden Village was a comfortable one and from there Walter cycled to school, where his teachers included John Redwood Anderson and H.H. Abbott, both of whom wrote and published poetry. He shared his youthful literary crazes for Shakespeare, Milton and others with his friend, Tom Divine, with whom he undertook many enterprises in his teens. During the last years of the Great War these included the compilation of a miniature handwritten magazine — *Shell Splinters*. This ran to twelve issues. The meticulously written and illustrated articles about the weapons of the time reflect the fascination such things have for thirteen- and fourteen-year old schoolboys in time of war. The seriousness is impressive.

Walter's notes on his Cambridge days at St Catharine's College (1921-1924) where he read English and French, show him transferring his editorial interests to the College magazine and now sharing his passion for English literature with his new and musically talented friend Miles Tomalin. Sharing enthusiasms was clearly always important to him, and was later to make him an infectious teacher. It was also to inspire his writings on art, his compilations of anthologies, his mounting of exhibitions.

Strachan's grandfather, Walter James Strachan had been, as he mentions, a passionate amateur watercolourist, who painted vivid seascapes. His often delicate sketches evoke the glory and romance of the sailing boats that plied up and down the Humber and along the East Riding coastline. Enthusiastic both about his own paintings and the natural world around him — he was reputed once to have stopped a tram in Hull so that the passengers could get off and look at the sunset — he undoubtedly passed on to his grandson an ability to respond warmly to what he saw and to share this response impulsively with others.

In his accounts both of his family and his days at Cambridge, Walter

Strachan hints quietly at two recurring themes in his life: the secure stable home, with supportive and proud parents, and the importance of close friendships. These were to set the tone for his own family life when he married Margaret Jason Wood in 1929 and formed friendships with such people as the engraver Stephen Gooden and the painter Percy Horton in the twenties and thirties.

The other recurring source of inspiration he evokes was encounters with exceptional men and women, writers, artists and others, who aroused his interest, admiration and sympathy. Sydney Cockerell, the Director of the Fitzwilliam Museum, whom he met at Cambridge, was an early example of this. Nancy Cunard, the poet and biographer of George Moore and Norman Douglas, and Jean Lurçat, the tapestry artist, would, decades later, be among many others.

Glimpses of Hull and Cambridge

Up to the age of seven or eight I was agreeably dominated by my sister, Marjorie, three years my senior. Lorna who was born between us and survived only a few weeks, was referred to by my mother as 'baby Lorna'. She was in heaven. I had no visual memory of her but I imagined her aloft when the sky was particularly blue. Later, it struck me that she owed her name to a favourite novel of my mother's.

Games and music. The promoter of both was our Auntie Beatie, my mother's young sister and a teacher. She had a humorous face and a long, witty nose. An omnivorous reader, she was still taking out five books at a time from the library up to her death at the age of ninety-eight. With a touch of badness, she early put my sister on to the most tearful reading — *Little Women*, *Uncle Tom's Cabin*. Observing Marjorie's weeping face, I turned, resignedly, to the books I had been given by my grandpa, Walter James Strachan, and my father: *The Scottish Chiefs*, *Rob Roy*. But I heard no trumpets blowing martial sounds. Nor could I make out a word of *The Poetical Works of Robert Burns*. My grandfather gave me this in three successive years for my birthday, January 25, which coincided with that of the Scottish poet. Partly in deference to his Caledonian obsession, my mother used to sing some of the 'auld Scottish songs' on family occasions: 'Ye banks and braes of bonnie Doon'. 'Flow gently sweet Afton'; 'My Love is like a

Red Red Rose', which I *could* understand — as opposed to: 'The Rigs wi' Aaanie'. What was 'Aaanie'? — I just accepted the sound.

My mother had a sweet soprano voice and was the leading singer in Eleanor Coward's Hull Ladies Musical Union. She went on tour to Norway. But when singing songs round the piano, as most of my relations did, she wasted her voice on banal sentimental songs by Fred Weatherly, characterized by a penultimate minor key, resolved in a happy reversal to the major. For my part I used to sing 'The Powder Monkey':

> But little Jim was booked,
> For as the fight was just near won,
> A musket bullet picked him off,
> Just as his song was done...

Eleanor Coward, with whom I later had some singing lessons, soon changed all that, but I'm afraid my relations didn't take very well to Lully's 'Bois épais'.

My mother's father, Captain John Gale, had been killed at sea when the mainmast crashed down on him during a storm. The shock to his young wife was so great that she became deaf on the spot and never recovered more than a minimal hearing. So 'Grandma Gale' kept her native Devonshire accent and mode of speech — she came from Brixham like her husband — unaffected by her long years in Yorkshire. John Gale had brought his fishing smack there to join the new Hull fleet. Even before the fatal accident, he had been shipwrecked off Heligoland with my mother and Auntie Beatie on board. They recalled being rowed to the shore by the German lifeboat on the day that Wilhelm II, 'Kaiser Bill', annexed the island. My mother talked about his white horse and his withered arm, which gave me a strange *frisson* as I listened in childhood years.

If family records go no further back than Grandma Gale on my mother's side, I know a good deal more about the Strachans. This is thanks to the longevity of my cousin, Charles Maxwell Strachan, the son by his second marriage of my great-grandfather James Strachan, and to a detailed 'Journal' kept by James himself from 1857 to 1859. The latter evokes a picture of mid-Victorian English life as seen by a first generation Scot to cross the Border.

His two brothers, John and William, emigrated, the first to

Canada, the second to New Zealand. My great-grandfather James, the middle brother, born in 1828, was more cautious. The Strachan family motto had been: '*Non timeo sed caveo*'.* James waited for an opening as an engineer at the naval dockyard in Portsmouth. His father had been born in 1778 and ran a leather business in Aberdeen. Great-great-grandfather James married Margaret Adam, 'School mistress of Banchory' [near the village of Strachan], as an existing sampler records. Our family's first teaching genes? After her husband's death in 1842 she continued to keep a close watch on her sons' fortunes.

James arrived in Portsmouth in 1846, aged seventeen. In the course of his work on naval vessels he met David Maxwell, ten years his senior, who had served his engineering apprenticeship with the Great Western Railway in his native Dundee. James obviously looked up to him and extended his affection to David's daughter. 'Sent to Janette a workbox, 2/6, a Christmas present' he solemnly records. Charles Maxwell Strachan, his son, told me in a letter how his father used to take her out in a rowing-boat on the Solent. I guess from the matter-of-fact tone of his Journal that he would probably have confined his observations to details of the passing ships or perhaps regaled the ten-year-old girl with an episode from *David Copperfield*, which he was reading at the time. Yet the fact that nearly a quarter of a century later, he married her, following the death of his first wife, Louisa, argues for some sort of romantic — if hardly Carrollian — attachment.

The epicentre, the omnium gatherum, for all social and educational activities in Portsmouth was the James Watt Institute. It catered for such leisure hours as then existed in the great age of self-help and self-improvement. Public readings were organized there or in St George's Hall. The Journal mentions James's attendance at readings from *Dombey and Son*, *The Christmas Carol*, Thackeray's *The Virginians*. He joined the Dockyard Library 'in order to obtain 3rd volume' of the then best-seller, Macaulay's *History of England*.

The only real entertainment seems to have been taking the children to see a ventriloquist in St George's Hall. Sundays were for church attendances — in James's case at a succession of chapels and churches of different denominations and services on which he

* 'I am not afraid but I am cautious.'

made careful comment. He finally settled for Unitarianism, in which church our family continued to be brought up.

When he moved to Hull some years later he became secretary of the Burns Club there. Two years after Louisa's death he married Janette Maxwell and began a second family. In partnership with his brother-in-law, Louis Calvard (a ne'er-do-well, who took to drink) he founded the engineering firm of Calvard and Strachan. His children from both marriages, my grandfather, Walter James, and Ada from the first, Charles Maxwell and Mary from the second, were brought up and lived their lives in Hull.

I met my great-grandfather Brittain, father of my grandmother, Kate, only on one occasion. He had returned to this country from America at the outbreak of the Civil War. He had been an expert in the then fashionable grain-painting. His visit to us in Hull is agreeably fixed in my memory because of the charming adopted daughter, Gertrude, he brought with him. She was not only, in my eyes at any rate, a great beauty in the tradition of the 'Gibson' girl of the famous magazine covers, but a *siffleuse.* Yes, cousin Gertrude Schmidt was my first and instant love. I never mentioned it to a soul.

In 1968 David Chalmers Maxwell, great-grandson of the David Maxwell who had left Dundee for Portsmouth, was responsible for making a book of family trees, covering seven generations, of twelve interconnected lines. He sums up in his 'Notes' on them. 'These are not families of eminence. Before the present day, the only person of note to be found here is James Chalmers (1782-1853), inventor of the adhesive postage stamp'. As an obsessive correspondent, I salute his memory. I am grateful, too, to James Strachan, my great-grandfather, who, by giving his young son, Walter, an unbirthday present of a box of watercolour paints, encouraged him to paint many excellent marine paintings in later life and make valuable records of the fishing vessels of the time on the Humber and off the Yorkshire coast. It was his example, applied to landscape, that persuaded me to try my hand at water-colour painting, an activity from which I have derived enormous pleasure.

University years are an island encountered in a voyage. For three or four years one lives in an isolated continuum. The atmosphere of Cambridge in the early twenties of this century was unusual. The men who should have been spending their last academic years there had either been killed or maimed on the battlefields of the Somme. A sprinkling of survivors arrived at the University on 'Special Forces' Grants'. They represented a minority of mature men who made us eighteen- or nineteen-year-olds seem jejune and callow. However, they were tolerant towards us, often our advisers.

At the Cambridge Union I used to listen to two exceptionally precocious presidents, S.V.T. Adams and R.A. Butler. Each seemed to us already a qualified parliamentarian. There were the 'draws' of celebrities from outside. We heard squeaky witticisms from G.K. Chesterton. I had loved his books and poems (*The Man who was Thursday*, *Lepanto*), the phoney mystique of 'We are the people of England, that never have spoken yet'. Having attended lectures on mediaeval England by the historian G.G. Coulton, I was especially interested in his polemic against Chesterton. The reply came in Hilaire Belloc's 'Remote and ineffectual don/ Who dared attack my Chesterton'. I was on Coulton's side for the simple reason that I extracted from him a brilliant Chaucer parody for the St Catharine's College Magazine, which I was editing at the time.

The Cambridge Union, as a club open to all undergraduates who chose to subscribe, was an agreeable haven. The luxury on Sundays of reading *The Observer's* 'garbage' — the detractors' appellation for articles by J.L. Garvin [its editor from 1908 to 1942] — and the erudite literary reviews, pages long, by Harold Nicolson, to buttered toast, brought by a servant in a green apron. All this in a haze of smoke — incense rather — of Balkan Sobranies. *The Observer* apprised us in our private world of rumblings in the world outside: the unemployment that was to result in the General Strike of 1926.

I doubt whether I discussed such things with one of my new friends, Miles Tomalin, who shared supervision with me under E.M.W. Tillyard, Milton expert and later Master of Jesus College. Tomalin, dreamy, uninhibited, natural to the point of eccentricity, appealed to me, still rather urban and conventional as I was. Each day by teatime Miles had donned his dressing-gown and reclined in his easy chair (I had only a college basket chair that 'talked' in the night), surrounded by his Vermeers and Pieter de Hooches — reproductions, of course, but framed Medici prints were then a luxury; he claimed to have bought them with money saved by not smoking. We often talked of early music and poetry and light verse (he had pieces published in the undergraduate magazine, *Granta*, later in *Punch*) — and young women, consisting of a Girton undergraduate called Hope and her friend and chaperone, a plain foil whose name escapes me. We played tennis with them of a not very high standard.

Miles had turns of phrase that sounded strange to me as a Yorkshireman: 'no more he does', 'nor it is', 'but my dear Walter…' He talked about the Dolmetsch family and their pioneering of old instruments. Romantic, he bought a two-stroke motor-cycle and voyaged round local villages like Ian Hay's *Knight on Wheels*, in search of the 'not impossible she'. Sometimes with me on the pillion. We looked at Audley End House, then owned by Lord Howard de Walden. Or we escaped academe in the canoe Miles hired to explore the higher reaches of the Cam. Now and then we drifted to the bank while he played his *vielle à la roue*, the bagpipe-like drone of whose strings drew unwanted attention from more barbarous punters.

We might be discussing the Reid Lectures Walter de la Mare was giving on 'Childhood and Poetry'; or the more interesting of our lecturers — Forbes of Clare (who lectured in pyjamas); pedantic, intolerant Brian Downs (a distant relation of mine), who turned away undergraduates in plus-fours from his brilliant lectures on Ibsen and Strindberg; S.C. Roberts, racy on Dr Johnson; Cook, making Greek drama palatable to non-classicists; dry but intriguing G.G. Coulton. All this meant for us a shared, not too exam-orientated study of English Literature, rather than 'galloping in a horse and chaise through Saintsbury's *History of English Literature*', as 'Q' (Sir Arthur Quiller Couch) had described and deplored it.

It was in his Trojan, that most eccentric of all cars, with solid tyres and multiple gears, that Miles was to drive to my wedding in Bradford in 1929. It aroused some amusement in Rolls-Bentley and Daimler land — and among passers-by, as it jerked over the characteristic West Riding streets paved with granite setts, a progress which necessitated a periodic tightening-up of nuts and bolts. It was typical of Miles's unselfconsciousness that on the wedding eve he should have entertained the wedding guests, impromptu, with selections of recorder music, played, I was told, on a variety of different recorders, which he drew in turn from their leather case. My father-in-law, Jason Wood, a surgeon, and others present were charmed. More accustomed to listening to formal subscription concerts, they never forgot that evening.

I made two important links with senior members of the University during my Cambridge years. Colonel F.J.M. Stratton, Fellow of Gonville and Caius College and Professor of Astrophysics, had served with the Signal Service of the Royal Engineers in the First World War. He happened to be president of the Cambridge Unitarian Church, of which I was honorary secretary. He frequently entertained me to a wonderful breakfast and talked so rapidly that no one could do more than catch the general gist. Because I sang lustily in the chapel choir, he credited me with a musicianship I was fortunately never called on to display. Thanks to him, my father enjoyed, as his guest, more of top table than ever I did.

The second was Sydney Cockerell, Director of the Fitzwilliam Museum from 1908 to 1937, whom I got to know through what masters at school had reported as my 'inquisitive mind'. I plied him with questions about favourite authors who featured prominently in the Museum: Hardy (whose executor he became), Shaw, Conrad, and also, more closely, about his link with William Morris. I elicited from him an article in his own hand on 'A Young Man's Visit to John Ruskin' for publication in the St Catharine's Magazine. I was to meet him again later at his house in Kew.

Miles Tomalin was one of my eminently unworldly friends. Richard Thompson was as definite, opinionated and defiant as Miles was dreamy. He read Modern Languages and played rugger. His conversion from Science Part One to Spanish Part One was spectacular. Had no one ever learned Spanish before? He dressed Spanish, ate Spanish, punted up and down the Cam with cries of '*olé*', as if he were at a bullfight. He cut a fine figure, broad-chested, narrow-waisted, with a trim pair of shoulders whether in rugger vest or lounge suit. He was courageous on the field: fell on the ball before formidable opposition, which resulted more than once in concussion. Essentially an Alceste — no compromise. Stripper of pretentions — noticeable in the seemingly trivial matter of names. There was a plethora of double-barrelled and hyphenated names in our college. Dick Thompson would have none of that. To F.D. Field-Hyde — 'Get rid of the ball, Hyde! Don't be so damned selfish!' So on the rugger field, as elsewhere, cutting men down to size from the tallest, Webb-Peploe (six foot seven) whom he called simply 'Peploe', down to Delves-Broughton: 'Hi, Broughton, pass!' In our second year there was a Siley in the team. No mercy: 'Silly' it was.

All these *trivia* stick in my mind precisely because my father, used to the Boothroyds, Ratcliffes and Dunkleys of Yorkshire, was fascinated by these, to him, attractive affectations. Although I did not know half the said personalities, Father would quiz me during the vacations. 'How's Wyatt-Wailing? De Lart? Webb-Peploe?' and so on through the whole litany! But he enjoyed the directness of both Miles Tomalin and Richard Thompson, who made short vacation stays with us and were taken to see choppy seas off Flamborough Head or guillemots on Bempton chalk cliffs. It was the acid test for any Cambridge friends: did they like the sea? They better had! My father's library was full of it.

SEA-PIECE

written at Flamborough Head

Green, lank-haired boulders
lolling on monstrous shoulders —
the rock ledges, limpet-starred
the tide has bared.

A herring-gull
with curved, lethal
beak;
a kittiwake
uttering a thin call.

A toppling wave,
briefly held
in the sun
obliquely seen
from the cool chalk cave
the tides have
channelled.

A strange terrain
of betwixt and between,
neither sea nor land;
and a white ship sliding silently
beyond.

PART ONE

THE TEACHING YEARS: THE WRITER EMERGES

1924–1942

TEMERITY

Here locomotives slip into the night,
Guided by lamp and lever to their goals,
Each numbered coach a calculated freight
Precisely gliding on the moonlit rails.

With what conspiracy of phrase and image
Would we, with words our only vehicle,
Set travellers moving on uncertain voyage,
To destinations no one can foretell?

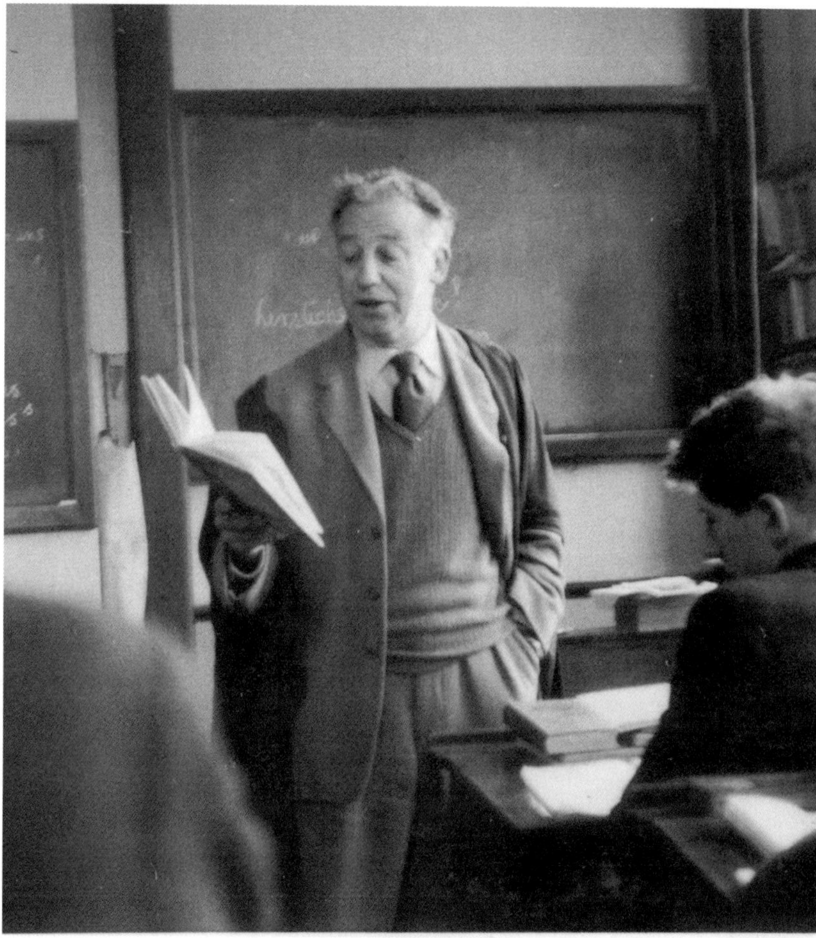

THE TEACHING YEARS: THE WRITER EMERGES

> 'I remember Walter Strachan best as a young and enthusiastic teacher of French and English in the 1920s. He introduced me to much of French poetry and literature... Art and architecture too; I think it was he who first gave me some knowledge of Van Gogh and Cézanne.' Bill Hughes

> 'He was certainly one of the biggest influences in my whole life, opening my eyes to art and architecture, starting me drawing, conveying his enthusiasm for French culture — so many things, and all given with that inimitable mixture of zestful enthusiasm and chuckling amusement. He's remained an inspiration ever since.' Paul Thompson

> 'My schooldays were immensely happy and fulfilling and it was almost entirely due to Walter, who taught me to appreciate so many beautiful things, whether it was a French romantic poem, a monumental sculpture, a Lurçat sketch, a new sample of calligraphy, an architectural quirk, another owl or an *objet trouvé*. But leaving school... and time and space made no difference — the same enthusiasm he imparted flourished over fifty years of fascinating and intimate correspondence.' David Wright

During the next eighteen years Walter Strachan's love of language and passionate responses to art and nature led him steadily towards writing, drawing and painting. In 1924 he had gone straight to Bishop's Stortford College, on the borders of Hertfordshire and Essex, to teach French and English. In December 1927 he took up a teaching post for a brief time at Giggleswick School in Yorkshire but was invited to return to Stortford, which he did in autumn 1928, as head of modern languages, a post he then held for forty years.

Even-handed in his dealings with all the boys he taught and coached in rugger and hockey, Strachan warmed particularly to those who responded to his own enthusiasm, both in the classroom and in the many out-of-school activities he encouraged. Over the years these embraced art, architecture, poetry, drawing, listening to music, play reading, modelling, calligraphy and typography and more besides. From the earliest days he formed friendships with ex-pupils (as well as with teaching colleagues) that lasted a lifetime. One of the first of these was with Tom Jason Wood, the son of a surgeon who lived in Bradford and was himself an old boy of the school. On a visit to Tom at home during the school holidays, after the latter had been seriously ill, Walter met Tom's three sisters, Dorothy, Margaret and Kay and was much struck by Margaret, the quiet one in the middle. Travelling across England by motor bike, he made visits to see her while she was completing her training as an infant teacher at Bedford and later in Sleaford. They were married in 1929.

Bishop's Stortford College had been founded in 1868 as a Nonconformist Grammar School for boys. But from the first the sons of Anglican parents were welcomed, not excluded. In 1900 F.S.Young, an old boy of the school, was appointed headmaster (a post he held till 1931) and changed its name to Bishop's Stortford College. An outstanding athlete and former scholar in Natural Science at The Queen's College, Oxford, 'F.S.Y'. proved to be an energetic, austere headmaster, devoted to building up the resources of the school and to encouraging hard work and personal probity.

Coming from a Unitarian background in Hull, Walter Strachan was more drawn to radical aesthetics and politics and the rationalism of Bertrand Russell than either Nonconformist or Anglican Christianity. As he got into his stride as a teacher he had, like many another at that time, to make accommodation with the official Christian pieties of the school as best he could. Clearly F.S.Y. appreciated Walter's personal qualities — he was eager to attract him back from Giggleswick — and in the early days, at an allotted period when form masters were expected to spend time with their pupils studying scripture, he allowed Walter to focus on the study of church architecture instead. This led to the founding of the school Architectural Society, which flourished under Walter's aegis for four decades.

Both under F.S.Young and his somewhat more liberal successor, Leo Price, again an old boy of the school, a brilliant athlete, a Noncomformist of great probity and in this case a mathematician (a former exhibitioner at Corpus Christi College, Oxford), the school was in some ways becoming a conventional small public school — but in other ways remained rather unconventional. Strachan wrote of Price in 1932: 'One rejoices in his sane and decent view of education. There can't be many heads who put the boys' happiness and the real value of education in the widest sense first. None of the publicist or showman or charlatan about him'. The school was a place where boys could be treated as individuals and brilliant, eccentric teachers could thrive and have a great civilizing influence on the boys they taught and on the ethos of the place as a whole.

As an assistant housemaster in his early years, Strachan came under the aegis of 'Tid', A.G. Tidmarsh, the somewhat larger-than-life music master and first Housemaster at the newly founded Robert Pearce House (1923). As well as encouraging music and drama, Tid taught some art and painted himself. Walter learned quite a lot about art from him in his early years, but more about the craft — and temperament — of the professional artist-engraver from Stephen Gooden, who lived in the town. He and his wife Mona, who had a strong literary bent, became good friends of Walter and Margaret in the late twenties.

Still more important for Strachan was the arrival in 1925 of Percy Horton as art master. Horton was a committed professional painter of landscapes and portraits who subsequently became Tutor in the School of Painting at the Royal College of Art and in 1949 Ruskin Master of Drawing at Oxford. He played the violin and was an exuberant amateur actor. He and Strachan shared an interest in literature, ballet and cinema as well as art. They also shared a love of nonsense humour. Horton was in many ways a free spirit. Born in 1897, he had been a conscientious objector in the war. He and Strachan collaborated over many school projects, and in 1929 produced a booklet of poems and graphic decorations by boys at the school entitled *First Offence*.

Percy Horton left Stortford in 1930 and Strachan clearly missed him greatly. From Horton he had learned much about looking at pictures and also drawing and painting himself. They embarked on a lifelong correspondence, frequently illustrating their letters with comic drawings, and continued to meet regularly. Both were avid readers. They enjoyed letting their hair down together and each offered the other a sympathetic ear over the daily aggravations of life at Bishop's Stortford College on the one hand and the Royal College of Art on the other.

Percy Horton's successor at Stortford, and a close friend of his, Geoffrey Rhoades, was also a committed painter of landscapes — and of fantastic arcadian scenes. He, too, encouraged Walter Strachan's painting. Strachan's particular friend and confidant among full-time colleagues at the school during the thirties, and referred to in his letters, was Norman Monk-Jones, who shared his left-wing sympathies. Wyndham Woodward joined Strachan's modern languages team during the mid thirties. He and his wife Iris, whom he married in 1938, and who painted haunting watercolour landscapes, became close friends. It was Newman Catchpole, a dentist, also a friend in those years who recurs in Strachan's letters, who later introduced him to Henry Moore.

During the twenties and thirties Strachan visited France a number of times: an exchange visit at sixteen in 1919; visits for language and culture courses in 1923 and 1924; later a visit to St Symphones, near Tours, where his hostess, Madame Madeleine Baudouin enthused him with the

Fables of La Fontaine and he taught her 'Tea for Two'; then a visit with Margaret to Paris in 1937 to see galleries, buildings (including Le Corbusier's Salvation Army Citadel), theatre and films, and again in 1938 with Wyndham Woodward where they saw *Les Enfants du Paradis* and Chartres Cathedral, 'the mediaeval glory of its stained glass pierced by bright sunlight'. The later memory of this last visit to France until 1949 clearly inspired a number of poems including 'Chartres'.* During the early thirties Strachan also went to Germany at least twice. Parties of German schoolboys and staff from the Dorotheenstädtisches Realgymnasium in Berlin visited the school in 1927, 1929 and 1931. The idea underlying F.S.Young's invitation was to make a practical contribution to international understanding. In 1930 F.S.Y. and Strachan accompanied a party of Stortford boys on a return visit to Berlin. Strachan was eager in those years to bring his German up to the standard of his French and made a further visit in 1935. Much of what he found there under the then recently installed Nazi regime was very disturbing to him, as he records in a letter to Horton.

In 1932 my sister Jean was born and I followed in 1935. In 1937 Walter Strachan began a ten-year period as Housemaster for Robert Pearce House, so the whole family had to leave our little home at 37 Thornfield Road and move into the school boarding house, a major upheaval for both my parents. In September 1939 the war brought a much greater upheaval, as it did for the whole country. In Strachan's case he was one of the older members of staff who remained to keep the school going while younger men, like Wyndham Woodward, joined the services. Naturally the summer of 1940 with the fall of France, Dunkirk and the Blitz on London brought fresh anxieties. In June our mother took my sister and myself to live in a cottage in the village of Water Yeat in the Lake District, close to the southern tip of Coniston Water. We stayed with her younger sister Kay and her three boys. Kay's husband, Alan, was away in the army. We remained there for eighteen months, by which time the worst of the Blitz appeared to be over. (It is recorded that during the autumn term in 1940 Bishop's Stortford had undergone 180 air raid alerts.)

For us children the days in the Lake District were magical. For our parents it was a period of painful separation and continuing anxiety. Ironically, Percy Horton was in Ambleside, a few valleys over from Water Yeat, to which the Royal College of Art had been evacuated, separated from his wife, Lydia, who was in London, doing war work at the Ministry of Food. During the school holidays Strachan was able to come and stay in Water Yeat, to spend time with the family and to discover and

*See Appendix.

paint the beautiful landscapes and buildings of Lakeland. Occasionally he was able to see Horton, who in the spring of 1941 came over to Water Yeat and made a portrait drawing of my mother, an event celebrated by Strachan in a poem.

It was during these early war years, spending many hours alone — as so many people did, whether in the services or on the Home Front — in his case fire watching and making sure all the boys got into the air raid shelter when the siren went — that Strachan read a great deal of poetry and also wrote a lot. France was much in his mind. He submitted his poem 'Paris Remembered' to Nancy Cunard for her *Poems for France* anthology in 1943 and in the later war years she was one of several writers who encouraged him with his translations of modern French poets, among them Péguy and Aragon.

The first of the chapters of Strachan's drafted 'encounters and relationships', which covers his early years in Bishop's Stortford is a brief account of his friendship with Stephen and Mona Gooden. Gooden was the first professional artist he came to know. What Strachan learned from him about the engraver's technique must have stood him in good stead two decades later, when he began writing articles about the work of French graphic artists. But he left no memoir of his friendship with Percy Horton and little account of the way his own interests in art and poetry were evolving in the 1930s. For this reason I have included here a chapter made up of extracts from Strachan's letters to Horton during the crucial years from 1934 to 1942 plus one to his former pupil and brother-in-law, Tom Jason Wood. These offer something of a portrait of Horton at that time and also show Strachan's own evolving tastes and his growing understanding of the concerns and struggles of the living, working artist. This must have nourished his sympathetic appreciation of the aims and craft of the many artists and sculptors whom he was later to meet and whose work he was to write about during the last forty years of his life. It was also a period when Strachan began modestly collecting original works of art, as his fascination and admiration for creative artists as people began to burgeon. Having bought a painting by Edward Bawden in 1940, he wrote to the artist. Bawden wrote back, surprised and pleased, 'It is a rare occurrence for a painter to receive such a charming testimony'.

In these letters we also see Strachan reaching out for his own self expression, first through drawing and painting, encouraged by Horton and Rhoades — if not by Gooden — and later through writing and translating poems. This creativity with pencil, brush and pen would greatly enhance his appreciation of the work of writers and artists whose work he was subsequently to interpret and champion in his writings and translations.

1 Stephen and Mona Gooden

The discovery some years after I arrived in Bishop's Stortford that there was a professional engraver living there was an exciting one. I knew nothing about engraving beyond seeing illustrations of graphic work in numbers of *The Penrose Annual*, business gifts to my father, but these were unlikely to have been copper engravings unless by William Strang. At Stortford, however, 'Tid' (A.G. Tidmarsh), the housemaster to whom I was the assistant, had initiated me into the mysteries of etching; I had even tried my hand on a bookplate. I soon learned from Stephen Gooden that engraving on copper was a very different matter and the most exacting of all autographic media.

The Goodens, Stephen and Mona, could not have been more welcoming when I paid my first of many visits to their cottage-cum-studio in Warwick Road (never did simple cottage have a

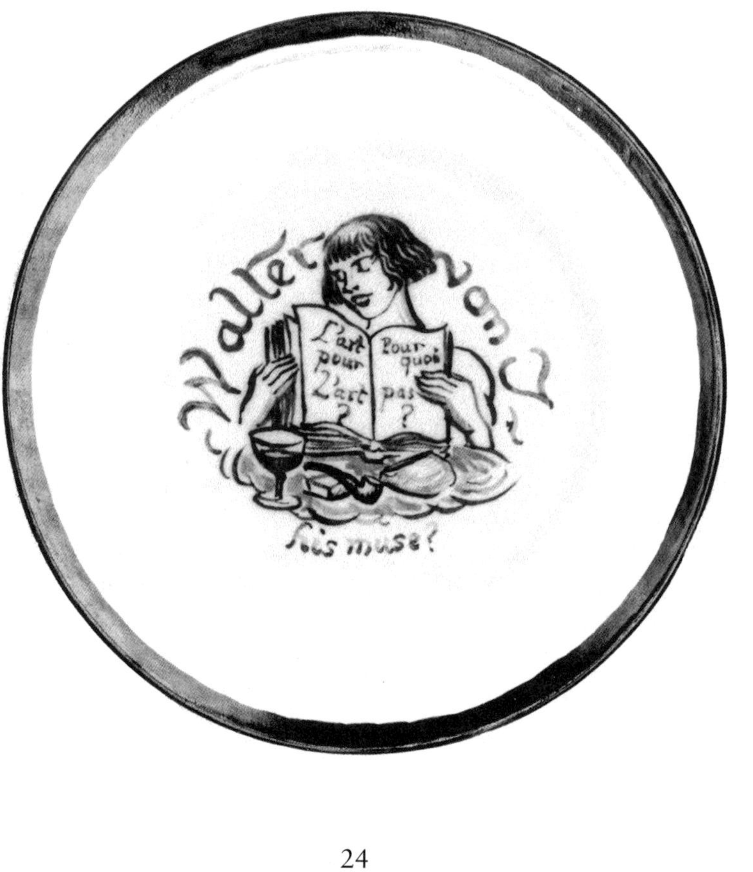

more exquisitely engraved letter-head). Stephen had a dark complexion, almost swarthy. His hair was a deep, shiny black. Give him a couple of gold earrings and he would have made the popular image of a pirate. Until he spoke — with the cultured accent of an Old Rugbeian and the background of a London gallery owner — a low, emphatic drawl, quick to make a satirical point. In contrast, Mona was fair, more than pretty, and there was great charm in a voice that had been formed in County Wicklow and refined at Trinity College, Dublin. She was very sociable, and we were soon, even at our first meeting, exchanging ideas on French literature: the sixteenth-century French authors were her speciality.

This was in 1929. The College art master, Percy Horton, was part-time; he taught only on Thursdays and Fridays, spending the night between mostly as our guest. I had exploited his willingness to talk to some of my senior pupils one Thursday evening, and it was natural for me to make it a social occasion and invite the Goodens to dine with us. So on November 7 (a date in my calendar) they came to hear Horton on 'Modern Art: Delacroix to Cézanne'. I should have remembered, even from my short acquaintance with Gooden, that he was an admirer of Ingres and, like that great exponent of linear draughtsmanship, a worshipper of line. I knew that Horton's equally fervent passion was for the leader in the other camp, Eugène Delacroix.

The talk had not got far under way when Horton was quoting Delacroix's dictum: *'Il n'y a pas de lignes dans la nature'**— volume is what matters, painting your subject from within. Up jumped Gooden: 'Line is the testing point of art' and, quoting the master, *'Faites des lignes, rien que des lignes'*.** The argument was on and hotly debated. My sixthformers were delighted. Surprised that two grown men could feel so passionately on a matter of art. It was in fact a form of the old quarrel of the Ancients and the Moderns. For Horton and most art historians modern art can be said to begin with Delacroix. These strong differences between Gooden and Horton did not affect the cordiality of our respective allegiances, except that Gooden expressed his opinions with increasing vehemence.

* There are no lines in nature

** Make lines, nothing but lines.

There could be controversy, too, about the next 'Thursday Evening talk', as we unbent to listen, partly in an atmosphere of cigar smoke. Gooden was holding forth on his own craft and demonstrating method and technique. He illustrated, symbolically, two essential points about engraving. First the thrusting action of the burin, like a ploughshare, the copper shaving being, as it were, the earth that is turned over. Secondly, everything is executed in terms of straight lines. Curves are produced by turning the plate, placed on a leather pad. The slow, deliberate movement of the snail symbolizes the necessary reflective action. He brought along his illustrations for La Fontaine, very relevant for my sixthformers who had the *Fables* for a set book. Gooden explained how he worked. He showed us examples in proof stage. Among the examples he showed, the boys were particularly struck by the humour in, for example, 'The Lion in Love' (1929), 'The Acorn and the Pumpkin' (1930) and 'Death and the Woodman' (1930).

Stephen took an interest in the architectural society I ran for the boys: outdoor visits in summer, talks and modelling in winter. He suggested giving a talk on 'Structure in Architecture', which resolved itself into a statement of three fundamental requirements before a building could deserve to be called 'architecture'; it must be a good shape; it must be suited to its purpose (a museum shouldn't look like a temple); it must be appropriate to its region or environment. He put his points over forcefully with the use of nothing more complicated than newspaper cuttings and photographs projected by an ancient epidiascope. The boys were impressed.

My relationship with the Goodens was enhanced by my devotion in the first few years of the thirties to the work of George Moore. I had at first no idea that Gooden had illustrated Moore's *The Brook Kerith* and *Peronnik the Fool* with original engravings. The subject of a gargoyle, one of the subjects he submitted for his ARA (1937), was inspired by a nineteenth-century church in Chelsea. He took this particular engraving to a sixth and final state and that version he dedicated to me. He had already generously given me the original drawing (always a prelude to each engraving) of a cat lying down.

When the Goodens moved from Bishop's Stortford to Belsize Gardens in London we used to meet for the odd meal in London, mostly at Vaiani's in Soho. And we corresponded. Mona wrote from 2 Belsize Studios, 29 December 1937: 'I hope we may meet soon and continue our discussions on the ancients and moderns!' Our friendship had romantic overtones. I had the first violets sent to her from Cornwall, and gathered wild flowers to parcel up and send her, the first primroses, then cowslips as they appeared in the local woods and meadows. It all seemed to fit in with George Moore's Irish tales, *The Untilled Fields.*

The Goodens must have known 'G.M'. quite well but were reserved about him — unlike Nancy Cunard, whom I met some years later and who loved talking to me about Moore's visits to Lady 'Emerald' Cunard at Pergenhall. However, I do remember one time meeting Mona Gooden rushing into the local fishmongers, confiding to me that she was looking for some exotic fish as George Moore was staying overnight with them. I should dearly like to have met the great eccentric and shaken his limp hand, especially as that time coincided with my intensive George Moore period. I had begun in 1930 with the romantic *Héloise and Abelard* (graphic descriptions of the people of Paris taking refuge in the upper storeys of their houses when wolves invaded the city.) Then *Memoirs of my Dead Life* and his autobiographical accounts of French artists of the Ecole de Paris, he himself being a *peintre manqué.* After *Conversations in Ebury Street* I read the two works that Gooden was illustrating, *The Brook Kerith* and *Peronnik the Fool.* Later I saw the edition of the latter published by Nancy Cunard at her Hours Press in 1928. I couldn't escape George Moore. A decade after that when the schoolmaster father of a French boy we had entertained, Jean Noel, was working on a biography of George Moore, I helped him to obtain a reproduction of a Max Beerbohm cartoon of the novelist which belonged to my brother-in-law, Tom Jason Wood.

We had given a farewell party for the Goodens when they moved. The time had come to burnish out 'The Cottage, Warwick Road' from the plate on his letterhead: sensibly he retained the supporting devices, too precious to sacrifice. On either side of a baroque label, beautifully elaborate, are nude figures astride seahorses. On the left a Venus: on the right a Triton blowing an 'unwreathed' horn. When, later, I told Steve I had taken up painting watercolours he remarked sternly, 'The cobbler should stick to his last'. Mona was more generous. She wrote (29 December 1937): 'I thought your linocuts very promising'.

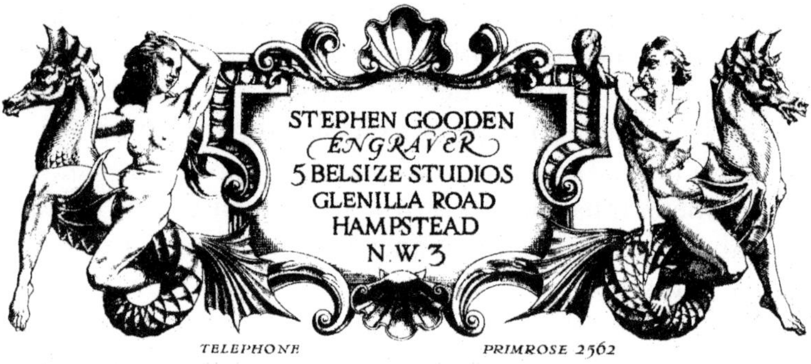

I was expanding from my first pencil drawings of 1931 under instruction from Geoffrey Rhoades, Percy Horton's successor as art master in 1930. In the meantime I had had the good fortune to pay visits to two local private collectors. One, a retired tea-planter, a Mr Tippe, had watercolours I greatly admired by Alfred W. Rich, and when he died I was able to buy my first painting, an Alfred Rich, 'The Chalk-Pit'. At the house of the other collector, Ernest Salaman, I saw Rowlandsons, a Paul Sandby and drawings by Chardin. Colour was tugging me away from pure line, but I never lost the insight I had gained through looking at Gooden's work: whether the witty depiction of a lion tearing at a sack, a light-of-foot milkmaid, or a cockerel perched on a key.

I preferred the engravings without a surround, yet Gooden was happy with the engraver's decorative conventions and used them to good effect, especially in his bookplate designs. He derived immense pleasure from the commission to design and execute two bookplates for Windsor Castle Library. He showed me the first sketches for this in November 1936. He was also responsible for two distinguished *ex-libris* plates: one for Lord Fairhaven, incorporating a long-horn bull, in 1951, and a final one commissioned by Sir Geoffrey Keynes for the Royal College of Surgeons' Library in 1953. (In *The Gates of Memory* Keynes illustrates the bookplate Gooden made for him in 1926 together with his emblem of the craft of engraving of 1932.) After the beginning of the war, Gooden was enticed away from illustrative work to use his skill on banknotes.

We continued a lively, if argumentative, correspondence. The style and messages are characteristic. I wrote to him about engravings of his I saw: I had been excited to acquire his early Cowley's translation of Anacreon and he had given me the *Peronnik the Fool* engraving at a dinner party at Belsize Studios in June 1938. 'You have progressed a long way in the art of flattery', he wrote in January 1943. 'The adroit enquiry as to the self-portrait on the silver cup shows that you are long past the 'prentice stage, and I, of course, can only purr complaisantly'. (The cup was part of the title-page design of *Peronnik the Fool.*)

More distressingly — and in the same letter — he castigates the 'French Pictures' (the Bomford Collection which was touring the country under the auspices of CEMA). 'Except for Cézanne, what a dreary lot of linoleum! What a shocking descent from Rubens to Renoir. Boudin will have his niche in Heaven next to Hollar for his sweet simplicity, but the rest are oh! so second-rate. ... Anyhow, I couldn't stand much of it and got away to the City where at least the ruins are of a later date and unframed' — a reference to blitzed London.

Gooden was in the forefront of those who recognized the great qualities of Eugène Boudin. And, from the evidence above, he would at least not have heeded Ingres' advice to his students when they had to pass through the Rubens gallery: *'Saluez, messieurs, mais ne regardez pas'.**

2 An urgent need to exchange ideas: letters to Percy Horton and Tom Jason Wood 1934–1942

Apart from this first letter, written on holiday in Wiltshire, all Strachan's letters to Percy Horton and Tom Jason Wood from which these extracts are taken were sent from his home at 37 Thornfield Road in Bishop's Stortford until 1937 when the school boarding house, Robert Pearce House, where he was housemaster, became his home. Percy Horton lived in London until the Royal College of Art was evacuated to Ambleside in the Lake District in 1940. Tom Jason Wood lived in Brighouse, Yorkshire.

* Salute them, gentlemen, but do not look at them.

Noon's Farm
Oxenwood
Nr Marlborough
Wilts (last day here)
Undated 1934

I feel so cheery, 'gentle Perce',
I almost wish to write in verse.
For true it is I'm in arrears,
No letter penned for years and years.
Excuse my style *'un peu'* sporadic,
Our life of late has been nomadic...
One week I spent among the Kilts
(I'm writing this, you see, in Wilts)...
We toured around like H.V. Morton
And not at all like Percy Horton,
Not like a packhorse on the down,
With easel, stool and paper 'Ingres'
Prepared for hours to sit and linger,
Until some fog should leave the air
(Unlike your old pal Carrière)
And paint the landscape far and wide
Oblivious of time and tide.
(I left a rhyme out, do not frown)...

It is remote here. I've tried my hand at distant landscapes. I've never been so quiet (except for turkeys). But the country's very lovely. I've been reading Ernst Henri's book on Hitler. Who is Ernst Henri? Is he reliable? It ain't half an indictment of old Thyssens and co!

Well, what of you? Have you had a successful painting holiday? I was in town not long ago to see F.S.Y[oung] cremated. Incidentally I went to *Ces Messieurs de la Santé* (Raimu) — very good — and looked up the Goodens and also did the Tate basement and Leicester Galleries...

37 Thornfield Road
Bishop's Stortford, Herts
1st Sunday after St.Valentine

St Percy: 'Not Angels but Engels'

Dear Percy

Many thanks for the letter and Manifesto.

At the moment I'm reading *And Quiet Flows the Don*, a marvellous title and a fine book. It has such a feeling of space about it. It inevitably reminded me of *The Storm over Asia*. In a way it seems to have borrowed from Eisenstein's film technique — odd revealing 'shots' alternating with rapid movement.

37 Thornfield Road
1934(?)

Dear Percy

Margaret and I got to the French Gallery today and thought it a fine show. We did enjoy it. You have got some good things there and we felt specially like running off with 'Cineraria'. Are you pleased with that? I thought that you'd got some marvellous colour in the foreground and the particular disposition of the books — in fact the composition of the whole most happy. What a good colour that citron! It's certainly the best 'still' in the show — and of yours, to my uninitiated eye, that I've seen... You've got some fine sweeping colour in the 'Kentish Landscape' which looked the most spontaneous and directly painted of any I've seen of yours. Don't you think you've got the distance particularly effective and pleasing in colour in it?...

The whole show is good and looks awfully well in those rooms (they are fine, as you say). I was very struck by Mahoney's 'House at Gt. Bardfield', Rhoades's 'Walcot, Charlbury', Rhoades's 'Bolton Street, Lavenham' and 'The Artist's Aunt'. Friedman's 'Farmer's Cart' and the latter's 'Landscape (No. 59)'... Margaret asks me to tell you how much she was impressed by your stuff. I couldn't get her away from your 'Woman Sewing' and the aforementioned 'still'.

We adjourned for lunch to Schmidts and, fortified by

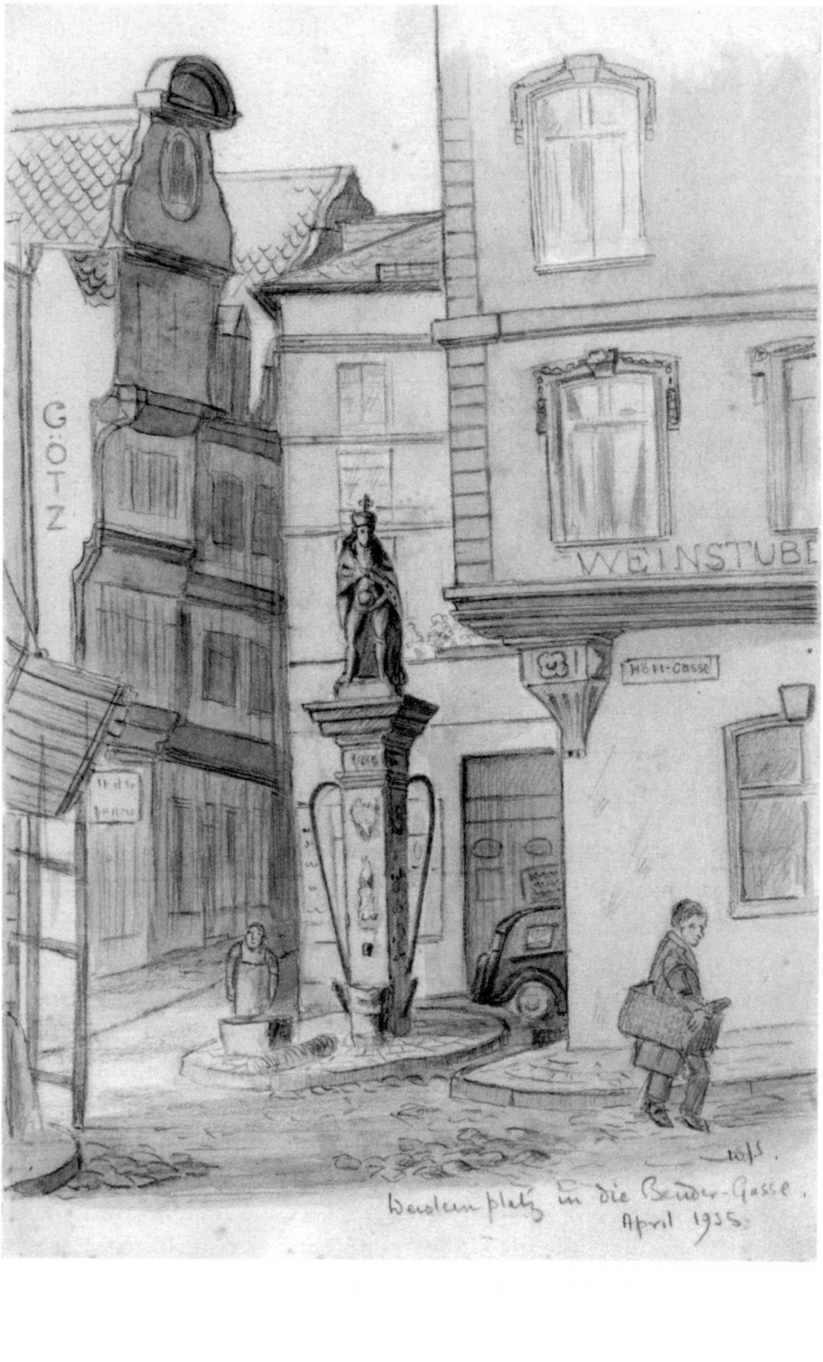
GÖTZ
WEINSTUB
HÖLL-GASSE
in die Bender-Gasse.
April 1935.

Kalbsbraten Garniert and Himbeerkrapfen and lager beer, went on to the National but only looked at very few — we'd really had enough for one day.

It is Wednesday evening — tomorrow I don the professional gown! I hate beginnings and endings. Stortford is looking lovely.

37 Thornfield Road
April 30th & May 1st 1935

Dear Percy

I would have written ere this but since my return on Wednesday night (last) I have been busy doing things while my memory of the German trip was still fresh. First, finishing three wash drawings of Frankfurt and secondly, writing an article on various aspects of Germany which I was fortunate enough to have brought before me. I was pleased with the former: two of them I did in the town — one a general view from the opposite bank of the Main, one of a street corner and one (the most successful) of a silver birch with a background of roof tops. The latter would have produced a marvellous wash drawing from your hand. The chief snag (to me) was a chestnut tree behind it (two in fact) which quickly sprang into full leaf as I drew them! But I did enjoy doing it.

I spent a good few hours in the Städel in Frankfurt (the picture gallery). It is very good — if not as good as Dresden or Berlin. I got to know the curator and saw a good many of the drawings they have stored there, including about thirty Rembrandts, which he let me pore over for an hour... The netherlandish school is well represented — some fine Van Goyen, some fine Brouwer — and a superb Van Der Weyden and the 'Madonna Von Lucca' of J. Van Eyck. Of the Modern French, two fine Renoirs, two Van Goghs, a lovely Courbet 'Winter Landscape', the best Sisley I have seen, a good Cézanne and a Corot portrait.

The family I stayed with were very helpful and I spent a lot of time with them for the sake of language... The father is a Papyrus decipherer, son training for law, one girl helping at home and a younger one of thirteen and of course the Hausfrau! I had the pleasure of hearing Beethoven's ninth, choral symphony (as well as hearing Goebbels speak!). I visited Homburg, Wiesbaden, and Aachen as well as some villages in the Taunus district.

I had an introduction to a certain Lismann, a German artist, in Frankfurt. He is a Jew and having to lie pretty doggo. I had a most painful *Kaffeeklatsch* with his (Christian) wife and nephew while they told me of their hardships. He is an elderly man, fought in the war and therefore should, according to the Nazi principles, be left to carry on. In theory he is, but no *German* can attend his classes. Of his kids (half Jewish) one he has sent to Paris as a sort of kids' nurse (although she was trained at a *Kunstgewerbeschule* and cannot return without being interned for a course of Nazi ideology!) The schoolmasters tell the kids that no one can hope for a job unless he belongs to the *Jungvolk* and then the *Hitlerjugend*.

No one with any Jewish blood is allowed to belong! (verb.sap) A distant relation of mine, who has been forty years in Germany, is giving lessons in English as hard as she can go, to these Jews who are awaiting a chance to clear out. I had even worse tales from a Jew in Cologne and he had the war service ribbons, *Ehrenkreuz*, and was captured on the Western front. All this, together with the fact that his family have been five hundred years in Germany, that they can prove, makes no difference. He said he has seen recent preparations for a new campaign: shields with: *'Juden ist das Betreten Dieses Ortes auf eigene Gefahr!'*,* and more threatening warnings still.

The fine war memorial in Frankfurt has been removed: 'too Marxist!' I saw the Nazi Party film *Der Triumph des Willens!* Two and a half hours of flag waving and Siegheiling. I heard the Mephisto of the piece — Goebbels — twice! All German talent in the films — Leni Riefenstahl, Emil Jannings — is used for *one* purpose — to teach Bismarckian precepts. Of course seventeen days is a short impression but I met and talked to many people. I cannot see much hope of any opposition being able to put it over. Hitler has on his side a hysterically zealous majority, merely

* 'Jews enter this place at their own risk.'

because he has delivered the kind of goods which they wanted — arms — show — nationalism — an excuse for submission to discipline and the submersion of the individual. I have sent my article off, as I felt I must get the stuff off my chest. I shall try the *New Statesman* or *Guardian Weekly*, tho' I suppose it's doubtful whether they will consider it worth the space.

I have brought back some most charming books on plants and flowers — butterflies, exquisite illustrations and a play, *Der Zerbrochene Krug*, illustrated by Menzel.

37 Thornfield Road
Jan 29th 1936

Dear Percy,

O Just, eloquent and mighty death! etc... '*Oraison Funèbre*' gloom — gloom — gloom.* Mass hysteria worked up by BBC and journalists... catafalques and plumes... and we semi-officials having to sport (*mot juste!*) black ties (and yesterday) funereal clothes, to sing 'Abide with Me' (all verses)!

My God! I'm driven to another escape — Monk-Jones and I are going to see a bad flick tonight: anything to escape from women whose sorrow, normally reserved for cats and Pekingese, is now expended, lavished, on the royal family!...

I enjoyed the books you sent me. My reading has been spasmodic — I've been sorry to have to interrupt my reading of [Romain Rolland's] *Jean-Christophe* (after Vol. IV), as I can't manage it in term time — even if one had the time, the quiet atmosphere is lacking!... Have you read anything of special interest lately? I'm looking for something for a 7/6 book token I had sent. It's no use for architecture and I'm not buying novels much. I thought, from Garrett's review in the *New Statesman*, that Clarence Day's *Life with Father* might be '*mon affaire*'. It's as well to foresee and (forestall?) the snares and snags for a bourgeois father! Somehow a bourgeois upbringing can never be lived down. I find in my own case that it's always there, however much one might *wish* it away!

* George V had just died.

Oh well, Percy, this is a poor effort — written, however, under extenuating circumstances — in the Common Room, with Colman, Hayward, Spencer and Craig talking commonplaces of the funeral cortège of yesterday!...

37 Thornfield Road
February 2 Sunday
[1936]

Dear Percy

This follows 'hard upon'! but I'm a little *'surexcité'!* I read in the *Observer* today that at the Walker Gallery there is a show of 300 watercolours of early English artists including Cox, the Varleys, Ward, De Wint, Edward Lear, etc., none priced at more than five guineas. Of course, I haven't five guineas in hand but I've considered ways and means of raising a few quids — eg I've sent off a list of some ten first editions I possess of various authors, from John Davidson to G.B.S, to a bookseller to see what I might raise and I've got an idea for an article for the *Christian Science Monitor.*

Now I wondered whether you've seen the above show and whether you think it worth my while coming up on Wednesday afternoon to see them. I suppose by now the best will be sold anyhow! No doubt many will be very slight. But I did like the Lears I saw at the Victoria and Albert and I have a special interest in him. If you could possibly look in on Monday and let me have a p.c. on Tuesday or Wednesday first post, I would come up Wednesday — I should only have a couple of hours — and go round! If you're busy and haven't time, just send a p.c. to that effect. I know what a hectic life you have!

I tell Margaret, *pour la consoler*, that this will be positively *the* last fling!

No time for more, all the best,

Walter

P.S.1)Do prices at these shows include frames?

2.Where is the Walker Gallery?

37 Thornfield Road
Feb.17th 1936

Dear Percy

The Walker 'do' had to go... I failed to realise the necessary capital and as you convinced me that I had let 'wish fulfillment' run away with me about the quality of the work likely to be shown, I half lost my enthusiasm. These things — bargains in really good works of art — don't happen anyhow in London galleries in this Year of Grace 1936! I realise that, though reluctantly! Anyhow it spurred me to an effort — an article on *Fathers and Sons*, which I've dispatched to the *Christian Science Monitor!*

37 Thornfield Road
9.4.36 'Bad Thursday'

Dear Percy

Well, the sun shines bright (and this was odd because it was an Easter Thursday night!) and it's all hands to the Pump!* Aye Aye, Sir. Avast you scum and spread the 'canvas' in the 'tops', ye lubbers!

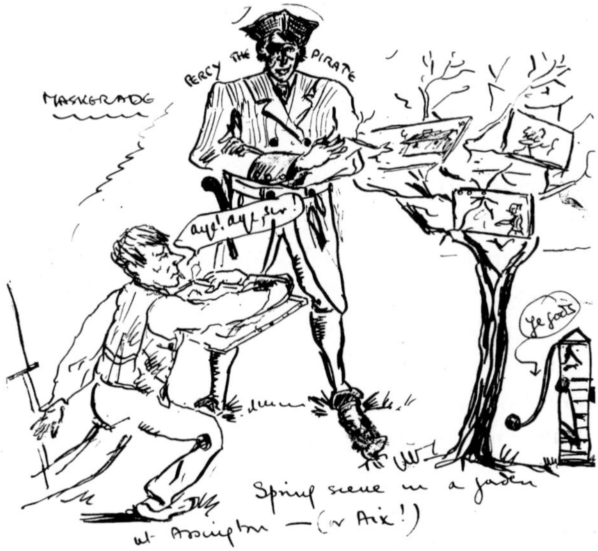

* A reference to Pump Farm, at Assington in Suffolk, where evidently Horton and Geoffrey Rhoades were to have a painting weekend. The mention in the caption of 'Aix' alludes to Cézanne's first floor studio in Aix-en-Provence, below which the fruit trees were said to be hung with rejected canvases, flung by the artist from his window.

I hope this weather holds out for your painting. The 'open' season begins a little later for *nous autres* amateurs.

Percy: In winter when the fields are white
I'll paint a scene for your delight.
Tid: In spring when leaves are getting green
I'll sketch within my limousine.
Self: In summer when the days are long
Perhaps I, too, will trot along.
Percy and Geoff:
In autumn, when the leaves are brown,
'Our eye is in', we put it down.

This was going to be a serious letter! about Mozart, Shakespeare and all them blokes — not to mention Edward Lear and Day Lewis! and now we are expecting our Easter guest at any moment and I ought to be about and doing, preparing the garage for its *ostensible* but (almost blunted) purpose(!) of taking a car. I must just say how much I enjoyed that Gainsborough Show! I saw the new Ingres, Constable and Rubens in the National the other day. The *latter* is absolutely a knock-out.

37 Thornfield Road
June 6 1936

Dear Percy

'A peasant slave am I!' Since the beginning of this term nought but a succession of trivial duties with a few bright intervals. Somehow a school of our type seems to exact the last farthing's worth and more out of all but the safe, unscrupulous ones. If I were an ardent Christian — or purported to be — and spent all my spare time coaching athletics — I should no doubt have more time and leisure. 'Assume a virtue tho' you have it not' is a singularly successful precept.

But one cannot enjoy the 'result' of such a philosophy, nor have their leisure without the attendant abasement. And so for goodwill one stays oneself. One might write a good version of *Pilgrim's Progress* from the point of view of the unimpeachable atheist who reaches his goal still preserving his atheism intact from all the temptations of Christian ideology!

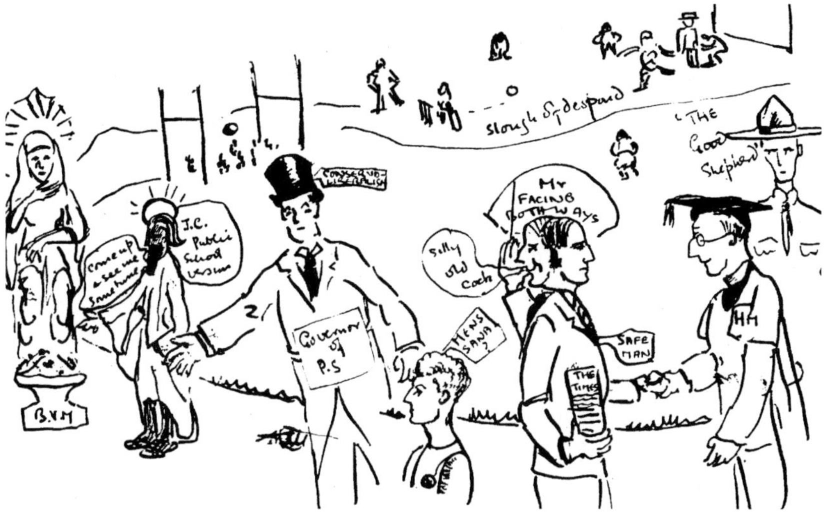

I haven't read much lately though I have to record volume VI of J-C (*Jean Christophe*, please!) behind me. It's a pleasure to read such well written stuff. It *is* sentimental in parts but on the whole very good.

Last Wed. a party of us went to the New Arts Theatre in Cambridge and saw the Vic-Wells ballet. Most enjoyable, especially 'The Gods go abegging' (a pleasing conceit) set to Handel's music (actually it is adapted mostly from the Alcina suite which I have in disc form!). Done in a Watteau setting and costume. Altogether a pleasant evening, for we had our *fête-champêtre* on the way back in the moonlight.

One cannot but regret with the 'passing tribute of a sigh' the elegance which (as they say in popular art history) was Watteau's!

Great God! I'd rather be
A pagan suckled in a creed outworn
So might I, standing on this pleasant lea,
Have glimpses that will make me less forlorn...
Or hear old Triton blow his wreathed horn.

Well — so much for neopaganism!

What do you think of the French situation — strike and all? I suppose the Action Française will be watching events pretty carefully. As for this country... with Sir Arnold Wilson's book (cracking up Fascism and Germany in particular) *que voulez-vous?* It's a *bestseller* too. Do you ever see Professor (Dr) Marach's stuff in the *News Chronicle* (I think)? He's a keen left winger and at our last '*so-genannte*' Peace meeting, when I was in the chair, he gave any apologists for Hitler a few straight lefts.

To Tom Jason Wood

37 Thornfield Road
Evening 30th & morning 31st Dec 1936

Dear Tom

I am missing our usual holiday '*échanges de propos*' and thought I would write a few hundred words on 'things that have interested me'...

... This term has had a good end for me in so far as we got a Modern Languages open scholarship at Cambridge. Colossal competition, of course. Your well-beloved, several times removed cousin, John Stubley, also tried for one. He is good but not up to that. Actually he's a very decent kid. He was my strong supporter in a recent debate at School when I was leading opposition to the motion 'That this House would welcome an O[fficer] T[raining] C[orps] in this School'. It was a full-dress debate with an outside proposer Dr Vernon Dockray Junior — a man whose chief claims to fame are: (1) a record time taking medicine; (2) being a Governor's son; (3) a big roaring voice and a commission in the Terriers. Anyhow the motion was lost 49 to 82 — a tribute to B.S. in these bellicose days, I think...

Some good books I have read recently:-

Novel on Yellow Paper, Stevie Smith. I can safely commend to one who appreciates nonsense literature because there is a streak of it underlying this weird book. Don't be put off by an unusual idiom...

Your Uncle [Fred Brooker] is taking Margaret and myself to the theatre shortly. We have chosen Granville Barker's *Waste*. Since reading and seeing *The Voysey Inheritance* and reading *Madras House*, I've had a wholesome respect for his stuff. It will be a treat for us both to be in town together — we don't often manage it. I 'exposed' (to the jeering public) two of the watercolours I did with Horton at Pump Farm this summer at the local show.

How's the cottage and garden? Jean and I have been collecting a lot of tree seeds and planting them in protected pots — lime, sycamore, ash, hornbeam etc. Trees fascinate me almost more than flowers. Have you thought of having a few saplings round your cottage or is it too exposed for all but mountain ash?... There's a very good new edition of George Moore at 5/- (five vols out now, including, I think, the fine *Esther Waters*. You *must* read it)...

To Percy Horton

Robert Pearce House
Maze Green Road
Bishop's Stortford, Herts
Boxing Day 1937

Dear Percy

I had hoped to be able to fix something up with you this term but you can imagine my first term has been pretty busy. I did manage to get up to see two minor classics *Le Roman d'un Tricheur* and *A Day at the Races* (in the *non*-Metro Goldwyn parts!) Did you see the latter? It might inspire a marvellous piece of bathos in a novel production of *Macbeth*!...

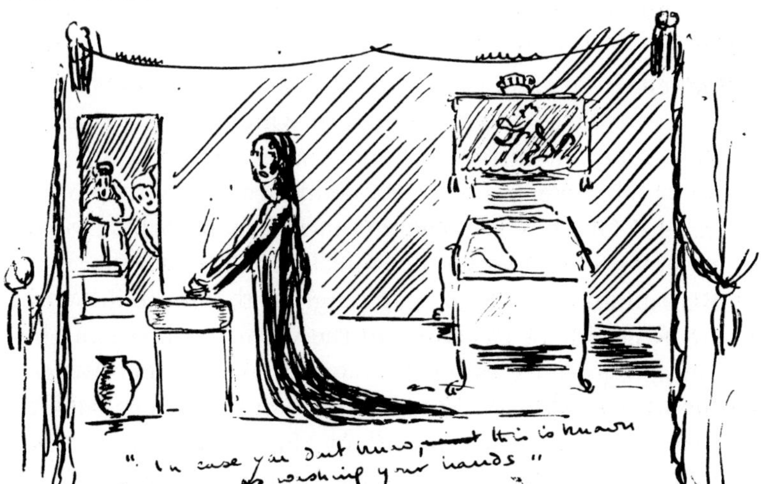

Lots of news of one sort and another — not *all* occupational! Have you read much lately? I've been sadly deficient there, what with lino-cutting with the boys in the Hobby Hut ... getting to know twenty-nine boys! not to mention family affairs and Geoffrey has got to a most fascinating stage: 'he lisps in numbers e'er the numbers came' — inventing Carrollian words of vituperation like 'blackimous'. Not that Jean is not interesting. She was telling Geoff yesterday about the new birth in the zoo. 'Wasn't it funny, A chimpanzee, Noel, was born in the zoo the same day as Jesus'. Geoff doesn't approve of the latter. 'I think he's beastly and blackimous!' ' So now, dear Christians...'

Robert Pearce House
10.3.38

Dear Percy

The country is marvellous now. The willows, in which we abound, look like *'gerbe'*, golden rain of the fireworks. We walked through Takeley forest where the hornbeams are so briarean and greenbarked. Then we saw a jay flash by in the sunlight. It would be a pity if jays disappeared. Primroses, anemones, celandine, pussy willow all out here now! 'The rathe primrose that forsaken lies'.

I took my architects to the seventeenth-century show. It was a great success. I've got a really keen lot. For once, I think, they are practically all keen on painting. We're doing practical work in the hobby — sculpting in plaster of Paris (supplied by Patcho [Newman Catchpole]) — making models etc. We're doing a census of windmills as a side-line and it's rather interesting, especially as about twenty-five per cent have disappeared since my ordnance survey map of ten years ago! One boy is essaying a model that works! Do you know any book on windmills? I feel I ought to get one.

I'm running a 'reading' campaign in the house just now, to stem the tide of thrillers, on the whole with reasonably encouraging results. Someone has managed *Esther Waters*. Someone else *The Trumpet Major* — it's a far cry back to the days when I was lending *all* my Hardys to Lower 5a!...

I hope I shall see you in the holidays after my Paris adventure. I return on *Good* Thursday!

Robert Pearce House
Dec 9 1940

My dear Percy

I wonder if my letter written on the eve of your departure ever got to you at Ambleside? I was very glad to hear that the prospect (in every sense of the word) is not too bad at your H.Q., tho' I wonder if the winter's rages have played havoc with your easels. Perhaps some future dealer will unhook your canvases from neighbouring conifers?...

I've been much concerned with architecture lately, having had to prepare a lecture for a girls' school in this district. A fearfully top-shelf affair in a huge country house!...It was a difficult business as the ages ranged from ten to eighteen and the 'tiny-tots' toddled out (by arrangement) at 7.30, halfway through! It was supposed to be an introduction to architecture and I dwelt largely on the structural ideas behind each new 'epoch' — beginning with essential principles, posts and lintels, the arch, the dome and finally the gothic revolution. I drew a good deal from good old Corbusier's *Vers une Architecture* and his analysis of shapes.

Actually I enjoyed myself and I only hope they found some interest in it. I did quite a few blackboard sketches and also took some of our home-made models. The place of the lecture was in the huge ante-room (pseudo renaissance!) and I had hastily to drop my illustration of a bad lecture hall with huge pillars everywhere, as that was precisely what I was up against (literally!).

Anyhow I am to have a 'rendezvous' with some of the girls at Hatfield Broad Oak Church in the warmer days to come! A mistress said perhaps I could show them round one day in the lighter months. 'Oh yes'! (girls) — 'Yes', said the Headmistress (probably hoping an invasion scare may intervene in the meantime!) 'in the *Summer*'. 'There's some very nice days in the *Spring*', chirped up some audacious County voice!...

We all hope we shall see you at Water Yeat in the holidays... Well — I now relieve the second watch, for this is written at the Observation Post and accounts for indifferent calligraphy!...

PORTRAIT-DRAWING

To Percy Horton

As I stand before this portrait-drawing,
Moved by its grave statement I am carried
To that other world, of blue Coniston slate,
Of whitewashed stone and deep windows lit
By a faltering lakeland sun, and live again
The excitement of the blank Ingres paper
Pinned on a board, pencil and sharpened chalk,
The pause, the look from a wary, practised eye,
The experiments with light on the posed head.
The disappointment too at the first assay,
Exquisite modelling — but something missed.
Then finally, after abandoned start — success.
Expression caught and fixed in a few firm lines.
The subtle mouth, the eyes' overtones,
Hair framing profile and sweeping back
From the clean curve of the neck, no line superfluous...

Then chatter, laughter as we went out
Through the paved garden and climbed to the
hill-framed tarn
And watched cloud-shadows sliding over its surface.

Robert Pearce House
July 3rd 1941

Dear Percy

... I've been having a marvellous week — alas drawing to a close this evening (Margaret is packing as I write) with Margaret here. We've just returned from an idyllic afternoon punting on the Cam in the sun. I got a charming edition of Clive Bell on *Proust*, stimulated thereto by the *New Statesman* article of last week-end (do you read it?). I see there's a new issue of Scott-Moncrieff's translation.

Margaret is brown and well and looks so young. I feel very proud of her. She was able to see the proof of the portrait photograph. I think it will be well executed — it's being very 'specially' done (I'm not sure how!) and I'll send you

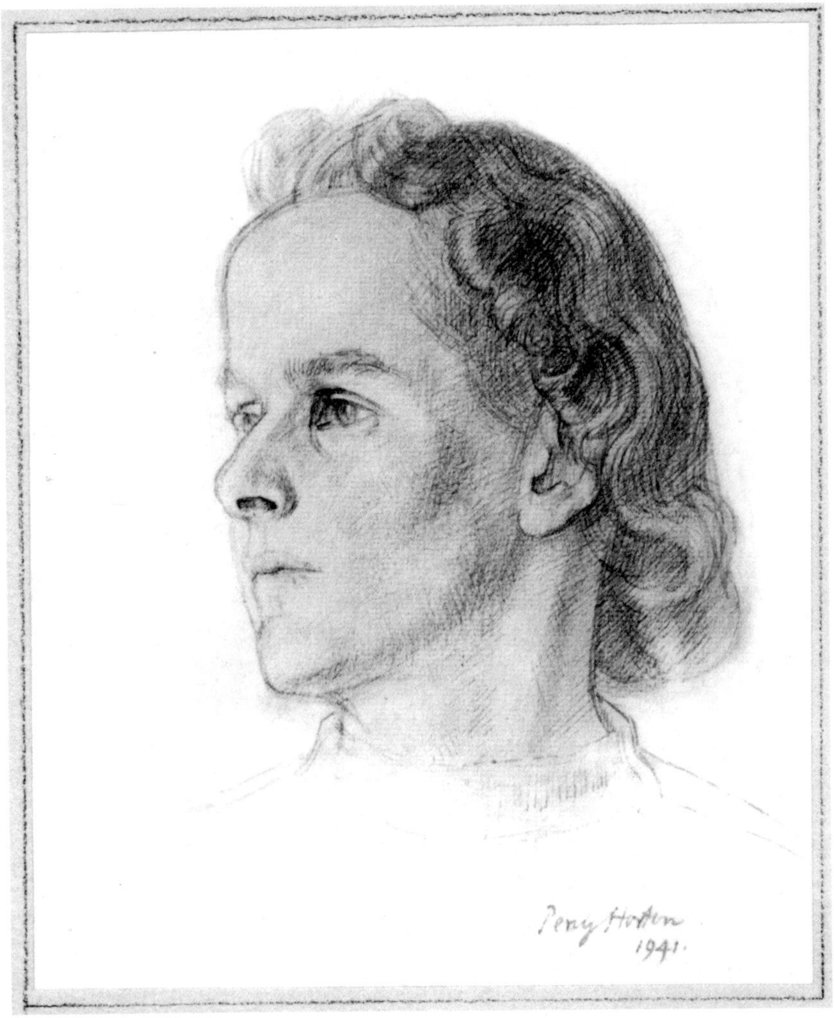

one eventually (Stortford-London liaison a bit slow!). I *shall* look forward to a visit to your Studio in the summer if and when I get up to the Lakes (awful farming programme may involve R.P.H. for a fortnight).

I've done a monochrome pencil and wash of a river subject which Geoffrey Rhoades likes. Iris Woodward (whom you met with us) did one of the same motif — amazing, they don't look like the same place! I shall enjoy seeing your stuff. How goes the R.C.A? Does '*pleinairisme*' relax the tensity?...

Well, what of the U.S.S.R?* — it hasn't had the effect of releasing the ban on the *Daily Worker!* But that was hardly to be expected! Still it gives a little more purpose to death! It's a hard world for those whose ideology is *'tant soit peu quarante-huitard!'* I've been lending the boys the Left Book Club Commune volume, but they still write in their essays about the 'mob' (as ye might say!).

On your recommendation I bought *Dominique* [by Eugène Fromentin] against the time when I have some leisure. Do you see *The New English Weekly?* I am to appear, I believe, in its pages at some not too distant date! It'll be a *'bon moment'* for me but I don't suppose very profitable!...

...Would you advise me to draw with charcoal? That is, when I want to be broader in effect. With my snatched time, it would be useful if I didn't always have to do careful drawing (despite Ingres' dictum!). I suppose for that little watercolour you gave me you used a brush straight off? It's a little gem...

Robert Pearce House
Oct 12 1941

Dear Percy

I can appreciate how *écarté* not to say *desorienté et perdu* you must feel up at Ambleside sometimes... I know that you've loved some of the natural features very well — that is evident in your pictures — but the strain, jar and jangle of communal life do get one down. I know so much from the more *comfortable*, but no less nerve-racking, life here in a school boarding house!... I'm still terribly restless and sleeping badly. I can't settle to read anything except verse (strange malaise!) and odd hours find me with MacNeice, or Auden or Campbell (Roy) in my hand or scribbling my own! on backs of envelopes. Is it a sin of advancing age to find so much of routine intolerable? I suppose essentially one submits or not! — and I've a hell of a lot of things I must do in my job — like attending chapel! When I do, I feel utterly sick and frustrated. Tonight I managed to shut my ears and

* Germany had invaded Russia in June 1941.

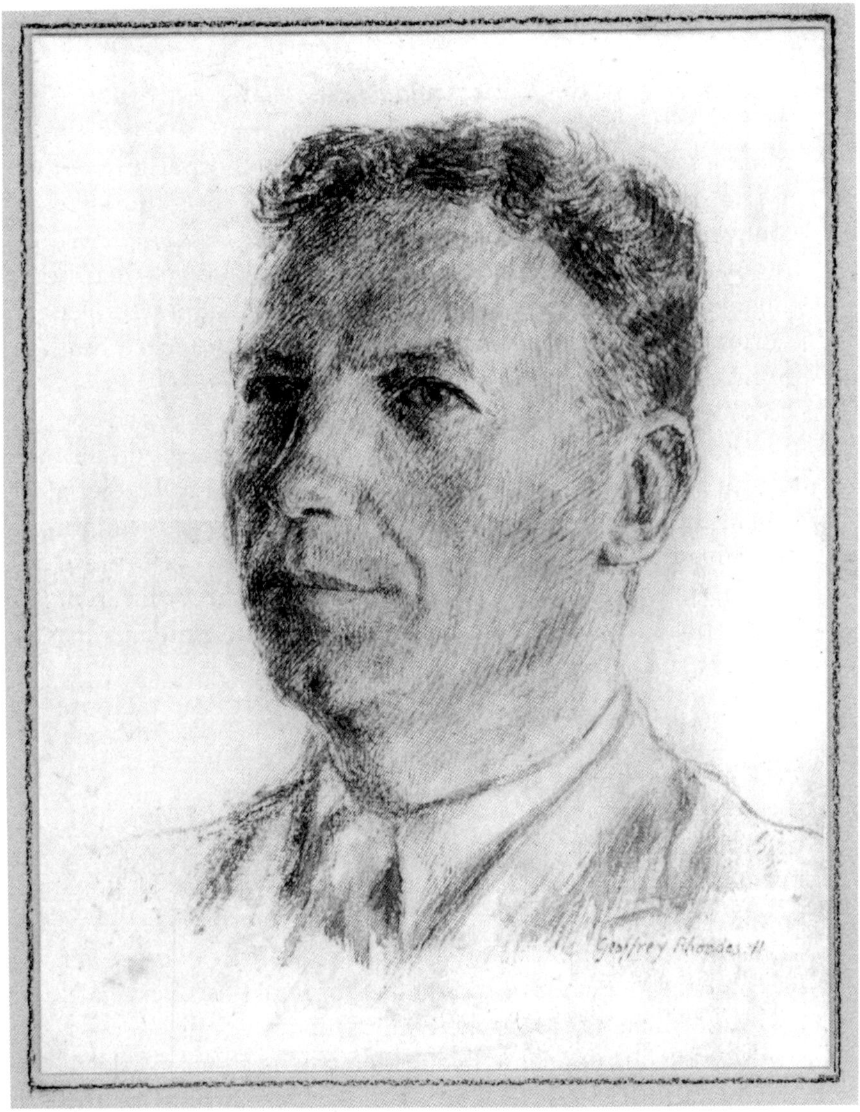

began to compose a sonnet — occasionally jotting down an odd line.

This morning I snatched an hour of frosty sunlight and began a water colour — two haystacks rather a John Nash subject of curves, also I can conceive it in his rather arbitrary tones.

I got to the Sickert Show one day. I *did* enjoy it. His pictures give me as much pleasure as any modern(!) I find his early, low tone ones actually appeal to me more than the later ones...

I also went to the Disney *Fantasia* — what a lost opportunity! The only tolerable things to me were *L'Apprenti Sorcier*, which was not treated too anthropomorphically nor in that awful Hollywood whimsicality vein! The Bach had glimpses that were not vulgar. The *Sacre Du Printemps* was an insult and entirely a cheap Wellsian reconstruction (unconvincing withal) of evolution. As for the Beethoven 'Pastoral' with female centaurs wearing brassières, need I say more!...

You will have seen that the portrait photo is enclosed and I do hope you like it and the general way it's been done. I returned three versions before being satisfied! I'm having a similar thing done with Geoffrey's of me* but fear it cannot possibly reproduce so well, being much more of a pot-pourri of drawing and wash drawing in two or three different shades of reds and browns. It 'comes off' but quite against the rules and canons!...

Robert Pearce House
Nov 6th 1941

My Dear Percy

I've just returned from Fire-watching as the 'All-Clear' has gone! My heart is often in my mouth, not because of this but because the renewal of Blitzes would force me to postpone the return of the family. No — they're not back — not till early next term, alas. So here I — and there you — sit like birds in the wilderness. I do feel for you — it's very hard and atmosphere is everything really isn't it?

I very much appreciated your kind words about my poem (poem?) and feel very encouraged. It is just for one's little circle of *'intimes'* that these things really matter and, like a flower, one expands in a warm and sympathetic atmosphere. Perhaps I'll be sending more anon. It's good to hear you're getting such pleasure out of the fiddle 'twenty years a'bowing'! — I can tell from my narrower and humbler part in the school orchestra** what the thrill must be to sustain a

* He had photographic copies made both of Horton's drawing of Margaret and Rhoades's drawing of himself, both made in the same year.

** Playing the double bass.

major part in chamber music.

I sent your letter up to Margaret, she will so appreciate your appreciation of 'The Woods'. My feeling for nature has come so much through her. One day I'd like to write in the vein of *A La Recherche du Temps Perdu* — that period of *tendresse infinie* which echoes through one's later years. Have you read Clive Bell's little essay *à ce propos* — I will send it with the *Dominique* and would like to have the *Proust* back some time, not too long ahead, as I pass it round to my Sixth Form. It's a nice little edition.

Do you see *Horizon?* Patchy, but has some good things now and again. [Augustus] John seems a bit hard-boiled in some ways unless he is *purposely* callous in his autobiographical notes? What a *disadvantage* to succeed too young! bad sign *nearly* always?

I've managed to do one autumn sketch in company with Iris Woodward, whom you met. Geoffrey quite likes it. He always says I owe much more to you than to him and I think it's true. Not that I think I'm good but it has given me *real* pleasure and revolutionised my life. I *mean* that. You see at Cambridge I always wanted to write but 'taking thought' wasn't any good and I've no illusions about my limitations; but the painting reanimated the little germ of that desire for expression and kept it alive and is bound up with this renewed pleasure in writing.

THE WOODS

I am drawn irresistibly to the woods;
For woods have secrets,
And they respond to my mood.
The mountains, too, have secrets,
But their secrets are cruel,
And less human
And the secrets of the hills
Are swept away by the winds.
But the woods harbour their secrets
Lovingly and with understanding.

The woods are delicate and mysterious;

They do not proclaim their beauty openly
Like the meadows;
They must be courted;
And their secrets are endless
Like a lover's
To whom the mysteries of his beloved
Are endless.

And the pattern of the carpet underfoot
Is intricate and full of surprises,
Like a beautiful character;
It is woven with an infinitude of tendrils
Hidden from the view,
And it is starred with wild-strawberry flowers,
Their brown eyes inviting confidence.

So I whisper my secrets to the woods,
For they have many of their own
And can understand.

[From hospital]
23.XII.41

My dear Percy

I am, as you will see, still in hospital. I had hoped to be home for Christmas but it is not to be and I'm sorry because of the children and Margaret... It's not that the 'op' I've undergone is serious — only bloody painful!... Margaret had a rotten time... However, she's more or less settled in and seen hundreds of people about food and milk and whatnot and got something going. We *shall* be glad to be all together again.

It's had a very deep effect on me this one and a half years and in some ways I can never be the same — for good or ill — a sort of emotional upset. I mustn't get too introspective, must I! But with all its snags, I prefer the *péripéties* of the emotional life. *A propos*, I've just finished two very different but nevertheless striking books, both of which you must have read, *To the Lighthouse*, Virginia Woolf, and *The Power and the Glory*, Graham Greene...

I've done a few poem-decorations in bed and written one poem (rather gloomy, nearly as pessimistic as 'Reading Gaol'

— I wish it were as good!!)

Robert Pearce House
Wed-Thurs Feb 4-5 (1942)

My dear Percy

I wonder what violent weather conditions have done at Ambleside! Perhaps they will seem less out of the ordinary than elsewhere where so much frost and snow is abnormal? Are you able to do a snowscape from your Studio window or are you clinging to the stove for warmth... It must have been hard settling down to the rusticated R.C.A. after a brief — all too brief — taste of London...

During my remaining holiday I did a few decorations, as a change from reading and playing with the children. I was stimulated thereto by two sheets of your cream Ingres paper! It called for a decorative treatment of another poem I've committed! and looks quite nice.* One day I'll try and improve my lettering. Actually Margaret bought me a noble and exhaustive volume on the subject (*Lettering:* Graily Hewitt) — rather formidable but I've enjoyed flirting with it for my birthday.

I sent the poem originally to the review *Poetry* but as they kept it, despite the usual stamped addressed envelope, I didn't feel free to try my luck elsewhere with it till some time had elapsed. The other day I sent it to the *New English Weekly* and had a note from Mairet to say that he liked it very much and if he'd had it six weeks back would have published it and would do so now, but for severe paper restrictions. I felt annoyed with *Poetry* but I suppose that's the sort of thing which must always be happening!

If I remember, I'll enclose it, as you kindly evinced so much interest in the last! I've ordered the complete Yeats with a book token. I don't like all of him but most is written with distinction. I've borrowed T.S. Eliot *1905-1935* — I find too much absence of feeling — too cerebral or satirical. MacNeice isn't profound but his imagery is more colourful and he's full of feeling. I can recommend, as at least interesting, his *Autumn Journal.* His selection in the Faber 3/6

* 'Autumn Mood': see appendix.

volume has some charming things in. One I have attempted to decorate, 'The Sunlight on the Garden'.

When it boils down to it my sympathies fall in with the romantic tendency (even when hid under various cloaks of cynicism etc, as in Hemingway, Spender, McNeice, or realism, as in O'Casey or the analytical cruelty of Proust.) I advertise the Miltons, the Eliots (I'm not juxtaposing them in merit), the Paul Nashes, but I don't feel in the same sympathy as I do with the Keats, the Sickerts, where there is always a *glow* and some human weakness!

I was so glad you were able to see your portrait 'in situ' and saw Geoffrey's of me. Margaret and I are very proud of our *Habseligkeiten* and she and the children are so glad to see all the pictures again. They come out with some trenchant remarks! Jean to me when she was worrying about me and Margaret dying and I had said: 'But *my* Father is still alive'. 'But *you* may be one of the early-dying ones and not one of the lasting-longer ones'! Home truths...

Robert Pearce House
13.V.42

My dear Percy,

I've started a sort of war-artist group among the boys in an attempt to stimulate their interest — they're to draw wartime features here in B[ishop's] S[tortford] C[ollege]! whether air raid shelters, poultry keeping (including geese nesting in the garden and so on!), the corps doing various things. The weather broke the day after my 'notice' but nevertheless quite a good response.

My umpteenth Modern Language assistant is here — another refugee, released from Canada. He's better than my last. He's quite interested in pictures and has among his *Habseligkeiten* a set of cigarette-cards (largish size) of *Moderne Malerei*. It's very good and, of course, rich in Corinth, Marées, Klee etc. England is represented by two Turners, and two Brangwyns! *Est-ce possible!* They will show up well in the epidiascope. The set is a rarity and Hitler banned it!

By the way I got to the watercolour show at the V & A and was so glad you'd mentioned it. I liked Ravilious's

'Farmhouse Bedroom' as much as any of his. His formula and recipe really suited the subject! John Piper's 'Cottage by the Rey, Gt Bedwyn' attractive in texture and colour and rather evocative. What do you think of Sutherland? I'm interested in him since his *apologia pro suam artem!* in *Horizon* in the Welsh letter... I wish I could have been with you but if you can spare a few moments to write your impressions I'd be grateful. I did notice that Bawden seemed to have flecked his paper in the ship on the slipway sketch in the same way as he had the clouds in ours.* I thought at first it might be accidental...

Robert Pearce House
July 22 1942

My dear Percy

We were so glad to see the notice in *The Times* of your picture of Dulwich... You've really forged ahead and are very surely building up a cairn which will be visible even to more distant spectators than the closer circle of cognoscenti. It must be a consolation to you in moments of depression — inevitable to any sensitive person — to think how *much* you have achieved.

When I was reading some very sad poems (the moderns are so much sadder really, because the sadness, instead of being rather *lusciously* expressed, like 'We'll go no more a-roving, So late into the night etc' or even de la Mare's 'Silence where hope was', is more between the lines and implicit in the *tone* of the poem) by Stephen Spender in *Ruins and Visions* — his latest, I couldn't help wondering how far it was a consolation to him, and similarly to MacNeice in his *Autumn Journal*, that they could externalise their emotions and distil their sadness into such memorable and universal form.

Artists by temperament are open targets for much more emotional sadness than the bulk of humanity, who can harden their hearts more easily. For an artist to harden up in some emotional crisis must mean a loss of sensibility and affect detrimentally the 'poetry' in his work? This problem

* The painting 'August 5pm' Strachan had bought in 1940.

interests me very much because I've been specially fascinated by the two poets mentioned and I remember in an early *Horizon* (No. 2) this passage by Spender: 'A great cause of weakness today is people putting less important things before those that are more important, for example, personal relationships before work and an objective philosophy of life'...

You'll be wondering when I'm going to give you any *news*! You must forgive me but I've not many people with whom I can exchange views on poetry! I've written a few fragmentary things lately which I can't think have any merit. Probably I only can produce occasional, tolerable efforts on the tide of emotion and my present mood is too conditioned by pettifogging irritations inseparable from war effects at B.S...

'Patcho' [Newman Catchpole] attends to Henry Moore's teeth and he is interested in the idea I've started among the boys of doing pictures of War effects on B.S.C. It's gone quite well and we formed part of a local exhibition. I've done three watercolours this term and one of Long Meadow (a commission for the brother-in-law Tom, whom you will remember — the *nice* one!)

I wish we lived nearer. I sometimes feel such an urgent need to exchange ideas etc with you in particular and no one else. Incidentally did you read E.M. Forster's lecture on Virginia Woolf? A delicate tribute... Also there's enthusiasm for *Le Rouge et Le Noir*, *L'Education Sentimentale.* There's no denying it, Percy, you've played the major role in my education — so jejune and such gaps when I left Cambridge! For to me *stimulus* has been everything. You opened up a deep mistrust of 'academism' in the bad sense. I hope to some extent I've been a *'personnage sympathique'*. Oh well, there's been a generation of boys grateful indirectly to you, and a few adults even!

Jean is full of fun and a dear thing. She's getting on quite well with her music. Geoffrey (the younger!) is coming on apace and it's a joy the way he reacts to ideas with flashing and humorous eye!

MIDWAY

Now as I stand between doing and remembering,
And you, not wholly surrendered,
Hover between home and the inevitable classroom,
And there are no disturbing loyalties
To cloud our understanding,
I would fix as best I may,
With the faulty apparatus of memory,
Your image, clear as a Spring-morning.

I would bear it with me like a charm,
Intact and precious,
Through the difficult years:
Your body, slender and trim,
Each part carelessly responsive
To thought and mood,
Your soft, untutored hand,
As with deft turns of the wrist
You spill brightness on to paper,
Or more deliberately draw
The crazy shapes
That people your world;
Your firm, unanswerable logic,
Turning in swift transition
To idle nonsense or fantastic rhyme
Running gaily off your tongue;
The sudden, abstracted look
That sends the years spinning back to babyhood;
Or the grave expression,
Reaching beyond the present;
The easy, unexacting affection;
The unclouded brow
In the disarray of sheets...

That I, through you, may return sometimes
To the beginning of things:
The mountain-stream
Where the water dashes
Cool and unsullied
And catches the frequent rainbow.

PART TWO

THE POETRY YEARS

1942–1948

ARMISTICE DAY, NOVEMBER 1944

Lying in bed, half-wakeful, wondering
How long this timeless war would dawdle past,
And, as night-fighters roared by thundering,
When a last 'All-Clear' would prove the last,
My thoughts inconsequently wandering
Among V.1's V.2's and all the waste,
Bomb-values scaling up, and pondering
What tonnage might achieve the final blast,
Turned to the toll of uncomputed things;
Unsalvageable joys that childhood missed,
Uncertainties that isolation brings
And no statistic mind has ever guessed,
The could and might-have-been that never were,
The lungs grief-choked even as the end drew near.

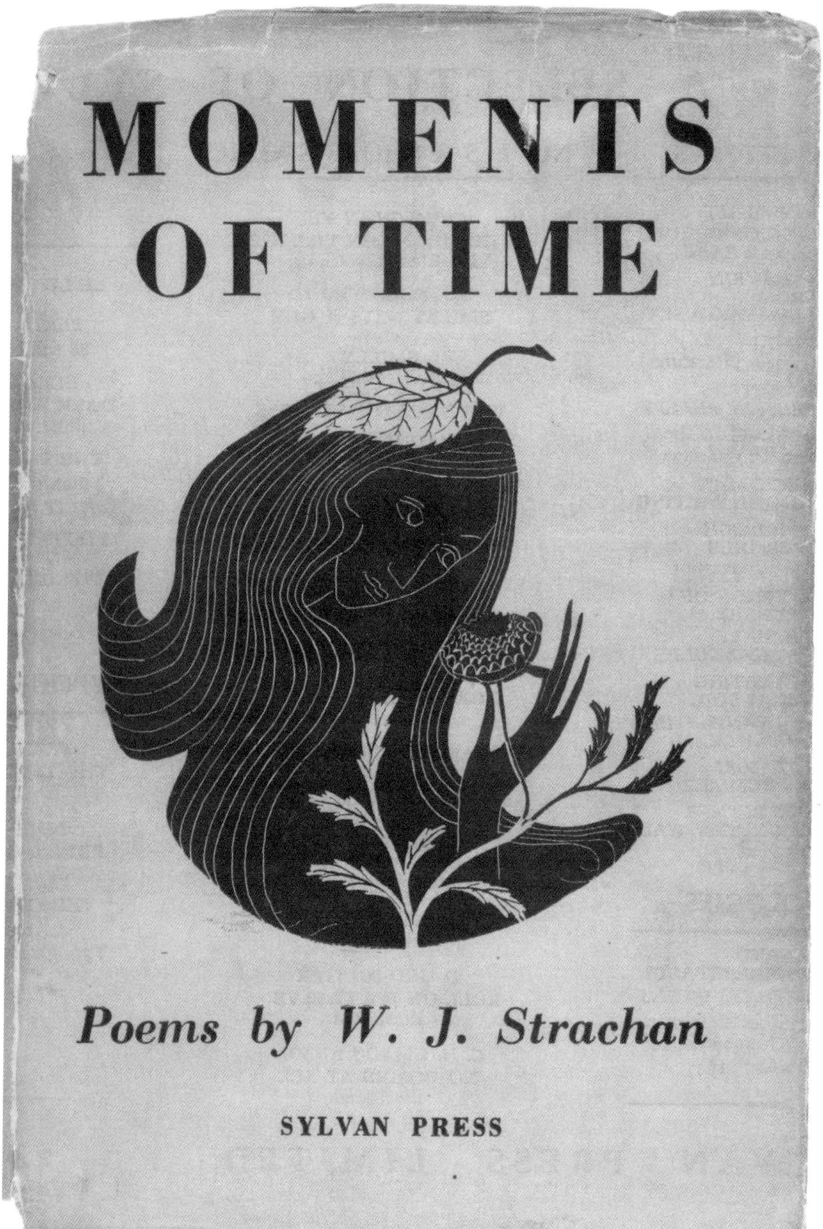
MOMENTS
OF TIME
Poems by W. J. Strachan
SYLVAN PRESS

THE POETRY YEARS

In December 1941 the period of Strachan's separation from his family that had lasted since the summer of 1940 (with remission during school holidays) came to an end, though the stresses and strains of war continued. On the literary front the floodgates had opened. Strachan wrote and published many poems in such periodicals as *The Spectator*, *Time and Tide*, *Our Time*, *The New English Weekly*, *The Adelphi*, *The Wind and the Rain*, *Poetry (London)*, *New Saxon Review*, *Decachord* and *Poetry from Cambridge in Wartime*.

After the war he continued writing poetry and his first volume of verse *Moments of Time* was published in June 1947 by the Sylvan Press, to be followed in June 1950 by a further collection, *The Season's Pause*, published by Secker and Warburg. The years from 1940 to 1950 saw his most prolific output of verse and it was out of this time that the friendships and correspondence arose with the three writers who form the subjects of the next three chapters, Sylvia Townsend Warner, Cecily Mackworth and Stevie Smith. Though still teaching French and German full time at Bishop's Stortford College — as he did until 1968 — Walter Strachan was now a published poet and could meet these writers on equal terms as a member of PEN (the World Association of Writers founded in 1921) and could sympathise from first hand experience with the joys and frustrations of the writer's life.

By 1948 he had also published his anthology of modern French poetry in translation *Apollinaire to Aragon* and in 1950 his first translation of a novel, Julien Gracq's *A Dark Stranger.* His translation work was thus proceeding alongside the writing of his own poetry. So it may seem a little arbitrary to separate 'The Poetry Years' from 'The Translation Years' — as I have done — not least because Nancy Cunard features in both. But I have ventured to make this distinction in arranging Walter's reminiscence of the writers and artists he first met in the forties and fifties, not least because much of the poetry he wrote in those years could be (and was) written before he was first able to return to France in 1949. His translation work, on the other hand, and, overwhelmingly, his writings on the contemporary *livre d'artiste* — and later on tapestry — became greatly dependent on regular contact with and visits to France, where he was to meet writers, publishers, artists and printers.

The titles I have given to each section of this book, and, even more so, the dates, should thus be regarded as more symbolic than literal. Helpful signposts, I hope, at a period of Walter Strachan's life when his interests as writer — and indeed as teacher — were rapidly multiplying and his championship of the work of other poets and of painters, sculptors, graphic artists and calligraphers was gaining momentum, both in the classroom and in the pages of magazines and periodicals.

3 PEN and Sylvia Townsend Warner

Sylvia Townsend Warner was one of a group of four women writers whom I met through the PEN Club. Two were intimate friends of Nancy Cunard, attracted by her magnetic personality and thereby drawn into her field of activity, if only as contributors to her anthology, *Poems for France* [London: La France Libre 1944]. Each had a strong individual identity, both in physical presence and in private and professional writing.

I would see them collectively — if scattered over the dining-tables — only at PEN dinners, but I encountered each one singly: Nancy Cunard on at least five occasions, as well as being her guest at Lamothe Fénelon in France; Cecily Mackworth many times, in London, Dorset and Paris. My only meeting with Sylvia Townsend Warner was on a visit to her house in Frome Vauchurch, Dorset, on one glorious and memorable summer day — and, as will appear, very fruitful. I met Stevie Smith on two occasions in the offices of *Harper's Bazaar*, when I was delivering an article. On one she reminded me with some asperity that I was taking her umbrella. This did not, however, interfere with an interchange of correspondence and the purchase direct from her for some paltry sum of a few of her zany drawings. Of Nancy Cunard she wrote: 'I think I met Nancy once and liked her very much, if it's possible to like a person very much you only think you've met'.

We were all members of the PEN Club (I was elected in April 1946, proposed by Cecily Mackworth, seconded by Nancy Cunard.) We were all francophiles and bonded by a common love of poetry. We had all published verse and translations. We had no declared philosophy beyond a vague 'humanism' but with a Camusian slant. The others, who were more active and less tied down by a job than I was, attended international congresses where freedom of expression and political independence were frequent issues and practically dealt with. The inter-relationship of these women is touching. When Nancy Cunard was exhausted after travel in Mexico she could stay in Sylvia's haven of tranquillity at

Frome Vauchurch. Some years later Stevie Smith writes to me joyfully anticipating her stay with Cecily Mackworth (the 'Marquise') in the château owned by the Marquis de Chabannes, La Pelise.

As our meetings extended into relationships by correspondence, I noted how each of the writers expressed her 'persona' in ways typical of her. Nancy Cunard's *staccato* when in her frantic hurry. Sylvia, the musicologist, moves along at an *andante moderato* unless, indignant about some book or acting, she tears off into an *accelerando furioso*. Stevie Smith's spidery statements always wind up with a formal 'Yours sincerely'. Cecily Mackworth, like Nancy, alternates between poised accounts of people and current events and a journalist's rush when she scribbles on any paper to hand, in one case some old music score. But always a firm hand. I suspect that Sylvia Townsend Warner's love of the baroque is reflected — though I am no graphologist — in her hand with the flowing tails to her descenders, 'g's and 'y's and 'f's.

Before I visited Sylvia at her home in Dorset, we had already established a close relationship. Between her first letter (25 February 1945) and the visit, I had received thirteen letters from her, and we had exchanged ideas on many subjects. It became apparent in the first letter that her urgent preoccupation was with the hungry children of post-Liberation Paris. She had heard from her friend, Nancy Cunard, of their near-starvation and the scarcity of vitamins and medicines. She herself set about collecting parcels of food and medical supplies for Nancy to take over as a privileged envoy. In the same practical vein she suggested that I, as a schoolmaster, might make links between English and French schools. To this end I collaborated with the director of the Lycée de Saint Jean de Saillie in the 16th arrondissement of Paris.

Our correspondence soon passed on to themes of mutual interest. I was able to lend her precious copies of *Poésies* 1944-5, from which I had translated poems for my *Apollinaire to Aragon*, and also, as they became available, copies of Cyril Connolly's *Horizon*. I had seen the tragic actress Korène in *Bérénice* on the occasion of a visit to London of the *Comédie Française* (her performance had moved me to write a poem); Sylvia had seen Marie Bell in *Ruy Blas* ('What an odd play', she adds; 'nineteenth-century baroque'). An observation of mine about André Gide reminded her of a sleepy conversation heard during her journey to the Madrid Congress of Letters, which involved an illegal crossing of the

Spanish frontier. 'Stephen Spender began arguing about Gide who at that time was in bad odour with the puritans. Anne Seghers [of the well-known publishing house] laid her head down and fell asleep. They were still furiously quarrelling when she woke... *"Mais qu'est-ce que vous avez contre ce Gide?"** she inquired in a tone of motherly patience. It was very pretty'.

Her wry comments are as entertaining as her anecdotes. Of Gide's *Les Caves du Vatican:* '... But still at the end of it I came off with the feeling that it is a mistake when authors' right hands do not know what their left hands are doing, however excellent this may be in Christians'.

There seems to be an agreeable dichotomy in one letter which contains a *bon viveur* attitude to wine: '... the most interesting white wine I ever drank was called St Nicholas de Bourgueil: *Côte du Rhône* ... it had the most fascinating husky-dusky-musky bouquet'. Then in the same letter: 'Yes, indeed, let us exchange *Apollinaire to Aragon* and the *Portrait of a Tortoise* [her selections from Gilbert White of Selborne with her illuminating introduction]. Chatto & Windus have gone and printed it rather preciously...', and the Puritan-Quaker strain: ' I shall be sorry when the paper restrictions lift and publishers can return to their fancies of printing on blotting-paper with two-inch margins'.

Her humour: 'I happened the other day to say that I was looking forward to seeing the *Rape of Lucrece* in company of county neighbours. After I had said it I realised that none of them had heard of it, and so they thought my anticipations eccentric'.

I can't think of anyone whose comments are more revealing of the persona. For example, her praise of the Third Programme: 'Did you hear the announcer, t'other night, remark, "We are now running twenty minutes late", as calmly as if we were in a train to Cork or Cadiz? That is what I reckon to be civilization'. Her next letter reminds me of our friend Cecily Mackworth's enthusiasm for Mallarmé and of her own background in musicology. She had made her early acquaintance with him 'entirely through music': 'And finding no obscurity in the music I found no obscurity in Mallarmé'.

Sylvia was not one to let go any use of a word that offended her respect for the word, its etymology, its precise meaning. She won-

* But what have you got against this Gide?

dered, for example, when I used the word 'aftermath' in a poem whether I knew that it was originally applied to a second reaping of a grass crop. After reflecting on her remark about 'episcopal blessing', describing chestnut leaves unfolding (an image I felt pleased about), I scrapped the word. 'I can't bear, even for a moment', she had written, 'that a blithe bishop should get between a chestnut tree and me'.

Her next letter (16 July 1947) concerned our family stay in Dorset and our visit to her house by the trout stream in Frome Vauchurch. She begins flatteringly with my poems in *Moments of Time* and concludes, 'I certainly like your sombre pieces best'. Then the switch: 'Please let me know when you are at Warmwell... for there is a house I want you to see. It belongs to a man called Norman Lupton, and he has a good collection of English pictures; mostly Cozens and Girtins and that school, and one or two of the Sickert period. He likes showing them, and so seldom has anyone in this part of the world who knows a Turner from a Bonington'.

Then the great day. First the pleasure of seeing the cottage: in vernacular Dorset style, honey-coloured limestone that Auden would have appreciated. An intensely green lawn benefitting by the occasional overflow from the trout stream that ran along the bottom of the garden. Cottage-garden plants, I think a responsibility shared between Sylvia and her companion, Valentine Ackland. We met the latter briefly; then she went off to her antique shop.

The children were with us, Jean aged fifteen, Geoffrey twelve. They still, with amusement, recall the seed-cake. They had heard me reminisce about the eternal seed-cake my aunts used to provide with the occasional relief of a madeira. Sylvia put them at their ease, walked with them to the bottom of the garden to watch the stream for any sign of trout. She looked very much as I had imagined her, with humorous grey eyes and hair severely styled. We talked about Dorset, which Margaret and I had fallen in love with from our first holidays there — two years running in 1938 and 1939 — at Charmouth. The second visit had been interrupted by my recall to duty as war became imminent with the news (August 31) of the evacuation of women and children from a London that anticipated immediate air-raids. Sylvia was interested to know that we were now staying in an isolated period house near Warmwell, formerly assigned to retiring abbots of Cerne Abbas. The chalk cliffs were quite close. By a perilous descent among a tangle of barbed wire, we were able to get down and find an uncluttered space to have a swim.

Conversation turned to art. We must, urged Sylvia, see the collection of Norman Lupton and his sister. The house of their design had been purpose-built to contain his pictures, chiefly — as she had written — early English watercolours. She accompanied us to the site, somewhat hidden away, which the Luptons had chosen on an ancient British camp. The building reminded me of a Corbusier villa. I seem to remember that there was independent access to the gallery by an outside staircase, which served as a fire escape. What impressed me most was the quantity of Wilson Steers, not so much of his elongated girls of Walberswick as of Constable-like landscapes. Could they have been of Hadleigh Castle?

I need not have been hesitant about our intrusion at short notice. 'He and his sister, both quite old, quite unmarrying, and rich', Sylvia had written, had 'set to and built a very good modern house and made a hillside into a garden. To do all this without the smallest intention of posterity, purely to please yourself, at that age, seems to me courageous'. In point of fact the pair may well have decided even by that date to bequeath the collection to the Art Gallery at Leeds, of which they were natives. The bequest dates from 1951. I happened on it in Leeds some thirty years later when I went to the newly opened Henry Moore collection, housed in another part of the Gallery. I was even more impressed on this second viewing by the magnificent Yorkshire scenes by Thomas Girtin. More than ever I appreciated Turner's observation 'If poor Tom had lived, I should have starved'.

After that meeting Sylvia became more real to me and our correspondence for the next five letters (up to 1950) took on a more intimate tone — a face to face chat. Then a very long silence. Sylvia had suddenly to give all her attention, medical and emotional, to the ailing Valentine Ackland, who died in 1969. I had a letter (13 February 1970) to say Valentine had died in the previous November. An odd coincidence, I thought, that it was written on the eve of St Valentine's day. But the five intervening letters were full of unforgettable asides such as: 'I am being distracted by a cockchafer which *will* fall on its back and expect me to put it right side up again. Nocturnal insects are always so confiding'. Then her eruption about Montherlant's *Le Maître de Santiago* (I had seen an English version with Sir Donald Wolfit's mouthings — the only way I can describe the sickly lines — at the Cambridge Arts Theatre.) Sylvia writes: 'I heard it on the Third, where I thought they made an execrable performance of it, all talking as if they had some form of religious lockjaw'. We were exchanging views on *The Order of Release*, an account of the relationships between Ruskin, Millais, and Effie Gray. Sylvia thought that Effie's years of conjugal misery had not been well handled: 'It left me with a strong sensation of someone dauntlessly grasping the dock and avoiding the nettle'.

In June 1948 she writes that 'the last sign' she has had from Nancy Cunard was a parcel of real West Indian sugar: 'till now I had always thought of it as some sort of grocer's mineral'. Lapidary phrases fall, unbidden, from her pen, a characteristic of her writing, particularly in her works of the zany *Lolly Willowes* kind. She shares with her Dorset neighbour T.F. Powys (*Mr Weston's Good Wine*) and with David Garnett (*Beany-Eye*) this strange power of evoking ostensibly ordinary country folk and endowing them with the kind of personalities possessed, on a more sophisticated level, by Shakespeare's fools.

When I first corresponded with her, she was at work on 'my interminable novel' *The Corner that Held Them* (1948), a moving story about sisters in a Norfolk nunnery. As in *The Flint Anchor* (1954), the sense of place is strong. I am surprised that writers like Beryl Bainbridge have not dealt with this aspect of her stories. I consider Sylvia's life of T.H. White the best piece of biographical writing of our time; she was just the person to understand that complex character.

This is not the place for assessing her considerable literary oeuvre. Verse writing was important to her. For *Boxwood* she was fortunate in having the wood-engravings of Reynolds Stone as an *obbligato*. He lived in Lytton Cheney, near Dorchester, and she and he had a friend in common, Roger Peers, the director of its County Museum. He had been a pupil of mine before reading history at Brasenose College, Oxford. A close link was forged between them. She became a Friend of the Museum and co-operated in many ways, I believe, in supporting musical events.

Her letters in the seventies have an elegiac tone, following not only the death of Valentine Ackland but that of Nancy Cunard in 1965. 'I often think of Nancy. She never left a blurred impression'. Then, turning to Museum matters, 'Roger Peers, is a kind friend to me. His conversion of the Dorchester Museum from its random dullness into a thing of purpose and excitement has been a long thrill to watch... The last time I saw him he had just been given a sower's 'fiddle' for his Dorset agricultural room. If, the next time I see him, he will have acquired a Phoenix in perfect stuffed condition, not a feather missing, I shan't be in the least surprised'. She ends the letter: 'A book on sculptors' drawings ... I shall look forward to it'. Even when overwhelmed with sadness and failing health, she had sustained her interest in my writings.

In her last letter to me (January 1978: she died in May that year) her critical spirit does not desert her. Commenting on the cover of the paperback edition — 'all I can find' — of *The Flint Anchor* (retitled *The Bernards of Loseby*): which she sent me... 'Even for a popular reprint [it has] a singularly unrepresentative view of its characters. I leave the pleasure of tearing it off to you'. She reverts to her full signature 'Sylvia Townsend Warner' as if asserting her identity which, to the end, every sentence, every witticism betrays.

Author's Notes

1 I received a message from Roger Peers in the summer of 1981 reporting on the very successful party held in the Museum in memory of Sylvia when the room dedicated to her and containing memorabilia was opened. 'It was a distinguished gathering of Sylvia's and Valentine's friends. I was sorry illness prevented your presence'. (I have given her letters to me where they can be seen in the Sylvia Townsend Warner Room.)

2 Valentine Ackland. A poet in her own right of published volumes of verse: She worked for a local doctor as secretary for some time and also ran an antique shop attached to the house where she lived with Sylvia. She had had a difficult life which is graphically described in her book *For Sylvia* which is a touching *confessio amantis* — a deep love for Sylvia, understood, appreciated, but not requited.

4 Cecily Mackworth

It is more than half a century ago. Cecily Mackworth is writing about the situation in Paris in 1940: 'I stood with Jeanne Bucher on the balcony of her art gallery and heard the distant thudding of guns in the eastern suburbs. Her stern old face turned quite white and she said in a low clear voice, "Now God is dead" — a hyperbolic pronouncement that echoed the feelings of all lovers of France the world over. Cecily Mackworth, living in Paris precisely to imbibe its cultural atmosphere and write about it, was caught up in the mass exodus, moving in an unorganized procession to escape from the capital towards the Spanish frontier. In *I Came Out of France* she describes the horrendous conditions of that unholy pilgrimage under continual fire from German Stukas. Thrilled by her account, I noted in my diary (15 January 1949): 'I can't believe, knowing her, all she went through'.

She repeats some of this report in her book *Ends of the World.* As she writes in the opening, 'One has to begin somewhere', and it seemed to me that, in the intricate pattern of my friendship with Cecily Mackworth, it would be appropriate to start with an episode that is history brought alive and that bears witness to her courage and tenacity. Also because part of her story involves meeting the tapestry artist, Jean Lurçat, quite coincidentally at a halt at Aubusson. He was looking after his Polish wife. They were joined next day by their son, Victor. Victor, eager to fight back, had managed to cross the Spanish frontier and get a passage to America where he joined the U.S.forces. It would appear that eventually he served with a parachute unit and asked to serve with the Resistance in the Lot. When I visited his father at Saint Céré in 1952 I could not risk opening an old wound by asking whether he had been shot down or had died in a parachute accident.

Cecily's retroview of the gloom caused by the fall of Paris among people in Britain, in particular those who had cultural links with France, explains the frenetic eagerness over here to learn about what was happening — or had happened — in the realms of books, theatre, cinema, art during those four and more years of repression and isolation. British poets and translators were amazed at the volume and quality of the poetry of the Resistance. Defiance and resilience were expressed in verse of high quality from many writers, notably Eluard and Aragon. During and just after the war we couldn't wait to read the acclaimed plays of Sartre, *Huis Clos*, *Les Mains Sales*, or to hear Gérard Philippe, whose performance in the title role in Corneille's *Le Cid* had set on fire young audiences bored by reading classic plays for the 'Bac'. And then there was Simone de Beauvoir.

Cecily Mackworth entered with zest into the dissemination of all this exciting news. *'Vive la nouvelle poésie!'* she wrote to me, accepting some of my translations of poems by Aragon and Apollinaire and sharing them out between her own collection, *A Mirror for French Poetry*, and Stefan Schimanski's *Transformation 4*. Thrilling for me, and leading to a commission to translate *Un Beau Ténébreux*, a novel by a young writer — pen-name 'Julien Gracq' — of surrealist proclivities, who is now included in the prestigious 'Edition de la Pléiade', along with such names as Camus and Gide.

Following the exchange of a few letters, Cecily and I had our first meeting in London. I made my way to Eyot House, Chiswick Mall, under a moon reflected in the dark Thames water. A strange reversal of Cecily's first return to unblacked Paris, from which she wrote on 11 November 1945: 'I cannot begin to tell you what I felt when I stepped out of the métro Denfert-Rochereau at midnight and saw the Lion de Belfort by moonlight'. My own excitement was over the prospect of meeting someone whose interests so coincided with mine and who seemed *sympathique* and open. We talked chiefly about my translations of the poetry of the Resistance.

Then a second meeting with Cecily. She had discovered a restaurant in Soho where, amazingly, they served duck and white Bordeaux — fie upon austerity! We went on to see the film *Days of Hope*, based on Malraux's novel about China, *L'Espoir*, and a documentary on Henry Moore whose Shelter Drawings were fresh in my mind. After her first visit to our home, she wrote in a charming thank-you letter: 'I wish you had been able to come to the Paragon(!) [i.e. Louis Aragon] party. It was great fun — frightfully distinguished, with Aragon dressed up as an Englishman *à la française*. He read one of his poems, very badly. I was introduced but couldn't think how to open up a conversation so just said *bonjour*

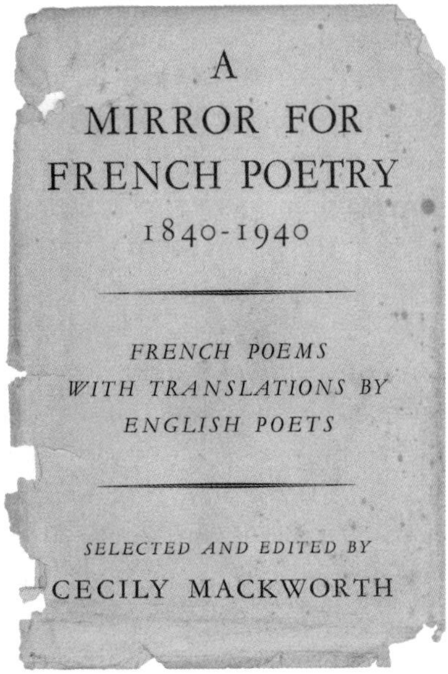

and passed on. One of Claudel's daughters was there in an astonishing Paris hat and I had a long talk to her'. The 'astonishing hat' period coincided with the Liberation. It would seem to have been an implicit defiance of the Germans, by then in flight, and women's exuberance and relief as life was becoming more normal. National feeling in France is often reflected in *haute couture.*

Because of Cecily's uprootings for foreign travel, she was always changing her address. One of her letters is headed '38bis rue Boulard', a studio temporarily vacated by the painter-critic, André Lhote. I was translating his *Traité du Paysage* and *Traité de la Figure*, and rue Boulard, an artists' quarter, became for me a pleasant place of pilgrimage to consult Lhote. His wife invariably invited me to lunch or supper and to see her archaeological collection. André never seemed to wear a suit but worked in pyjamas and dressing-gown. He was for ever losing his glasses, getting into a panic — 'I might as well be dead!' he would moan — until the patient Madame Lhote pointed out that the said article reposed on his, by now, fevered brow.

But here, back in England, a homely note. Cecily paid a visit to us at Robert Pearce House, at the College. We talked, discussed books. She was marvellous with our young children: she had the experience of her own young daughter, Pascale. She enjoyed the occasion enough to suggest a repeat visit, proposing this time to talk on Mallarmé — her pet poet — to my sixth form boys. She records it all in *Ends of the World*, from which I quote. 'We met at Bishop's Stortford where Walter was a schoolmaster... sixth-formers sprawled on the sitting-room floor in front of a blazing log fire... Talking to them about Mallarmé', Cecily continues, 'reading "Les Fenêtres"... I asked them, was it an example of Mallarmé's morbid pessimism, as their Short History of French Literature told them it was? They caught on at once, and a boy with red hair said no, because even if life does seem like *"un triste hôpital"* from time to time, one can always open the window and see *"les galères d'or comme des cygnes/Sur un fleuve de pourpre et de parfums dormir..."* We had tea, then inspected paintings and sculptures Walter collects from France, Italy and Germany... and something of Henry Moore's ...'.

It was an occasion that remained vivid in the memories of at least two of the boys in that audience. Forty years later Peter Rowe, by then retired both from the headship of Bishop's

Stortford College and of Cranbrook School, and Patrick Cullen, retired head of the German department at Christ's Hospital, were still talking about it.

I had been disappointed at having to forgo meeting Aragon, the key Resistance poet in my *Apollinaire to Aragon*. There was to be a second disappointment. Once again duty commitments and a nonconformist conscience prevented my accepting an invitation to meet Jules Supervielle, whose poems I had been translating, to his satisfaction. A consolation was the acceptance by the BBC of my translation of his short story, 'Simone's Levitation', for reading on the Third Programme. It was published, together with a review in *The Listener*. A third disappointment was failing to find my way to a rendezvous with Julien Gracq in Paris in the extensive annexes of La Closeraie de Lilas, as famous for its clientèle as the Café Royal in London. However, I did not fail to attend the dress rehearsal of his play *Le Roi Pêcheur.* I next saw Cecily in Paris in 1953, in the August of which I took her along to the engraver, Albert Flocon's flat, at 93 rue de Seine. He showed us his own copper engravings and work in various media by Johnny Friedlander, with whom he ran the Atelier de l'Ermitage.

One day when I was holidaying in Dorset with the family, there came a summons as peremptory as Nancy Cunard's to the Café Royal two years before: we were to meet Cecily on the beach at Lyme Regis at half-past eleven. This time Pascale was with her mother and the children set to and made a huge house of stones that to them looked indestructible. We adults joined in, enjoying occasional peeps at the Cob and Golden Cap. Cecily reminisced in a letter (13 October 1948): 'I am back from Italy. While I am playing house [in Paris] you are wandering on the beach seeking for treasure [our fossilizing] — a sort of blotting-paper image of our real lives... I wonder if there's still a vestige of that house on the beach at Lyme...'.

To me Cecily's most important contribution is her understanding treatment, in *English Interlude* (1974), of four off-beat French poets to whose work she brings her specialist approach. Her portrayal of the periods in England of Mallarmé, Verlaine, Paul Valéry and, especially, Valery Larbaud, is not only illuminating about their reaction to English manners but extends to the English circles, especially in Larbaud's case, in which they moved. The marvellously eccentric early twentieth-century writer Valery

Larbaud, who took the pen-name 'A.Barnabooth' from the place-name 'Barnes' and 'booth' from the booths which were to him an intriguing feature of the Crystal Palace. And what an endless supply of information and gossip he supplied to French editors of the time! A similarly bilingual Cecily Mackworth was just the writer to introduce this amazing quartet; each one with a different attitude to England and the English.

There is an air of confidence, justifiably, in her autobiographical-cum-travel book *Ends of the World* (1987). I find it refreshingly frank. The passages about the disillusions that inevitably follow certain childhood expectations, first published in *Orion 3*, are movingly written. The philosophy that seems to emerge is akin to that of Camus in *Sisyphe*. But the toil is not worthless. Implicit, too, is the transcendental value of great literature and art. I quote briefly from the childhood paragraphs. Her sense of being unique: 'Each birthday was a step forward, a flag planted in the soil of my own land. Every thought which formed in my brain seemed to me an absolutely unique event'. She had picked a white narcissus from the 'flowerbed on the second terrace of our Somerset garden...' 'No-one before me, and no-one ever again would see the sun glowing through that exact texture of white petal... it was one of the flowers of my island...! Well it was all a mistake. There was just a collection of cells, roughly coagulated in the shape we know as human... And death? I had thought a good deal about death and believed it to be the ultimate possession of my island... However, it appeared I had been foolish and that my death would merely mean the unnatural order of the cells returning to their natural order. But the trouble is that my *dulce et decorum* island has become a habit... I have created my own monument'.

Cecily Mackworth's plea can perhaps be for the transcendental power of the word: 'It can have an occult power to wrench soul from body'. This reminds me of Herbert Read, who compares this feeling to the vision of the mystic. Blaise Pascal attributed all our trouble to our inability to stay quiet in a room. The contemplative life has not been for Cecily Mackworth. Travel and work. But Cecily's doubting mind can find consolation in the contribution she has made and is making to scholarship and entertainment in at least two countries.

DUALITY

For C.M.

Did not Pascal attribute human ill
To inability to stay put in a room,
And Marcel Proust exclude the noises off
With walls cork-lined so that he could,
Easing asthmatic cough,
Unwind slow-motion pictures of the past
For his distressful pleasure?
But what had Pascal been without the silences,
The eternal silence of the vast spaces,
Beyond the walls?
Most conscious he of what to us is dead
Whose feeble antennae wave about
Half atrophied,
Responsive only to the big sensation.
Of what Proust stored in his short lease our minds
Scarce store a tenth. Not that events mattered;
They were but the foam. The undertow,
The hidden swell, the sea's mysterious currents
Were what he charted.
The internecine wars of jealousy,
The quests for happiness, that Holy Grail
That puzzles the blond heads of Anglo-Saxons
Who sink their problems in a cross-word clue,
Discuss their duties, when to buy and sell.

I think of this and how we live who wish
To deal in words and traffic in impressions,
You who sway like a water-weed in the stream,
Whose roots, flimsy, suffice.
For you, my dear, these things are not so simple,
Who feel a two-fold tug,
Not always able to move or stay behind.
Though we shall argue in our duologue,
I who chiefly stay and you who wander,
I shall remember your impulse to play houses,
Under a kitchen table or on beaches,

You, mine, to get away from walls and fixed places,
To write poems in trains, on café-tables.
Both perverse to what our instinct teaches.
We shall meet at those points where dual forces
Cancel each other out.
Our work shall be their final resolution,
We who must map our individual courses.

5 Stevie Smith

Although my relationship with Stevie Smith ('Stevie' mockingly after the famous jockey Steve Donaghue because of her riding on a London common) was less close than that with her friend, Cecily Mackworth, it was important at the point in my life when I discovered her poems and her drawings for them. I have already called the drawings 'zany', but how otherwise to describe them? It will appear from a letter which I will quote later that I was the first person ever to wish to acquire originals of some of them.

It was at PEN Club dinners at the Rembrandt Hotel in Kensington that I was to hear more of that cutting, nasal voice which had challenged me when mistakenly I picked up her umbrella. She would release some shaft of wit, some devastating put-down, and Baroness Budberg, who for some reason was often seated opposite me, would look surprised but not enough to drop her monocle, which seemed glued in. At first this voice, issuing from so diminutive a figure with straight lank hair and anachronistic fringe — Irving Wardle recalls her scurrying through the *Observer* offices like a tiny Beatrix Potter mouse — was off-putting. But my voice is my fortune, sir, she said. It became more widely known from BBC poetry readings when, as before private audiences, she would burst into a banshee wail to suit a particular poem.

For the origins of her virtuosity as a performer and, to some extent, her idiosyncratic drawings, we have to go back to her childhood education at Miss Hum's enlightened academy, Palmers Green High School. Girls' high schools in my and Stevie's time were mostly havens for middle-class 'gels'; and Palmers Green, with its high standards of English teaching and poetry reciting, was the ideal place for Stevie and another girl destined for fame, the actress Flora Robson. Stevie must also have owed to the school her love of French literature, and hence her remarkable gift for incorporating passages from French poetry to great effect in her own. She translated 'Athalie's Dream' from Racine's tragedy, but more often plays around with the language as in '*Le Singe qui swing*'.

She had little if any tuition in art, but no teacher seems to have reproached her for her eternal doodling — her comic portraits of school companions — or called it a waste of time. The school's firm discipline did not in fact inhibit the girls' free expression.

In contrast, the home background was less happy: real happiness or contentment dates from when her aunt, Margaret Spear ('the Lion of Hull') took over Stevie and her elder sister Molly, materially, domestically and more or less financially. Their mother was always ailing, and did not get on with her seafaring husband. The family almost welcomed his absences at sea which, during the First World War, were prolonged. So there was little influence from that quarter, despite Stevie's occasional indulgence in a little romancing about him and about his father who, up to his bankruptcy, was quite a figure in the Hull shipping world.

Stevie's biographer, Frances Spalding, consulted me for background information on the Hull of that period. My own parents were contemporaries of the Smiths, and I must have passed their Victorian house in Park Street on my way to the Park Street Unitarian Church. But whereas my father used to bring dockland alive for me on our walks, the Smith family apparently offered little reason for any such romancing. Nor is there a hint of romantic nostalgia in anything Stevie reports about her aunt. 'I will tell you about her. She is looking like a lion... This lion has a very managing disposition, is strong, passionate, has enormous moral strength, is a fine old Fielding creation'. In Stevie's character, too, there was a northern, spartan, puritan element.

Her father worked for the Wilson line: 'Hull is Wilsons and Wilsons are Hull', to quote her biographer. Park Street, Hull, was a good address, but financial stringencies caused them to look elsewhere for a house. 1 Avondale Road, Palmers Green, in North London, it was, and there first the Smiths, then Stevie and her aunt, and finally Stevie alone lived until their deaths. On one occasion Cecily Mackworth sallied out to Palmers Green to see and, I

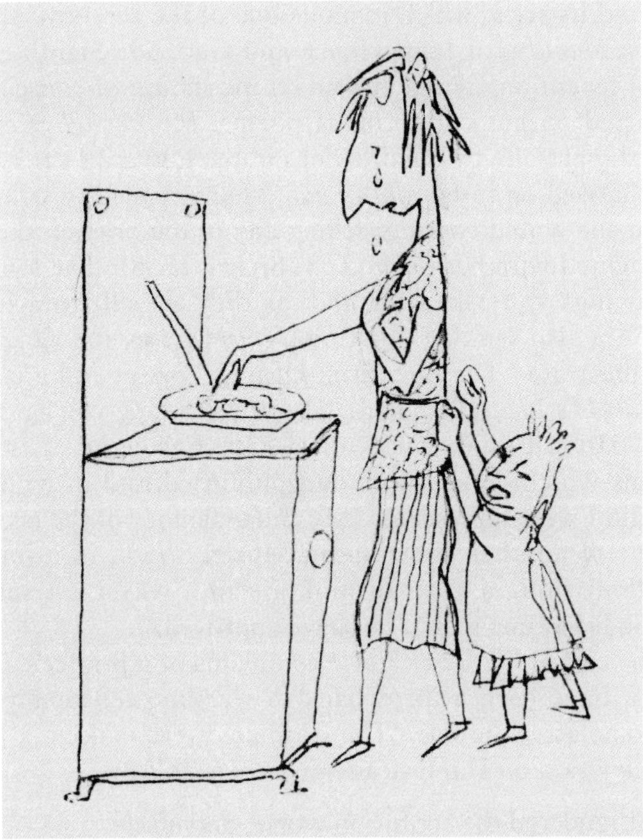

suppose, interview Stevie. In her *Ends of the World* she reports her impressions of the spartan furniture, particularly of Stevie's bed and bedroom with no bedside lamp. She found Stevie touchy and aggressive, a mixture of naivety and sly wit. 'She was always exhausted'. True, she lived on her nerves, and the faults Cecily finds in the person become important ingredients, indispensable in her verse.

Stevie (christened Florence Margaret) gives a frank and only partly disguised account of her persona as 'Pompey' and of her friends, acquaintances and employers in her *Novel on Yellow Paper* (white was reserved for her official work). For most of her working life she was secretary to Sir Frank Newnes of magazine publishing fame. Her work was not arduous, her employer not exacting. An ideal situation for the compulsive writer she had been since childhood. The success of *Novel on Yellow Paper* is due to its gossip and its style, which reminds one of the eccentric author of *Tristram Shandy*, of James Joyce and Gertrude Stein's effective tricks of repetition unified into an erratic stream-of-consciousness.

I started on her collection of poems, *Mother what is Man?*, attracted especially by the drawings in the Edward Lear tradition. When I moved on to *Harold's Leap*, I felt impelled to write to her to ask if she would consider selling any of the original sketches. I was delighted with her reply (22 February 1958): 'I've looked out the drawings you asked for and, as they are all from *Harold's Leap*, I am also sending one from *Not Waving*, the King Arthur one to illustrate "The Blue from Heaven" poem and a large one from *Harold's Leap* (Pad, Pad)... I enjoyed seeing you again at the Owens' party'. I think it was to celebrate *Springtime 2*, a volume of poems which Peter Owen had published and in which both Stevie and I were represented. My chief memory of the occasion is the sight of another contributor, Muriel Spark, in a long pink dress, flourishing a glass of pink gin in a way I am sure Miss Brodie in her prime would not have approved.

At the end of her letter Stevie complains of a printer's omission (could it have been a throwback to wartime censorship?). The lines 'come after the line "The Germans were making a particularly heavy raid on Hampstead" and are as follows:

What rendered the confusion worse, perversely
Our bombers had chosen that moment to set out for Germany

Sickening, isn't it?' She was ever watchful for errors and her second thoughts must have been a printer's nightmare. I have some of the first editions from her in which she has written in corrections or changes.

In her next letter (7 March 1958) she writes: 'You really are most noble to patronise the Arts in this forthright splendid way, most people just content themselves with saying "Very nice"! So I am grateful and will perhaps leave you a wodge of scrappy other drawings when I die (which I feel sure will be before you do)'. In fact I made a later request to buy a few more drawings, but by then her fame had spread, and BBC Television had collared the lot. But, to my knowledge, they are still unexposed.

Some publishers and editors whom she approached with batches of poems and drawings were keen enough on publishing the poems but balked at the drawings or severely restricted the number. While the nonsense drawings of Edward Lear or — say — Nicholas Bentley's for Belloc's *Cautionary Tales*, for all their crazy subjects, betray the hand of the trained artist, Stevie's are unprofessional. She herself admits problems in coping with the lower limbs. Compare these formless appendages with the vestigial legs of Lear's Yonghy-Bonghy-Bò. But hers is never child art nor even, like Dubuffet's, a parody of it.

Her next communication (28 March 1958) enclosed *errata* slips for me to pass on to my daughter Jean, whom she had met in the *Observer* office 'and anyone else who has the book, as I tremble to think of any single copy going around un-corrected!'

By 1959 Stevie was becoming known nationally. Her readings of her own poems were popular among the intelligentsia, and the BBC joined in to produce a play with a surrogate Stevie. She wrote (23 May 1959): 'I am so glad you liked that creepy broadcast... I took rather against the Female Character (*Me*, I mean, not the young actress who played it). We sounded, as written by me, a bit like a dotty deb! Still, can't be helped. It was just an experiment'.

Her letters are illumined by some touches of wit, often of a mock self-deprecatory kind. A propos languages, for example (she had taught herself German): 'Everyone seems to think I'm polylingual. A Swiss prof wrote a long piece, very flatteringly!, about me in the *Neue Züricher Zeitung*, very tricky that was, but I recognized my name and the titles of my books. I'm sure you're right about "les chants désespérés". I believe I lifted it, probably inaccurately, from Huxley's *Texts and Pretexts* — must turn it up'.

My final exchange of letters with her was about her poem 'O Pug!' — a favourite with me and one or two of my calligraphers. There is an element of 'Not waving but drowning' in many of Stevie's animal poems.

She was always looking at herself from outside: the title of the posthumous collection (1981), *Me Again*, is very apt. She sometimes had to face an unsympathetic audience, unused to her bursts of tuneless song. But her fundamental self-confidence about the merit of her work, especially after she had been awarded the Queen's Medal for Poetry in 1969, two years before her death, enabled her to face these uncomfortable moments.

PART THREE

THE TRANSLATION YEARS AND FRENCH BOOK ILLUSTRATION

1948–1960

PARIS TWIN-GALLEYS

From time of swamp to perfumed Lebanon
Paris, twin-galleys here at anchor rode;
And then through tale of palace come and gone,
Of private griefs of glory spread abroad,
Of Roman emperors, of Napoleon…
When our forefathers harnessed to the load,
Who kings had borne and thrice a people's throne,
Hung over slanting oars with shoulders bowed.

We, too, are chained to this, the well-worn seat,
With body, mind and soul must ply the oars,
Bent, broken, bruised but not effete,
Slave on these galleys here between her shores:
Our soul the phoenix rising from defeat,
Our body crouched by Notre-Dame's grey towers.

Translated from the French of Charles Péguy

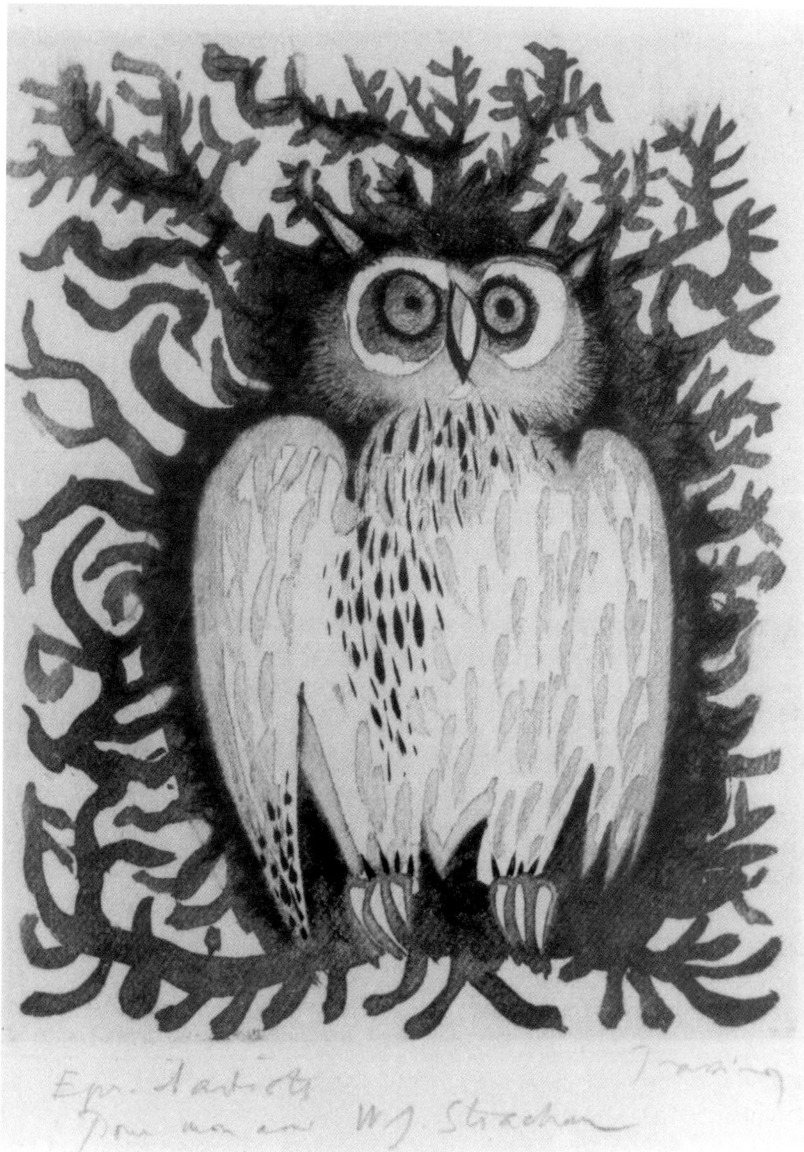

THE TRANSLATION YEARS AND FRENCH BOOK ILLUSTRATION

During the early war years, from 1940 onwards, Walter Strachan had devoted much time to reading and writing poetry. But alongside his own poems, his committed interest in French life and French culture had led him to begin translating poems by a wide range of twentieth-century French poets. Following the publication of his first volume of poems *Moments of Time*, his anthology *Apollinaire to Aragon*, containing his own translations of poems by thirty modern French poets, was published by John Cullen at Methuen in 1948.

The end of the war in Europe in May 1945 — though it left a continent ravaged by appalling privations on both sides and still reeling at the discovery of atrocities perpetrated during the war years — could only be welcomed for the relief it brought — the slow return to some kind of cultural normality: the lifting of the ban on flying kites, the return to public view at the National Gallery of great paintings that had been stored away in safety since the beginning of the war. Such events were recorded in Strachan's own poems,* as hope for the triumph of the human spirit, emerging from the darkness, dared to raise its voice.

But already in May 1945 just a few days after V.E. Day (and also at the National Gallery in London) Strachan had encountered, as he later recorded, tangible evidence of the resilience of the human spirit, expressed in words and images, in what was to prove one of the great revelations of his life. This was the exhibition of twentieth-century French illustrated books — *livres d'artiste*, limited editions illustrated with original autographic prints. These ranged from books created early in the century to editions produced in France during the long years of the German occupation, both by established artists, such as Derain and Picasso and by a younger generation of *peintres-graveurs*, who were to flourish after the war. It was above all in the 1950s, when he was able to return to France, that Strachan pursued his quest, to study and spread the word about this thrilling range of artistic and literary creation — a triumphal marriage between words and images that he seemed to have been searching for all his life.

Meanwhile translation, at first from French and later from German and finally from Italian (which he decided to learn round about 1950), became a major activity of this period, as a simple list of his publications at that time shows. Having begun with poetry and the volume *Apollinaire to Aragon* in 1948, he published translations of two

* See appendix.

important books on art by André Lhote, *Treatise on Landscape Painting* (1950) and *Figure Painting* (1953). He published five translations of novels from the French: Julien Gracq: *A Dark Stranger* (1950); Hervé Bazin: *Grasping the Viper* (1950) and *Head Against the Wall* (1952); Georges Bernanos: *Night is Darkest* (1953); Jacques Chardonne: *The Wife of Jean Barnery* (1955) and *Pauline* (1956). He also translated an autobiographical book by Jean Cocteau: *My Journey Round the World* (1958).

During the same dozen years he also published translations from the German of two works of fiction by Hermann Hesse: *The Prodigy* (1957) and *Demian* (1958); as well as a volume, *Modern Italian Short Stories* (1955), which he selected and translated, two volumes by Cesare Pavese: *The Political Prisoner* (1955) and *The House on the Hill* (1956) and a volume by Vera Cacciatore: *The Swing* (1959).

As a teacher of modern languages, Strachan had always been committed to offering his pupils the stimulus of exposure to the best literary texts in whatever language, not a practice shared by all teachers. This was reflected in the publication of two educational editions: *Ici Paris* (1952) and *Ici les Provinces* (1956), selections of French literary texts, edited by himself, and an edited edition of Albert Camus: *La Peste* (1959), the first of the series Twentieth Century Texts, which for many years he was to edit for Methuen.

There are three chapters in this section, all with overlapping themes. Strachan's account of his friendship with Nancy Cunard, which began in the years of the war, also covers many aspects of his own writing (and teaching) life during the forties and fifties. His passionate interest in typography and italic handwriting, fostered among his pupils, is a recurring theme. Following this chapter, I have included an edited version of the account he wrote for the catalogue published by the Taylor Institution, Oxford, on the occasion of the inaugural exhibition for the W.J. Strachan Gift (made in 1987) of his collection of complete books and *bonnes feuilles*. This tells in impressionistic style the story of his discovery of the French *livre d'artiste*, evoking the energy he devoted to making the books known in Britain through his writings and exhibitions. It also refers to some of the many friendships with artists, writers, publishers and printers that arose from this. The third chapter in this section refers across to the previous two. It is Strachan's account of a visit to Jean Lurçat's studio at Saint Céré in the Lot in 1952 at the time when he was staying with Nancy Cunard. This visit first fired his interest in modern French tapestry, about which he wrote a number of articles and gave many lectures, culminating in his last public lecture (on Jean Lurçat) at the Victoria and Albert Museum in 1990.

6 Nancy Cunard and Post-War France

> 'Anyone who says "Nancy Cunard" to me alerts my goodwill'. SYLVIA TOWNSEND WARNER

It is now (as I write this), an impossible twenty-six years since Nancy Cunard met her tragic death in Paris in 1965. Yet I am still haunted by memories of my twenty-year friendship with her. Her fascinating personality springs to life whenever I dip into my archive of letters, postcards, scribbled notes etc. Some are lengthy typed letters, characterized by the misbehaviour of her ancient machine with broken-off 'Y' and holes punctured through flimsy paper by the letter 'O' which makes the sheet look like a pianola record. When handwritten, a nervous script, not without calligraphic qualities, as befits a hand practised in typesetting on her own press.

My correspondence with her dates back to November 1943 when she was preparing her anthology *Poems for France.* One translation I submitted which she particularly liked was too late for inclusion. This was my translation; 'Paris Twin-Galleys' of Charles Péguy's poem 'Paris Double-Galère'. However, at her suggestion I sent it to Raymond Mortimer who published it in the 'Liberation of Paris' issue of the *New Statesman* (26 August 1944). I followed this up with my translations of other French poets of the Resistance, Eluard, de la Tour du Pin, for Nancy's comments. She liked them.

Then the magic summons from her address in Jermyn Street: 'Café Royal, Regent Street, at 6.15p.m., in the big café on the ground floor. *Mon signalement:* old beige large coat with high fur collar. Will this suit? Work making everything impossible; but look forward to meeting you. N.C'.

At the age of forty-nine, she could not quite be the famous beauty who had attracted such literary figures as David Garnett, Aldous Huxley, Harold Acton and Louis Aragon. But no wartime clothes could conceal that tall, elegant figure. Her headdress, stiff kiss-curls, the ivory bangles that clothed her slender arms were as much her dress and style as the strange three-cornered hat and draperies were of her friend, Edith Sitwell. But much less self-conscious. The bracelets were part of her African collection. Nothing however could deflect attention from her eyes which seemed to change colour: early admirers described them as 'deep blue' or alternatively 'green as jade'.

She had doubtless inherited the beauty of her mother, Lady Cunard, the American wife of Sir Bache Cunard, and a celebrated hostess who entertained the famous at the large mansion, Nevill Holt in Northamptonshire. Sir Thomas Beecham was among her regular guests. But of all this I was ignorant at the time, and the matter in hand was poetry and translation — and France. France was still recovering from the effects of the German Occupation. How could we writers and academics help in practical as well as cultural activities?

One of the outcomes of our businesslike chat over a simple lager was that I got in touch with her friend, Cecily Mackworth, who was preparing her anthology of translations. She suggested I translate Apollinaire's long poem 'Zone', a work that opened a new attitude to the material and treatment of poetry: a kind of sophisticated primitivism, akin to that of Douanier Rousseau in painting. We also discussed typography, which I fostered at Bishop's Stortford College. So it was exciting and stimulating to hear her talk about her own press, The Hours Press, the subject of her book *These Were the Hours*, [published posthumously in 1969]. Exciting but disquieting. Exciting because of the writers she had published, Samuel Beckett (his first separately published work, *Whoroscope*) and Harold Acton (*This Chaos*) among them. Disquieting, because Nancy had just heard that the premises in Réanville, Normandy, where all the press material was housed, had been raided and ransacked by the Germans, only a few Hours Press titles surviving in the rubble.

Very soon there was a follow-up to this encounter; she would visit us at our home in Bishop's Stortford. She came in the middle of a severe winter spell on 7 January 1945. The day before I had been tobogganing with the children. The same day my translation of Aragon's 'Nuit de Mai' was accepted by *Modern Reading*: good news to greet Nancy with. I met her at the station and realised her imperative need for a rum — a *romolo*, she euphemistacally called her favourite tipple. Margaret produced a lunch of veal olives and we washed it down with the last bottle of claret available in the town. Immediately after the meal, Nancy squatted on the floor and chatted with twelve-year-old Jean and nine-year-old Geoffrey

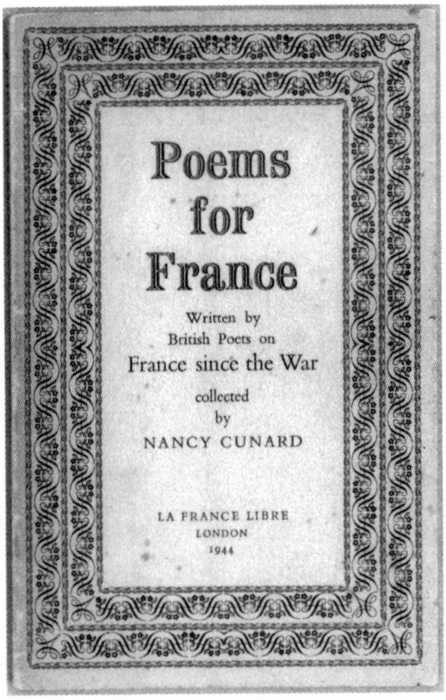

— no talking down to them on her part. In the middle of her reminiscences the children announced the emergence of a butterfly from its chrysalis.

Then tea and talk of poetry, English and French, until it was time to take her to her 6.45 train back to a Liverpool Street still in war-time blackout.

Nancy was a catalyst to me, as she was, I believe, to other young poets at the time. 'I want a poem from you', she told her novelist friend, Irene Rathbone, when they were talking about her anthology, *Poems for France*. Irene Rathbone: 'But I'm not a poet; you are mistaking me for someone else'. Nancy: 'I mistake you for no-one. I've read a poem of yours. Your only one? What do I care?'

Nancy took an interest in my writing on typography; I had just begun reviewing books on it and related subjects for *Tribune*, whose literary editor, George Orwell, had accepted my translation of Aragon's 'Dunkerque': I used to receive letters from his acting secretary, Barbara Hepworth. Nancy also followed my acceptances of English poems in the 'little reviews' which were a feature of the war and post-war years. She wrote that she had loved the day with us. It was the start of a friendship, based on shared interests, which lasted right up to her final postcard of 1965, the year of her death.

In 1941 I had written a sonnet (published in *Time and Tide*) prompted by the tragic suicide of Virginia Woolf.* Nancy compared her editorial and printing-press activities with Virginia's for the Hogarth Press. Virginia and Leonard had warned her: 'Your hands will always be covered with ink!' At any rate the Woolfs believed enough in the poetic merit of Nancy's own text, *Parallax*, to launch it as their first publication. Nancy was amusing about her publisher. 'Having known Virginia', she wrote, 'one should read James Joyce with a strong drink — what Stulik used to qualify as "hearing the anchels sing"'.

* See appendix.

Parallax impressed T.S. Eliot enough for him to include a section inspired by Nancy's poetry in *The Waste Land* but omitted, on Ezra Pound's advice, from the final version. In her realistic poems such as 'Gens d'Espagne' she showed her sympathy for Republican Spain and the ordinary Spanish people. Her own taste was rather for the surrealist poems of her friend, Tristan Tzara, inventor of Dadaism. She was thrilled to hear that he liked the translation of a poem of his that I proposed to include in my *Apollinaire to Aragon*. It was recited in the poet's presence at a session in the rooms of Miron Grindea, editor of *Adam*, in Emperor's Gate, Kensington. Tzara gave a lecture on his pet theme '*Langage et Poésie*' which few, including Cecily Mackworth and myself, could follow. But he liked my translation, and I met him again in Paris, and have the original limited and signed edition of his poem, *Les Miennes*, illustrated with etchings by Jacques Villon.

In a long article, written for *Horizon* in 1945, Nancy covered almost every aspect of post-Liberation France. Ever practical, she had taken supplies of vitamins for underfed French children and did some organizing in that direction, helped at this end by Valentine Ackland and Sylvia Townsend Warner. Her report on cultural life in Paris emphasised the courage of intellectuals under the Occupation. She told how Paul Eluard had escaped capture by taking refuge in an asylum. She paid tribute to the Jewish poet, Max Jacob, tortured and killed by the Gestapo. But she dwelt on the new creative spirit: the Sartre play *Huis Clos* (noted for the line *'l'enfer c'est les autres'*), the popularity of the plays of Albert Camus, the liveliness of the arts. Picasso and Derain had remained in Paris, Picasso absorbed in his aquatint illustrations to Buffon's *L'Histoire Naturelle*, Derain with novel colour woodcuts for Rabelais' *Pantagruel*. It was heartening news after the four years of silence.

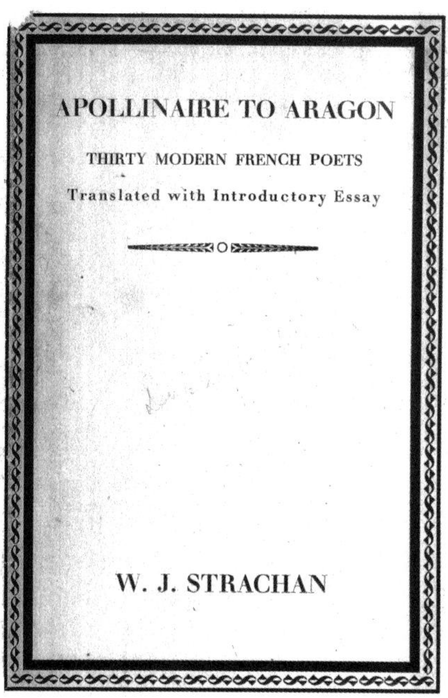
APOLLINAIRE TO ARAGON

THIRTY MODERN FRENCH POETS

Translated with Introductory Essay

W. J. STRACHAN

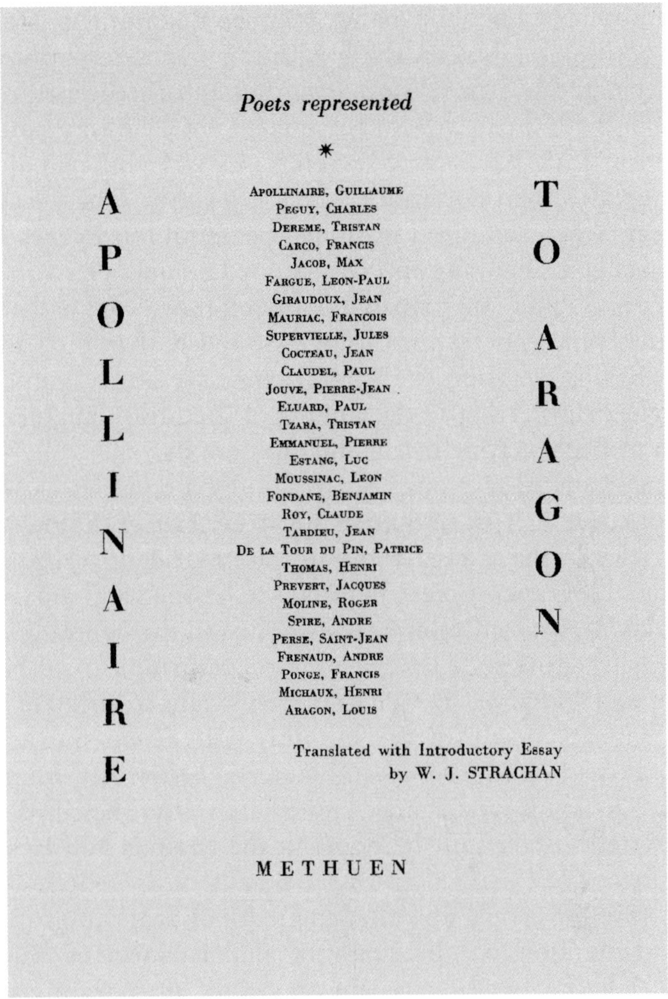

Poets represented

*

A P O L L I N A I R E

Apollinaire, Guillaume
Peguy, Charles
Dereme, Tristan
Carco, Francis
Jacob, Max
Fargue, Leon-Paul
Giraudoux, Jean
Mauriac, Francois
Supervielle, Jules
Cocteau, Jean
Claudel, Paul
Jouve, Pierre-Jean
Eluard, Paul
Tzara, Tristan
Emmanuel, Pierre
Estang, Luc
Moussinac, Leon
Fondane, Benjamin
Roy, Claude
Tardieu, Jean
De la Tour du Pin, Patrice
Thomas, Henri
Prevert, Jacques
Moline, Roger
Spire, Andre
Perse, Saint-Jean
Frenaud, Andre
Ponge, Francis
Michaux, Henri
Aragon, Louis

T O A R A G O N

Translated with Introductory Essay
by W. J. STRACHAN

METHUEN

Apropros book-illustration, Nancy had been struck by the copper engraving on our walls, signed and dedicated by Stephen Gooden. It came from George Moore's *Peronnik the Fool*, of which she had published an edition in 1928, two years earlier than Gooden's.

The re-opening of communications with France, at first for journalists and officials, made possible for me a reunion with an old friend from my stay in Tours in the 1920s, Madeleine Baudouin, now on the staff of *Le Matin*. She announced her visit to London and, in due course, we were lunching at Brown's Hotel in Albemarle Street, which so many French people favoured. We talked about her new husband, Jacques Renault. As Madeleine was working on a project to do with the theatrical world the fact that her name was now Madeleine Renault threatened to cause confusion with the actress of the same name. She wanted the permission of J.M. Barrie's ex-secretary, Lady Cynthia Asquith, to adapt a play or plays of his for French television. First we talked of past years when she, speaking in her beautiful *tourangeau* French, had long ago excited my enthusiasm for La Fontaine's *Fables*. Her reading had made me realise how much more sophisticated and witty the French poet's versions of Aesop were than the Latin originals. On this occasion she was wearing the extravagant type of hat I referred to earlier in the context of Claudel's daughter. It was quite a problem getting her in and out of taxis.

Nancy Cunard was once referred to by a reviewer as 'A Rebel without causes'. It is, of course, not true. Her anthology *Negro*, her articles in the *Guardian* about maltreatment of Republican prisoners by Franco's men, her defence of Spanish bank workers on strike in post-war Spain are evidence to the contrary. 'Strike, strike', she wrote in a letter to me on returning from her fact-finding tour of Spain. 'People are always right to strike in the last resort'. In an article in the monthly *Our Time* she wrote an appraisal, with all the first-hand material before her, founded on her visits to south-west France immediately after the allied victory, of the intellectuals and their role in the Maquis and Resistance generally.

It is rare for people absorbed in great political causes to devote love and attention to individuals not similarly involved. But not so Nancy, whether writing to me on behalf of a restaurateur in Mexico about how Piccadilly got its name, or putting me in touch with a French schoolmaster who wanted to arrange an exchange of correspondence, or — this most vital for me — tackling her former lover, Aragon, to get his written permission for the inclusion in my anthology of my translations of his poems from *Crève-Coeur* and *Les Yeux d'Elsa*.

I was delighted when one of the original poems of mine she liked appeared in *Modern Reading* as, by a happy coincidence, did a poem by my former teacher, John Redwood Anderson, by now an established poet. There was nothing, it seemed, I could do in return, but I was able to find a copy of 'The City of Dreadful Night' by James Thompson for the poet Joë Bousquet, now permanently bedridden as a result of a serious wound received during the 1914 War. Although physically incapacitated, he had been able to help in the Regional Resistance in Carcassonne. He wrote me a pathetically grateful letter in English: 'Will you receive, dear Sir, a thousand thanks, and never forget a lying [sic] man, in Carcassonne, who is in love with England and loves the dearest Nancy Cunard'. I was moved to write a poem about him that found its way into my first volume of original poems, *Moments of Time*.*

Still under the sign of NC and in marvellous 1945, the year that brought peace and relief to millions, I had luck in my private life. Trivial-seeming, but evidence of Nancy's pervasive goodwill. November, out of the blue from Paris, a long letter from an American journalist, Morris Gilbert. It ran: 'Nancy has told me of the interest instilled by you among your pupils about *Le Canard Enchaîné*, and it struck me as so remarkable that I felt you would not mind if I wrote about this extraordinary paper, in case your students don't know the details...'. It was ten years later that Nancy summed up this extension of her interest in my pupils. 'Do you know', she wrote, 'that I have your boys constantly in mind for *These Were the Hours*: that's some of the public I'd like'.

Nancy Cunard at Lamothe-Fénelon in Lot, France

On January 2, 1947, Nancy wrote to me from Paris, that she was demented at not having a place of her own. Then, November 16, that same year: 'I now have a HOUSE, a nutshell, absolutely complete with every discomfort and inconvenience and a veritable network of fissures... My little old woman of the Lot totters about, stone-deaf, competent, undeterrable!' This was Madame Achille, on whom Nancy depended. I encountered her on my visit there some years later in 1952. Madame Achille was still with her in 1955 when Nancy reported in a PS to a letter of June 20. 'There's a *divertissement* for your amusement next year. Get Madame Achille (surely you remember her) on to the question of *assurances sociales et allocations familiales* — a perennial red-hot subject. She has me in convulsions of laughter while I type this. It is all seventeenth-century; '*allez-vous embardouiller ailleurs!*' is

* See page 102.

what she roared at the tax-collector, *'on a bien assez d'emmerdements dans cette maison sans vous!...'**

I certainly remembered Madame Achille and her mutterings about the strange hours Nancy kept (rising just before lunch etc) *'Mais, zut, ce n'est pas normal!'*** My visit there was memorable.

'You must meet Pierre Betz (director of the *Revue artistique et littéraire, Le Point*)' she insisted, 'he is very *sympathique*, and knows everything about this region. And you'll love his *Edition Le Point*'.

It was my first morning. I had arrived from Paris by train at 5am. However, fortified with coffee and a couple of croissants, I took a bus to Souillac. After a halt to visit the church of *Saint-Marie*, with its Byzantine cupolas and strange sculpture, a carved stone figure, popularly known as 'the dancing prophet' (Isaiah), I made my way to the *librairie*-cum-office where Pierre Betz, briefed by Nancy, expected me.

He was a tall, burly man who had an arm injury, the result of a wound received on the Marne in World War 1. He gave me a warm welcome and seemed eager to pass on information about Lascaux, which I was planning to visit. He talked to me about the researches on the subject — the archaeological and aesthetic importance of the writing of the Abbé Breuil. Next the *Edition Le Point*. He handed me a few issues — most had been sold out (*épuisés*). However, he found one or two, to which Nancy added as they came out.

My last is No. 60 and was published in 1960. Betz had launched the review in 1936 and there were four numbers a year. They were bound in plain boards of various colours and their dimensions, 30 by 20cms, suited the sepia photographs and occasional colour reproductions. *Le Point* is basically thematic and each issue carries on the inside back cover the titles of all the preceding numbers. Sensibly, Betz narrows the treatment of artist or subject to one aspect. We have, for example, *Les Ateliers de Maillol; Le Corbusier* in the Marseilles *'habitations'; Aspects de la Musique contemporaine.*

If most of the themes pass beyond national boundaries, for number 57 he focuses our attention on that most French of all gallic

* [Roughly:] 'Go and tie yourself in knots somewhere else! We've got enough buggering about in this house without you!'

** 'For heavens sake, it's not normal!'

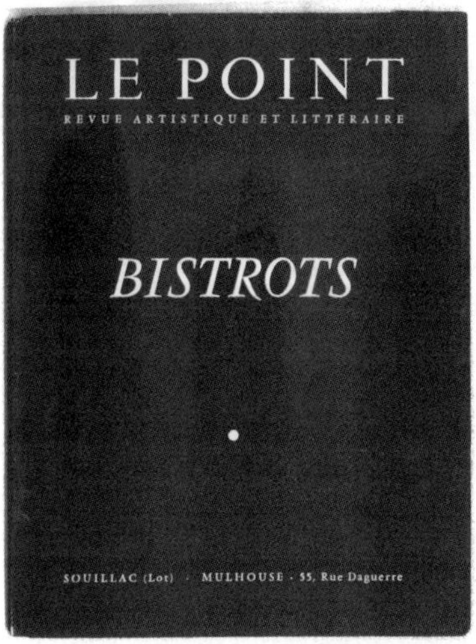

institutions, *Les Bistrots*. It is introduced by Paul Reverdy in handwritten verses *'Gravure sur le zinc'* (on the 'counter' along which — be it taxi-driver or meat-porter at 3am or tourist at midday — one's drink and change is unceremoniously pushed.) Unless, as in the photograph, we have been invited to drink *à la santé* of bride and bridegroom in the *Hôtel du Commerce*. Bravo, Betz! You and your colleague at Belfort remind us of the vast field of French culture which, in your company and that of your expert authors, we happily revisit.

My stay at Lamothe gave me insight into Nancy's routine of work — mornings bashing on her typewriter sacrosanct — work on the many books she was preparing simultaneously, combined with articles and translations. Sylvia Townsend Warner had once reported on this Lamothe routine, when Nancy stayed with her in Dorset for a rest: '... she ate her way through a great many overhanging jobs... every time I went in with a little glass she was translating into or out of a different language...'.

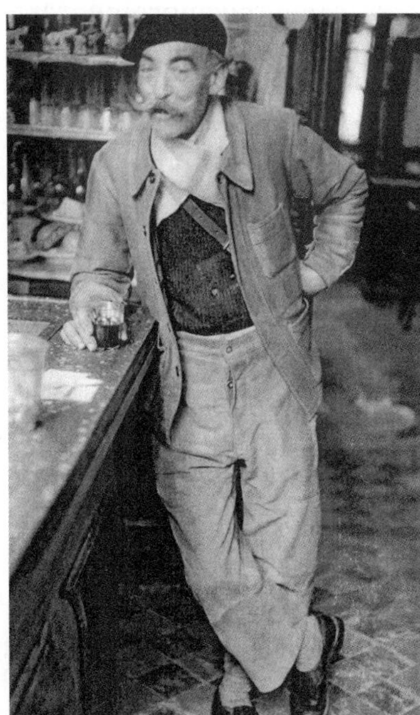

In the afternoons — open-air, long walks. On one she accompanied me most of the way across country to the château where lived Fénelon, the famous author of *Télémaque*, a moral tale for the edification of the child who was to become Louis XV. I imagine the still-existing moat round Château Fénelon gave the name 'Lamothe-Fénelon', eight kilometres away. One agreeable resting-place was in the cool air underneath a grove of sweet-chestnut trees.

She spoke about her friend, Géraldine Balayé, of Radio Toulouse who, thanks to Nancy, broadcast some of my poems and translations from that station. I was able to help Géraldine with certain information about Robert Louis Stevenson whose *Travels with a Donkey* she was translating into French. Another visitor to Lamothe, the American journalist, Louise Morgan, was fascinated by what Nancy had told her about my success in introducing the italic hand into Bishop's Stortford College. Subsequently Morgan devoted an article to myself and my calligraphic pupils in the *News Chronicle*, with a photograph of the handwriting of one of them, David Wright.

I had already planned a two-day visit from Lamothe to the Château Les Tours Saint-Laurent where Jean Lurçat lived and worked, which I describe in a separate chapter. Nancy lent an eager ear to my account of the visit.

In the summer of 1952 my *Ici Paris* was published, an anthology of passages about historic and contemporary Paris by famous authors in which I had in mind the needs of my own pupils. Nancy wrote enthusiastically (29 September 1952): 'Your LOVELY *Ici Paris* came this morning. Opened it at the Hitler story and just read this aloud to Géraldine in ecstasies about it'. Then, about her own proposed travels: 'I am in a dither. Will seven suitcases hold all? I am off next Sunday or Monday for six months, to Venice, Vence, Italy, Tunisia — Work. The Douglas book [*Grand Man*, a book about Norman Douglas] progresses...'.

Around 1952 or 1953 I suddenly returned to my Italian. I had been reading some contemporary Italian short stories by Moravia, his wife Elsa Morante, Silone, Bacchelli and others, and had translated some of them. Several were accepted by magazines such as *Harper's Bazaar*, and *The Listener* published with illustrations Papini's story, 'The Day that was not Returned', which had been broadcast. Then the publisher Peter Owen commissioned me to translate novellas by Cesare Pavese, whose work, though praised in his own country and in France, was not then known in England. When Nancy heard about this, she wrote expressing surprise at the fact that Italian was one of my languages. And from then on she took an active interest in the translations I was doing, and was enthusiastic about the collection of stories I translated and introduced, *Modern Italian Stories* (Eyre and Spottiswoode, 1955). I planned to be in Italy that year and Nancy was ready with names of residents I must meet when I was in Venice and Florence.

During the early fifties I had introduced Nancy to Henry Moore. She had been eager to meet him, but my first proposal in 1949 to take her over to his house and studio at Perry Green had come at a time when she was beset with worries about the settlement of her mother's will. When she and Henry Moore finally met in January 1952, the rapport was immediate. It was the meeting of two minds passionately interested in primitive Mexican art: Moore's obsession with the Chacmool reclining figure became the major inspiration of countless reclining figures. They had in common their familiarity with primitive Cycladic and other figures, seen during their visits to the Musée de l'Homme, in Paris. (The Musée de l'Homme, revisited after the War, had been the subject of an article by Nancy in the *Burlington Magazine*.) Moore was fascinated by her African ivory bangles, as — predictably — was Irina Moore who, Henry insisted, was the collector of their show-case artefacts.

In one letter the two preoccupations I shared with Nancy came together. She knew so much about Italy and the Italian language that I took the liberty of posing some questions that had arisen in my translations of Pavese. 'You *are* a wonder! Fancy asking me all these *Italianismi*. But I'm sure I can procure the answers from Hume Thorne who is Professor of Italian at London University... Ah! what pleasure you have given me in making me know Henry Moore. I think he loved Mexico. He is lunching with me tomorrow...' In the same letter Nancy refers to her projected book on African ivories — she had twenty-eight ancient examples, as well as those which she wore on her painfully thin arms. Her research entailed visits to German and English museums. She discovered that the Cecil Rhodes Museum in Bishop's Stortford housed Lobengula's ring, which the Matabele Chief had given to Queen Victoria. She planned to meet me at the museum, and asked me to get my best boy draughtsman to make a drawing of it. I asked Christopher Hewett to undertake this.

Nancy's verdict was that it was a beautifully made drawing.

She combined this visit with contacting her friends, Constantine and Theodora Fitzgibbon, who lived in a farmhouse about four miles from Henry Moore's house at Perry Green. Whenever an opportunity arose, Nancy paid visits to Moore, putting up at an ancient hostelry, the Red Lion, at nearby Much Hadham, from where she walked across fields and stiles to his studios.

Nancy continued to be interested in what she called my 'Italian side'. She reported back on her friends' reactions to my visits and on my first Pavese, *The Political Prisoner* (Peter Owen, 1955). Her note about *Modern Italian Stories* shows how faithfully she was following my literary progress. As an assiduous worker, she admired tenacity in others; hence, 'The thirteenth book. All in eleven years after *La Double Galère**...'

By the latter part of 1955 Nancy was at work on her 'ivory book' and had 'done' the German museums, Moore, as ever, in her mind. She commented that she had seen a lovely Henry Moore in the Museum of Basle. She asked me if I knew of a magazine which would publish an article on the Hamburg Museum. The re-opening of public galleries across Europe was one of the excitements of those years after five years of visual deprivation. My poem 'National Gallery Revisited',** was included by Patric Dickinson in one of his BBC programmes. In September 1956 Nancy's book about George Moore, *G.M.* was published by Rupert Hart-Davis. The event was echoed in our correspondence with her reversion to the field botany Moore had taught her during his visits to Nevill Holt. I asked her questions arising out of my reading the book. 'The white flower must be star of Bethlehem'. In her May 1st letter, another allusion to George Moore: 'The first picnic today in the very blue and yellow of spring that G.M. noted years ago'.

In Rome Nancy made the acquaintance — at my suggestion, although at that time I had only corresponded with her — of the writer of novellas, Vera Cacciatore. She called on her in her fastness, the Keats-Shelley Memorial House, of which she was keeper, in the Piazza di Spagna. 'You will like each other very much... She is a dear and so erudite... The Keats House brings tears to my eyes, even as ever did his poems...' By a happy coincidence I had a colour lithograph done by the artist wife of John

* 'Paris Double-Galère', the poem Strachan had translated in 1944.

** See appendix.

Redwood Anderson, which I presented to Vera Cacciatore when we met. It was a view of the Memorial House from the Piazza di Spagna.

Ominous in that letter, written on the brink of 1957: '... ill with bronchitis. Hell! Ill-heated hotel at great expense'. She mentioned that Jean Guérin — who became an important support to her later — was to do her portrait. There had been several portraits of her by well-known artists. She wanted to know which portrait of her by Wyndham Lewis I had seen. He had done several drawings of her while staying with her in Venice in 1922. Kokoschka did a painting of her two years later in her flat on the Ile St Louis, Paris. 'I had a squint at it one day and loathed it...' Brancusi had done a typically reductive portrait. They all found it difficult to do justice to her elusive beauty and restless personality and seemed content to fall back on their individual idiom, Lewis his linear rhythms, Kokoschka his expressionism.

The Henry Moore connection continues with the story of the 'ringstone', with a hole through and therefore pertinent to Moore's exploration of the hole in sculpture and the see-through view. It was very heavy, and when my son Geoffrey and his friend Paul Thompson, visited Lamothe in 1956 on a walking tour — 'two gentle, striding giants', Nancy called them — they had no room in their haversacks. Nancy (in a letter bewailing her illness: 'I am so ILL all the time'): 'I have a lovely "ring" for Henry Moore that even HE cannot have seen the likes of. A little heavy to send. HE won't get his lovely creative finger into it. Out of the sea. In stone of course. Stonehenge period'. Finally Irene Rathbone got it to London to be picked up and taken to Moore's, where I've seen it as recently as 1984 when I was working on my book, *Henry Moore: Animals.*

Archaeology, stones. Thoughts on these subjects became obsessive as, ill and ever less physically active, she emerged into nostalgic longings to be back at Nevill Holt, reliving her childhood with her cousin Victor; when already she was picking out attractive stones in the gravel in front of her cousin, indifferent, sophisticated — but adored. I mentioned a similar addiction — to finding 'fools' gold' in the gravel of my childhood home. Her reaction, in a dramatic note headed 'Nice — Clinique. Last of twelve nights, I think (yes, it was)' and 'Villa Pomone, St Jean Cap-Ferrat, Night, 2 Feb 1965': 'My dearest Walter... So it was for YOU I was picking up every one of those darlings...' Her sketches of the examples are firmly drawn. No hint of the *pulso nervoso* which she said spoilt her calligraphy. She is feeling nostalgic about her childhood, much of it spent with her cousin, who was more interested in his dogs and the prospect of 'tea and cake in and on silver' than watching Nancy grubbing in the gravel.

In the same letter she complains: 'I am so ill. Well, I cannot be or do as before'. Then back to the ring theme: 'Ha! What a ring. It is more or less the shape of an Avebury sarsen, but it does have two holes in its blessed base...' Then, in September of that same year, 1964: 'This moment a delicious letter from Henry Moore, saying how much he likes the stone and that it has many meanings, and that maybe he may use one of them one day. I knew he would see it that way'.

In the following year a young American professor, Hugh Ford, and his wife were at Lamothe helping her prepare her book on The Hours Press. Then the news came that she had fallen and broken her femur. On a postcard, typically crammed with messages, depicting 'The Helmet' excavated at Sutton Hoo (an indication of thoughts turning homeward) she wrote (17 February 1965): 'I am uplifted by the thought of living in England come late summer'. In a PS: 'Henry Moore will be enthusiastic about the x-ray photographs of my hip'. Her way of laughing it off or black humour? Her suffering never halted her mental energy nor her interest in outside events. She continued to foster my 'Italian side', sent me books on Italian history; wrote twice in praise of my translation of Fogazzaro's novel, *Piccolo Mondo Antico* [published in 1962 as *The Little World of the Past*] (she found the title odd for the treatment of the Italian rebellion against Austrian domination). She followed up my calligraphic interest, finding my pupil David Wright's hand (reproduced in the *News Chronicle* article) 'exquisite', and putting me in touch with an Italian priest scribe in Rome, Don Vergilio, who failed to understand how English boys could be interested in taking the *corsivo umanistico* of the Renaissance as a model.

In 1963 Nancy had announced her intention of composing a poem of epic proportions, a kind of poetic compendium of her interest in prehistory, mediaeval romance and nostalgia about her childhood. She invoked my help in matters of prosody and scansion. I answered her questions and commented on the slices of the work, *The Vision*, as it progressed. The writing totally absorbed her during a time of great physical pain. *The Vision* is a strange *omnium gatherum* of her nostalgia for the past, oddly mediaeval, coming from this former *avant-gardiste* poet, the author of *Parallax*. Part of the new sequence was devoted to 'Fish-Dream': 'Cosmo lay down in the hay, and the horse by his side' — a mediaeval fantasy, which goes uneasily with her evocation of the legendary farm-labourer ('Barnaby' in her version) who fell asleep on a haycock and slid into the river Nene, being woken by bumping his head against the stone bridge. 'Where am I?' he called out. 'Wansford', came the reply from the bridge. 'Wansford, in England?' I refer to it because Nancy's father, Sir Bache Cunard, to whom she was devoted, lived for a time at an inn called the Haycock in Wansford on the old A1, doubtless to escape from the endless parties his wife Emerald was giving in the big house. Nancy was reliving her childhood when, watched by her father, she canoed on the Nene.

Nancy Cunard's reputation will stand on the biographical studies of two men, Norman Douglas (*Grand Man*) and George Moore (*G.M.*). The former was of great importance to her during the second part of her life, as George Moore was to her during childhood. She attended the burial of Norman Douglas in Capri. She blames her lack of Latin for her bafflement about the inscription under the name carved on the grey-green stone, '*Omnes Eodem Cogimur*', which can be rendered, more or less, as: 'We all come to it'.

Nancy's final months of illness and agony from her broken hip have been chronicled in the biography written by Ann Chisholm. A tragic end, alleviated by the care and support of one of her many loyal friends, Raymond Michelet. In her very last communication to me — and indeed to anyone — in February 1965 she commended me to contact Raymond Michelet, whose address she noted on the postcard. He would give me any help I wanted in connection with my work on the *livre d'artiste*. Under the circumstances of her desperate suffering I found this unbearably moving.

THE GRIEF OF A POET

To Joë Bousquet

Don't write any more of World War one -
Most of the blighters that fought and won
Are dead and gone...

And dead and gone and stale as old crust
That tale of Flanders mud and rust
Since all went bust.

But what of that Frenchman who lies on his bed
Who never got up since abandoned dead...
Quite, quite, they said.

Who kept hope alive though white with pain
When the same bloody business started again,
And fought with his brain,

A help to men in a sorry plight,
And in those dark days his only light
Thompson's *A City of Dreadful Night*.

A poet's purge for a city's crime,
Ultimate agony done in rhyme,
Prolonged to our time.

For 'city' read 'world'... (oh, yes we know it)
But there's comfort for men who still go to it
In the grief of a poet.

7 The Livre d'Artiste: Genesis and Growth of a Collection

My collection of *livres d'artiste**, represented both by complete books, and by *bonnes feuilles*', i.e. sheets of illustrations and texts, passed by artist and printer as 'perfect', was largely given to me by the artists themselves, their printers or their publishers. Other examples were furnished by specialist French private galleries and bookseller-publishers. This collection is the end-product of a more than thirty-five-year love affair with the genre, the creation of the artists of the Ecole de Paris and their promoters, from Ambroise Vollard onwards.

Before my encounter with the genre I had long been interested in book-illustration, particularly when allied to fine printing, as manifested in English books published by such famous private presses as the Kelmscott, the Golden Cockerel, the Gregynog and Ashendene Presses and others and more recently the World's End Press. When, in the early forties, there was a revival of interest in the Humanistic or Italic handwriting, my own interest began to centre round the relationship between calligraphy and typography, more particularly in the combination of these arts with illustration.

It was in 1943 at Bishop's Stortford College that I mounted the first of many displays showing contemporary work in this field and borrowing examples from many generous sources. R.B. Fishenden started us eager learners off with specimens of Czechoslovakian typography, Charles Gimblett — opthalmologist and enthusiastic collector of Kelmscott Press books — lent us notable titles to leaf over in the College library, while Henry Moore — whom I had got to know in 1942 — lent us letters from well-known artists, including Eric Gill and E. McKnight Kauffer. Will Carter, typographer and letter-cutter (founder of the Lion Rampant Press), Beatrice Warde of the Monotype Corporation, Berthold Wolpe, designer for Faber and Faber, Robert Harling and Sir Francis Meynell gave us, in the course of the years, the benefit of their expertise in these arts, in talks characterised by their informality.

My interest in the French *livre d'artiste* was thus latent and soon declared itself; indeed, as it turned out, Robert Harling was the first editor to accept, for the magazine *Image*, my first article

* Now permanently housed in the Taylor Institution Library in Oxford.

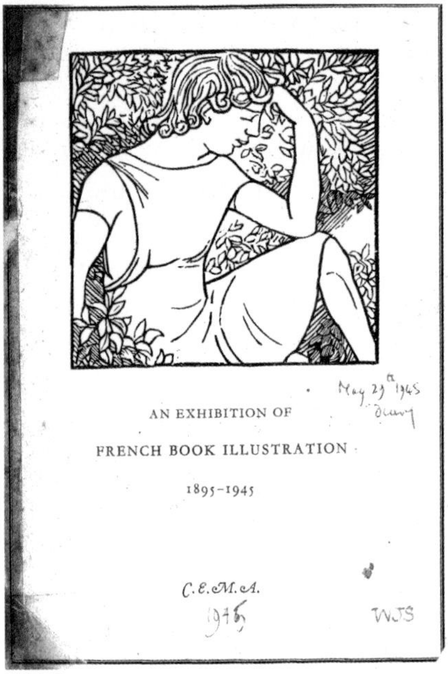

which dealt with three French artists in that field, Gischia, Clavé, and Houplain. In fact it had been my enthusiasm for the parallel English activities that had led me to take a party of boys in May 1945 to see the exhibition *French Book Illustration 1895-1945*, presented under the auspices of CEMA (the forerunner of the Arts Council of Great Britain). The catalogue contained an enlightened introduction by the late Sir Philip James.

For me the experience of seeing Bonnard's lithographs to Verlaine's *Parallèlement* (1900) and Picasso's sugar-aquatints to Buffon's *Histoire naturelle* (1942) (like Derain's *Pantragruel* with its brilliant colour wood-engravings completed during the German Occupation of Paris) was one which I can only describe as overwhelming. These and other book-illustrations such as Roger Vieillard's copper-engravings were a revelation. How could I have missed knowing about this genre, the *livre d'artiste*, which had been flourishing for half a century? A whole new and exciting field was open to explore. Once I got to Paris, Albert Skira's *Anthologie du livre illustré par les peintres de l'école de Paris* (published in 1945) became my bible.

My research was the more interesting inasmuch as it coincided with a period when I was translating, for my anthology of Modern French poems *Apollinaire to Aragon* (1948), several of the poets, Henri Michaux, Paul Eluard, Francis Ponge, Tristan Tzara, whose work was already published in *livre d'art* form. I encountered all of these poets at one time or another, inspecting the progress of the printing of their books at the various specialist printers.

My early meetings with artists — with Léon Gischia, Jacques Houplain, Albert Flocon, Mario Prassinos — resulted in friendly cooperation. They gave me '*bonnes feuilles*' — sometimes complete books — as material for my articles and for showing to the Keeper of the Victoria and Albert Museum's library to encourage a policy of new acquisitions in this genre. Fortunately *Typographia*, *The Studio* and *The Connoisseur* were keen over the years to publish articles illustrated from my growing collection of 'originals'.

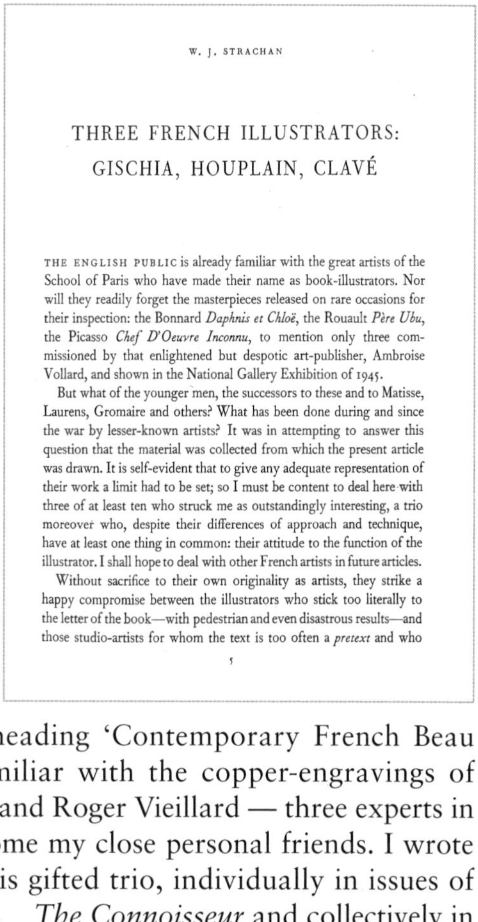

W. J. STRACHAN

THREE FRENCH ILLUSTRATORS:
GISCHIA, HOUPLAIN, CLAVÉ

THE ENGLISH PUBLIC is already familiar with the great artists of the School of Paris who have made their name as book-illustrators. Nor will they readily forget the masterpieces released on rare occasions for their inspection: the Bonnard *Daphnis et Chloë*, the Rouault *Père Ubu*, the Picasso *Chef D'Oeuvre Inconnu*, to mention only three commissioned by that enlightened but despotic art-publisher, Ambroise Vollard, and shown in the National Gallery Exhibition of 1945.

But what of the younger men, the successors to these and to Matisse, Laurens, Gromaire and others? What has been done during and since the war by lesser-known artists? It was in attempting to answer this question that the material was collected from which the present article was drawn. It is self-evident that to give any adequate representation of their work a limit had to be set; so I must be content to deal here with three of at least ten who struck me as outstandingly interesting, a trio moreover who, despite their differences of approach and technique, have at least one thing in common: their attitude to the function of the illustrator. I shall hope to deal with other French artists in future articles.

Without sacrifice to their own originality as artists, they strike a happy compromise between the illustrators who stick too literally to the letter of the book—with pedestrian and even disastrous results—and those studio-artists for whom the text is too often a *pretext* and who

5

As I returned to Paris each Easter, there were ever new discoveries, new connections. I had got to know Michel Ciry and his etchings for *Madame Bovary* were given full coverage in the first article I wrote for *The Connoisseur* — ultimately one of a dozen pieces (published between 1957 and 1970) under the general heading 'Contemporary French Beau Livre'. By 1954 I was familiar with the copper-engravings of Abram Krol, Albert Flocon and Roger Vieillard — three experts in that medium who had become my close personal friends. I wrote on book-illustrations by this gifted trio, individually in issues of *The Connoisseur* and collectively in the *Connoisseur Encyclopedia* of 1959.

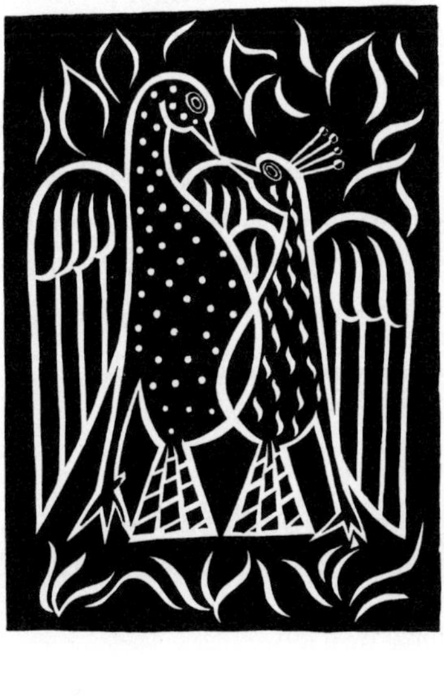

One of the most fascinating personalities on the scene — he later made an international reputation for his tapestries — was Mario Prassinos. I recall early meetings with him in his studios, at 18 Villa Seurat (among the cluster of various artists' studios) when we talked not only about his sulphur-aquatint technique but also about his friendship with Albert Camus, who had recently been killed in a motor accident and about the writings of Gisèle Prassinos, his gifted sister. He showed me his 'proofs' for *The Raven* of Edgar Allan Poe, wood-engravings and aquatints, which we persuaded Erica Brausen to exhibit at the Hanover Gallery, London in 1951. The Heffer Gallery, Cambridge, to which I took *'bonnes feuilles'* of Krol's mixed engravings for *The Ballad of Reading Gaol*, immediately set about arranging for an exhibition (1962, with a second one in 1967). Otherwise the only way I had of getting *livres d'artiste* seen was by lecturing on them in colleges of art — annually at the Cambridge College of Art and Technology from 1972 to 1985. In 1963, thanks to the initiative of the then Ruskin Master of Drawing, Percy Horton, I persuaded the Ashmolean Museum to mount a full-scale exhibition of my collection up to date. Other exhibitions were to follow.

I had had many other fascinating encounters in Paris by then; for example the visit to Prinner's sculpture-and-etching studio, particularly intriguing since at least at that time (1950) his (or her) sex was in doubt — although not the merit of Prinner's carvings or of *Le Livre des Morts des Anciens Egyptiens*. My meeting with the sculptor Henri-Georges Adam, destined to be considered one of the great French sculptors of his time, at his studio in the rue Christine (a name long familiar to me from Maurice Chevalier's famous song 'Valentine'!) was intimidating. On the other hand the warning pinned to the door of Marcel Gromaire's studio in the rue Sarraute, *'Pas de journalistes'*, belied the welcome I received when the painter saw my enthusiasm for his *Macbeth* etchings. I visited him in Paris in 1957. I was rather nervous. He had a reputation for brusquerie. However, we got on well.

I was impressed enough by his pen drawings of recumbent nudes to venture to ask if he could find me a small sketch (my ceiling was £100). He invited me back; the floor was covered with such drawings (I had seen them in the rue Bonaparte marked from £600 upward). 'But'... I stammered.

'Choississez n'importe lequel'
'Mais à combien?'
*'Rien. C'est un cadeau!'**

I was accorded a cordial reception not only by the artists but by the craftsmen involved in the printing of illustrations and texts.

* 'Choose any of them.' 'But how much?' 'Nothing. It's a gift.'

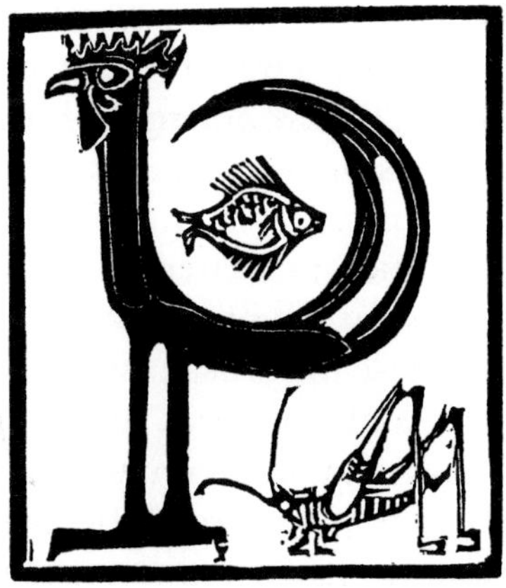

Every year I visited the Imprimerie Fequet et Baudier in the rue Falguière — the best source of news about *'les nouveautés'* — which they were often able to offer me, mostly *bonnes feuilles*, their own hand-set texts and relief wood-engravings.

During my visit to Paris in 1950 I met the highly respected *maître d'oeuvre*, Henri Jonquières, a free-lance typographer, from whom year after year I learned an enormous amount about the production side of the *livre d'artiste.* We quickly became friends, and he made me a willing collaborator in the production of *Prométhée* (André Gide's translation of the play by Goethe), since it involved continual discussions, on this side of the Channel, with Henry Moore, who was to illustrate it, about details of the lithographic proofs. These were produced at Mourlot Frères, the most famous lithographic studios in France, at that time in the rue Chabrol, later, of cathedral proportions, at 43 rue Barrault. Visits to both these *ateliers* were always exciting, since one was always liable to meet artists of the book, surveying the printing of their illustrations — Singier, Manessier, even Chagall. It was at Mourlot's that I watched the craftsman Henri Deschamps at work on the stones (there, no zinc plates as substitutes), correcting and registering works by the famous (including Moore's lithographic drawings for *Prométhée*). Fernand Mourlot, known as 'Chef', ruled like a king. He knew all the most famous artists, national and international, whose work entered his *atelier* (and later produced a book about them).

This is not to underestimate the amount and high standard of lithograph printing executed at the Atelier Desjobert, where the colour lithographs for both Aïzpiri's *La Sauvage apprivoisée* (Shakespeare) and *Le Cid* (Corneille) and Zao-wouki's for *La Tentation de l'Orient* (Malraux) were printed. Among the *taille-douciers* (who print metal engravings) the Atelier Leblanc shares the honours with that of J.J.J. Rigal and the famous Atelier Lacourière et Frélaut, printers of work in all graphic media. There I was thrilled to see work (previously unknown to me) by Terry

Haas, a fine Czechoslovakian-born artist and, (too late for inclusion in my book *The Artist and the Book in France*) by Vincent Guiro, whose aquatints for his *Psaumes messianiques* anticipate his present career as a sculptor. Sculptors, indeed have contributed illustrations to many *livres d'artiste.* The success of a Terry Haas exhibition at Heffers (1965) demonstrated that the English public only need the opportunity to see work by these *peintres-graveurs* to realise the artistic value of their *livres d'artiste.*

It is obvious that space forbids a year-by-year chronicle of new discoveries, new contacts, the viewing of the latest publications in the genre, but inevitably some years — as I study my notebook records — stand out particularly. An early one was 1952. There was the unforgettable first visit to the studio of the painter, Roger Chastel, at St. Germain-en-Laye. Aided by Jean Signovert, he had just finished the printing on his own press of all forty-two double-spread aquatints in two colours (illustrations and initial letters) for a *Bestiaire*, for which Paul Eluard chose poems of his own for the text. I witnessed the Herculean work and strain involved in carrying out this monumental book. I began to regard masterpieces in the genre with a new respect and awe, since they are almost always ancillary to the artist's easel-painting or print-making. My article on Chastel's *Bestiaire* had the happy result of bringing me a special print on Auvergne paper of the owl which I had admired in the book. Contacts in the art-world of Paris are close and friendly, and I was marked down as an owl-man, in consequence of which I have gradually been given dedicated owl prints and originals in every medium from pen and ink to enamel which now adorn my *'cage d'hiboux'* (the well of my staircase) from most of the artists of the book I have written on. I can count my years not 'in coffee-spoons' but in *oiseaux de nuit.**

It so happened that I was to receive another owl, *'la chouette de bonne espérance'* (in his typical surrealist vein) with a calligraphed original poem from Jean Lurçat, following a meeting with him at the Château Les Tours de Saint-Laurent at Saint Céré that same spring. My purpose in going there was to see his book-illustrations, some of the best surrealist inventions in my collection,

* The Owl collection was the subject of an article I wrote for *The Connoisseur*, August 1972. [Editor's note: The collection was bequeathed to the Victoria and Albert Museum and can be viewed on request in the Prints and Drawings Room: see Appendix.]

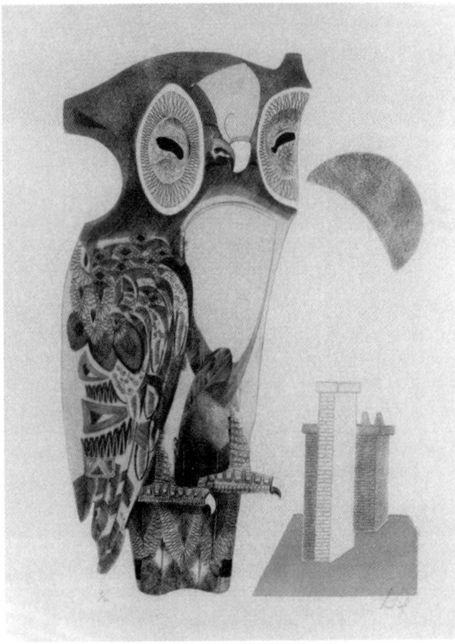

comparable to those by Coutaud and Bellmer and more varied. But there I enjoyed seeing the tapestry woven for the Palais des Nations from Lurçat's design. Hanging in the vast mediaeval hall it dominated the scene.

French tapestry from that moment became for me a parallel interest. I discovered that many of the artists who had contributed to the book were also *peintres-cartonniers*. The first of these that I met after Prassinos, was Gustave Singier, who took me to see one of his tapestries that hung in a court-room of the Palais de Justice. Many years later I visited the weaver, Plasse-Le Caisne, at whose atelier I saw tapestries he had woven from designs by Manessier and at once recognised one that he had used in a lithograph for *Les cantiques spirituels*. Through Antoni Clavé I met in Paris — and later in London when I reviewed his exhibition — Jean Picart-le-Doux, who, like Raoul Ubac, was celebrated as a pioneer of the New Wave of Aubusson tapestry designers.

The step from intaglio-engraving to sculpture is a natural one and has been taken, among others, by Vieillard, Hajdu and Ubac. To illustrate Pierre Lecuire's *Règnes* the sculptor Hajdu produced *estampilles* (uninked forms of relief) and for *Alentour de la montagne*, poems by André Frénaud, Ubac engraved on slate.

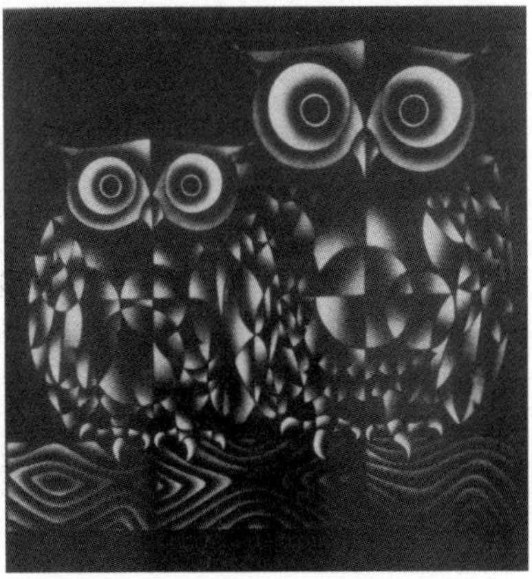

All the time I was looking at new works I was conscious of the past tradition, and as part of renewing my knowledge of it, I took advantage of an offer by Madame Daragnès, widow of the artist and painter, to take me to

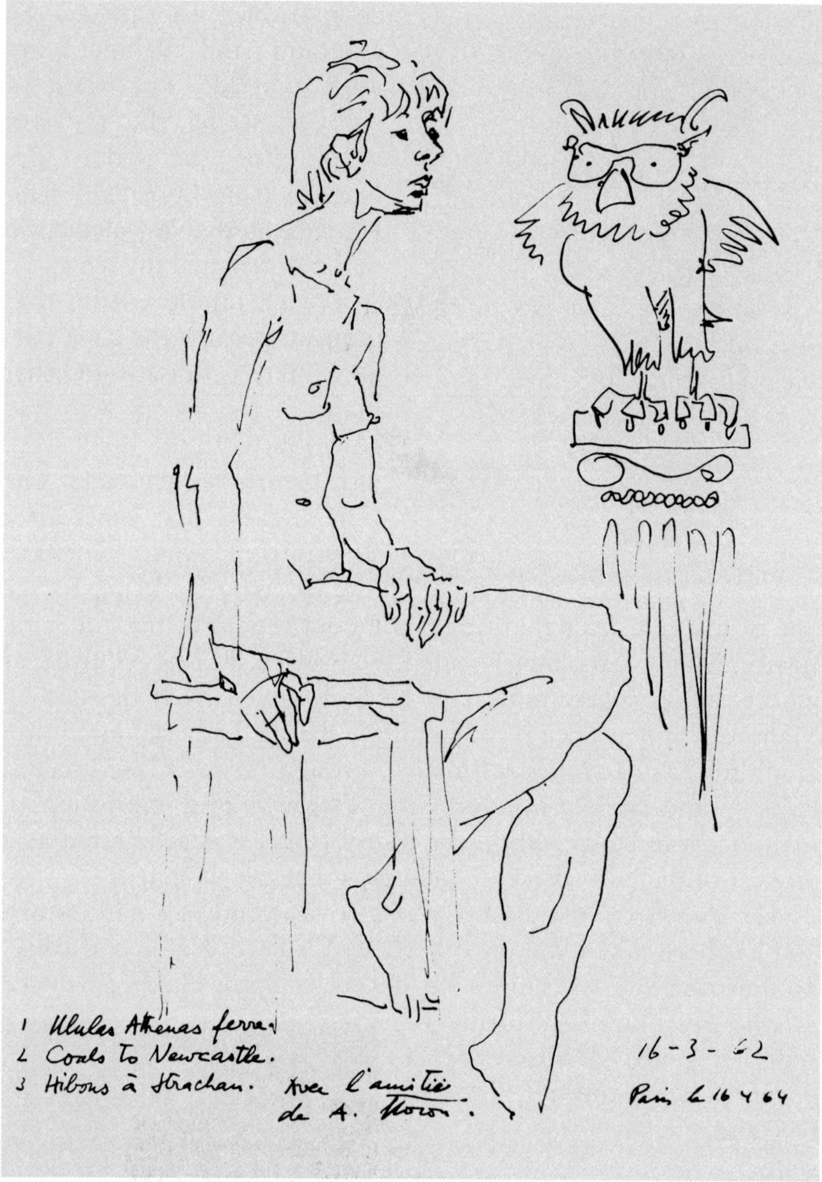

see the famous illuminated *Très Riches heures du duc de Berry* (1409-1416) at Chantilly. Thanks to her intervention, Monsieur Polignac brought the precious book out of its case and turned over some of the pages, exhorting us not to breathe on the gold-leaf of this illuminated book. A leap of 400 years into the early nineteenth century and a chance offered by the owner, Anton

Zwemmer, allowed me to turn the pages of an ancestor of the modern *livre d'artiste*, the French translation of Goethe's *Faust*, with lithograph illustrations and captions by Delacroix. A third refresher came when Henri Floury showed me his famous 1898 edition of Jules Renard's *Histoires naturelles* with lithographic illustrations by Toulouse-Lautrec — a fine prelude to the beginning of the century and to Bonnard's lithographic illustrations to Verlaine's *Parallèlement* of 1900.

In the light of these experiences, it was fascinating to see developments in that same medium in the illustrations by André Minaux whose paintings I had seen in a Tate Gallery exhibition:

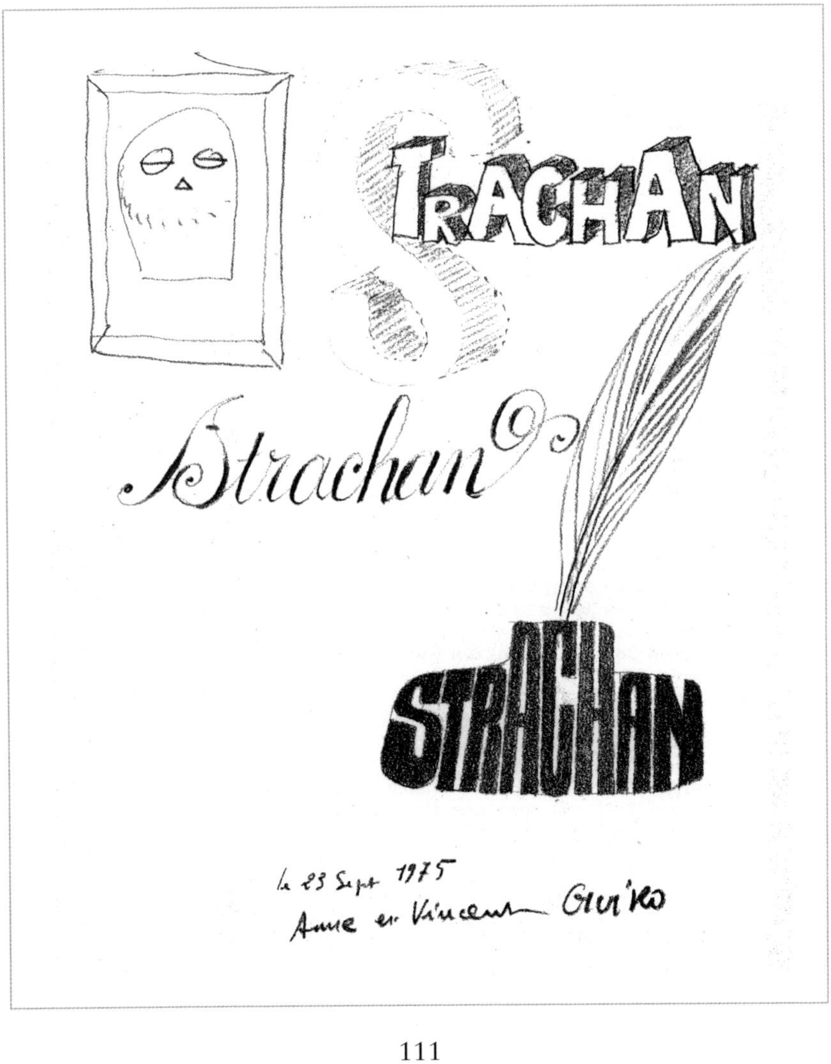

'Four French Realists' (1955). The lithographs for his early titles *Trois fabliaux du moyen-âge* (1956) are in a vein of somewhat poetic realism, a vein he continued in *Le Petit Ami* (1960). But — matching the text — his two-tone lithographs to books by Marguerite Duras (*Moderato Cantabile*) and Hervé Bazin (*Vipère au poing*) explore a more symbolic language: faces become masks-objects-symbols.

Several events happened to stimulate my research. I had seen Dubuffet's *Matière et Mémoire*, anti-romantic, like his *Métromanie* — *'art brut'* in a lighter style — and Picasso's masterpiece *La Maigre*, the latter at the villa of Colonel Sicklès, the most celebrated and wealthy collector of *livres d'artiste* in France, if not the world. Every work to which he directed me from the couch where he reclined was an *'exemplaire de tête'* — one of the strictly limited number of copies on different paper from the ordinary edition, and many of the books, in unique bindings, executed from maquettes made by famous *relieurs*, had a copper-

VICTORIA & ALBERT MUSEUM
SOUTH KENSINGTON, LONDON, S.W.7

Telegrams: VICALEUM, LONDON S. W. 7 *Telephone:* KENsington 6371

Ministry of Education

In any reply please quote:

Your reference: 64.

12·30 pm

The Library,
15th July 1965.

Dear Mr Strachan,

Please accept my apologies for this letter which arrives nearly a week later than I promised, but I have been caught up with a sudden rush of work concerning our autumn exhibition of Victorian Book Illustration and had to put everything else on one side for some days.

It was very pleasant to see you last week and I thank you once again for your kindness in bringing so many sample pages for me to see and for all the trouble you take in writing to your friends in France, I have now examined the list again which you left and here are the items I would like for the Library:

written –1. Aizpiri. Le Cid. approx. 800 NF.
" –2. Gantner. Cécile. 450
" –3. Matta. Les Voix. approx. 900 NF. — recd & approved
– 4. Cortot. Charge du Roi. approx. 300 NF. recd & approved
–5. Gischia. La S.Jean d'été. approx. 900 NF. recd.

engraved plate let into the front cover. I believe the collection has been dispersed.

I came away feeling impressed but more than satisfied with the books and *bonnes feuilles* I myself possessed, though no one would disdain owning one of these books in a binding designed, say, by Georges Cretté, whom I called on in the rue Pierre Nicole in 1957, a street where nowadays [1987] I am received by Pierre Lecuire. Subsequently I visited Pierre Martin, met Paul Bonet at Sautier's, and, in his Gallery, Creuzevault, all top-line binders. Later I was to meet Thérèse Moncey, who had designed, *inter alia*, the binding for Lurçat's *Géographie animale*, in company with Marcel Galland, president of the *Bibliophiles comtois*, who had commissioned Bernard Gantner to illustrate *Cécile* by Benjamin Constant. A happy encounter (I recall Monsieur Galland asking me in Simpson's, in the Strand, — where he insisted eating only English dishes — 'what wine do we have with treacle pudding?') also brought me a specially commissioned mysterious owl (ink and watercolour) from Gantner himself. I had already, as unofficial voluntary ambassador to the Victoria and Albert Library, been instrumental in their purchasing, as well as the *Cécile*, another book, Malraux's *Tentation de l'occident*, illustrated with lithographs in colour by Zao-Wouki, commissioned by the same bibliophile society.

Contacts with members of such societies and with successive Keepers of the Victoria and Albert Library on my return from these forays became part of the pattern of my Paris visits. The three Keepers: Arthur Wheen (to whom I first showed items in 1949), then John Harthan and finally Ronald Lightbown were all sympathetic to the selection of *'bonnes feuilles'* I brought back to show them and their visits to my home or mine to the Museum resulted — to the French artists' delight — in the Library acquiring on average three *livres d'artiste* a year.

Among the bibliophile society representatives, Madame de Harting of the Société Cent Une always had items to show me in the Galerie Champion, where I saw works illustrated by Masson, Laurens, Dali, Piza and others. It is impossible to list all the bibliophile societies but the importance of their role in maintaining the standard of work commissioned should be stressed. I must be content to cite as examples two particularly outstanding books commissioned by the Bibliophiles de l'Union française. The first is 'La Présentation de la Beauce' (Péguy), a marvellous *'livre manuscrit*', with monumental lithographs in colour by Manessier, and *Idea e spazio* by Egle Marini, with etchings in colour by Marino Marini.

It will be noticed that such societies are by no means exclusive to Paris; very active societies in the provinces include: Les Bibliophiles de Provence (*Gargantua* — Clavé), La Société normande du livre illustré (*La Sauvage apprivoisée* — Aïzpiri) and internationally Cent Bibliophiles de France et d'Amérique (*Ombre de mon amour* — Vertès). Prolific publishers of *livres d'artiste* are Brunidor, masterminded by Robert Altmann, and Les Impénitents, now up to their twenty-ninth commissioned book. It was Altmann who mounted an impressive exhibition at the Musée d'art moderne de la ville de Paris, in 1969, *Le livre comme oeuvre d'art*, where I first saw *On déplore la* (Guido Llinas) and *Ressemblance* (Charles Marks), copies of which Altmann generously presented to me.

Along with the Gallery Galanis, one of the galleries most renowned for publishing works illustrated by their painters is the Galerie Maeght. The Adami *Sang* has been described, but my debt goes back to their director, Louis Clayeux, who was responsible for the publication of five *livres d'artiste* in my collection — the Atlan (*Description d'un combat*), the Coutaud (*Ma civilisation*), the Chastel (*Le Bestiaire*), the Miró (*Parler seul*) and the Adami (*Sang*). This is not the place to acknowledge all my long list of indebtedness implicit in this account but, because of their help and co-operation throughout my researches and their great generosity, I cannot omit special mention of Marcel Sautier — bookseller and publisher in the rue des Saints-Pères, whom I first met in 1950, and Pierre Lecuire, typographer-poet, who (I see in my 'agenda') arranged a first rendez-vous with me in the Hôtel Récamier, Place Saint-Sulpice, where I habitually stayed, on April 7th, 1960 at 4.00 p.m.

Sautier put me in touch with Goerg and other artists, and presented me with some of their works. He was amused, moreover, by my interest in 'birds of the night' to the extent of obtaining for me original, dedicated versions from two artists he knew. As for my relationship with Pierre Lecuire, the inclusion in my collection of '*bonnes feuilles*' from his latest work to date, *Bestiaire* (1985), illustrated by Tal Coat, who died just before its publication, bears witness to its intimacy and continuity. From the start, I was impressed by the quality of Lecuire's mind, his feeling about typography, his flair for choosing the artist who would be the perfect match for the particular poem he was composing. It is relevant here, given the close connection between the Taylor Institution and the Ashmolean Museum to which the Christopher Hewett legacy — which includes Lanskoy's *Cortège* — has gone, to recall that I had the pleasure of introducing Hewett to Lecuire. More than a decade later Hewett's Taranman Gallery in Kensington mounted an exhibition of all the pages of the aforesaid *Cortège* — dazzling colour stencils from *'papiers coupés'* by André Lanskoy.

The personalities of the artists I met were as varied as their work. The restrained dignity of Pierre Guastalla is echoed in his charming etchings to the poems of Louise Labé. The idiosyncratic nature of Gianni Bertini's *'art informel'* fitted in with his eccentricity. At an electrifying interview with him (this amazing ex-professor of mathematics at Bologna University) he talked about the *'strip-tease poétique'* he had set up. Sheets of poems fell like leaves (*feuilles* in a double sense) as each page was read out. I was requested to sign my name on a wall covered with the scrawled signatures of a host of famous artists and guests with many flourishes and paraphs.

The colourful exuberance of Walter Spitzer matches his lithographic illustrations; the dedicated seriousness of Albert Flocon's obsession with line and perspective reflects his thoughtful purposefulness, explained partly by the war experiences he had undergone as an alien; Johnny Friedlander's ironic attitude, perceptible in his persona as in his engravings, seems, with hindsight, a cover-up against the sufferings which had been his lot as a German P.O.W.; Abram Krol, Jewish escapee from Poland, had to learn a new language as well as engraving technique, which he happily acquired in the sympathetic atmosphere of Atelier 17 under Hecht and Hayter. His war experiences are implicit in the choice and expression of his book-illustrations, in particular those for Wilde's *The Ballad of Reading Gaol* and Racine's *Athalie*.

Thanks to several visits, I got to know well Mario Avati, the greatest living exponent of *'la manière noire'* (mezzotint); he was honoured nationally by the use of an engraving by him recently on a French postage-stamp. Robert Blanchet, who has the equivalent reputation as a wood-engraver, was trained under the great

Jacques Beltrand who recreated Dufy's original watercolour illustrations to Dorgelès's *Les Vacances forcées.* The 24 originals for this required no fewer than 472 colour-blocks, all printed on Blanchet's hand-press. Now, the latter's son, Gérard, has taken over the *imprimerie*, combining this activity as a printer with his own as a creative artist. I had cordial meetings with Jacques Ramondot, one of the ten artists in my series of monographs. The first of these had been devoted to the charming painter and composer of music, Michel Ciry, whom I had met at his home at Chatou, exclusively focussing on his etchings — one hundred and fifteen of them — for the two-volume edition of *Madame Bovary*, which in their imaginative insight transcend any caption-type illustrations. Yet figurative language such as Ciry's has become less common in the genre. Innovatory techniques and experiments with new materials keep the art fresh and receptive. We have Ubac introducing slate as an engraving medium for the book-page. Vasarely in *Discours de la Méthode*, a variety of new materials including aluminium. Fiorini has successfully combined etching and lino-cut in single illustrations, Hérold and Max Papart have experimented with deep-engraving combined with designs printed 'blind'; Hajdu has produced the 'sculptured' book; Ania Staritsky her exploitations of the potential of specially made hand-papers.

It was, incidentally, an odd experience to find myself looking for Max Papart's studio in the rue Pernéty in 1969, where twenty years before I had interviewed Prinner. On reflexion, this was not surprising, since the fourteenth arrondissement is very much an artist's quarter. So too is the sixth where I used to visit Sautier, Krol and Jonquières and consulted the galeries Jean Bucher, Denise Renard, Jacob and the Galerie de Seine, not to mention the seventh with Avati and the Galerie Adrien Maeght. Topographically, then, the '*Rive gauche*' with Vieillard, Lecuire and the atelier Leblanc, was my chief hunting ground, but with essential incursions across to the '*Rive droite*'. There I went to the Galeries de France, Galanis, Maeght and Louise Leiris and to Frélaut et Lacourière's atelier at Montmartre, and to Beaudin's and Ramondot's studios. Such became the general pattern, interrupted by exciting expeditions outside the centre of Paris to J.J.J. Rigal at Fontenay-aux-Roses and Robert Blanchet at Boulogne-sur-Seine, always rewarding.

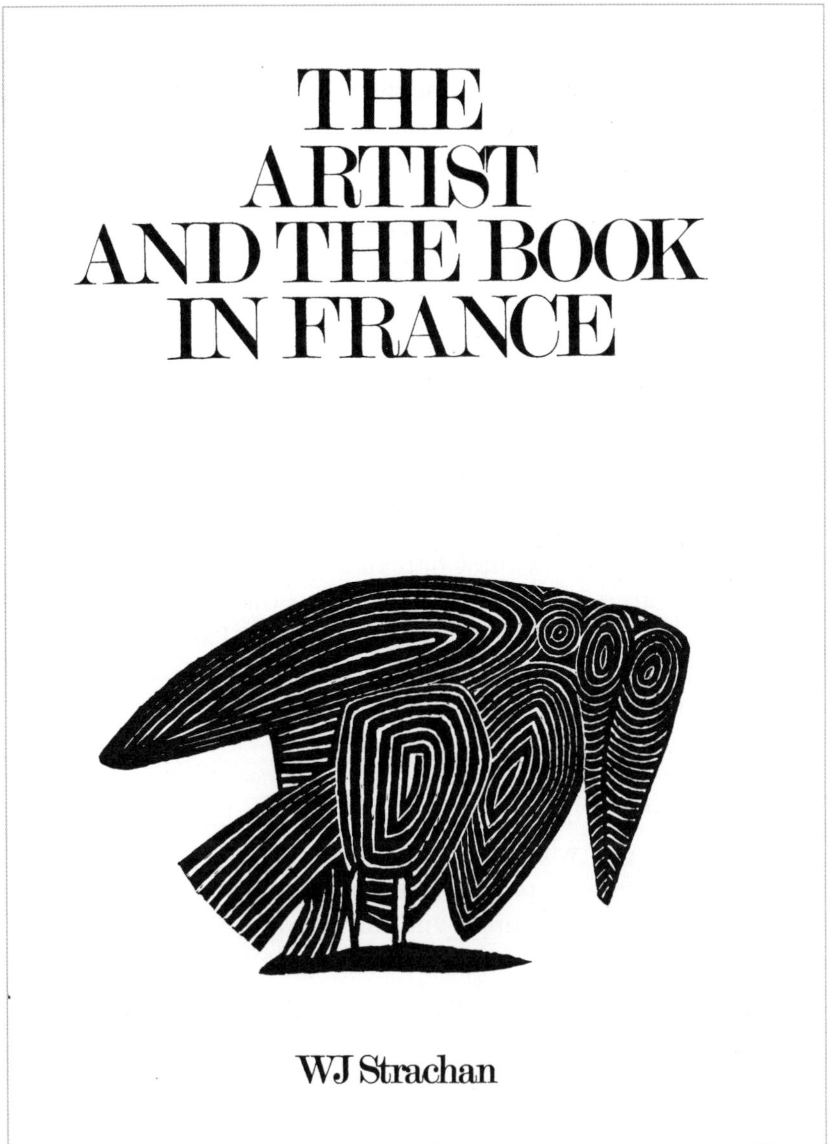

My whole long quest was interrupted from time to time by other activities, such as visits to French sculptors and to the publishers of the modern novels I was editing for an educational series. But these trips became more purposeful when I discovered that, following the initial exhibition of my collection at the Ashmolean in 1963, other galleries and museums (in Edinburgh, Bradford, Sheffield, Leicester and Cambridge, as well as the universities of Durham, York, Sussex and Norwich) welcomed the opportunity of putting on an exhibition of *livres d'artiste*. Only a book could now do justice to the material and, such as it was, the knowledge I had accumulated. *The Artist and the Book in France* was published in 1969 by Peter Owen. A further updating article was published in *The Private Library* in 1981, and some of the work described in that article is also included in the collection now permanently housed in the Taylor Institution Library, bringing the story to a happy, originally totally unforeseen, conclusion.

(1987)

8 A Day with Jean Lurçat

At the time when I paid the visit described here to Jean Lurçat at his home and studio in the Château Les Tours Saint-Laurent in 1952, he was already known worldwide for the part he had played in the revival of French tapestry in the 1940s. Paradoxically this happened during the '*drôle de guerre*' (the phoney war) and under the German occupation. We in England knew little about it until the Exhibition of French Tapestry at the Victoria and Albert Museum in 1947. There we were able to see examples of sections of the '*Apocalypse*' at Angers dating from the last quarter of the fourteenth century, which had so impressed Lurçat on his visit to that town in 1938 as to revolutionize his whole conception of tapestry. We saw how Lurçat and his fellow *peintres-cartonniers* had transformed an art form which, during the reigns of Louis XIV and Louis XV, had virtually been transmuted into the creation of oil-paintings in wool, involving literally hundreds of coloured wools, as the weavers matched the original colours in a painting.

The new tapestries treated the work as wall-decorations, two-dimensional, with perspective and skyline suppressed. Dom Robert, for example, substituted superpositioning for perspective in his treatment of moving animals — doubtless influenced by the way the deer or '*bovidés*' had been depicted in the newly discovered Lascaux Caves near where he lived at the time. Tapestry once more, as at Angers and the Musée de Cluny (home of the *Dame à la Licorne*), became an art in its own right, fulfilling Lurçat's definition: *'La tapisserie est principalement une chose de l'architecture'.** (It so happened that his brother was a distinguished architect.) The examples of tapestry shown at the Victoria and Albert Museum in 1947 illustrated the new direction. Marc Saint-Saëns, with reduced numbers of *'tons'* [tones] but using strong colours, produced a dramatic 'Theseus and the Minotaur', Marcel Gromaire created an architectonic evocation of Paris.

In 1933, curiously enough, a German, Madame Cuttoli had started the idea of having paintings by prominent contemporary painters such as Picasso, Braque and Léger transformed into tapestry versions. 'Oil paintings in wool', was Lurçat's derisive comment. His own reforms went deeper. He revived the mediaeval practice of including *légendes* and bannerets in the weft, as in his composition *'Liberté'* (1943), a tribute to those who died in the Resistance. His disciple, Jean Picart Le Doux, used tapestry as a homage to the Spanish Republican poet, Lorca, incorporating the well-known line about him, *A las cinco de la tarde.*

Never again will such valuable works as the *Apocalypse* and *La Dame à la Licorne* be allowed to be moved from their permanent homes. But the Victoria and Albert exhibition served an important purpose in 1947 in informing people in Britain about the new movement of which most of us had known little. In my case it prepared me for the meeting with the great pioneer.

My purpose in seeking the meeting with Lurçat was in fact to discuss his illustrations for books. The opportunity to interview him came at a good moment. In 1950 and 1951 I had been engaged in research in Paris on several artists who had illustrated *livres d'artiste:* Flocon, Gischia, Roger Chastel, Mario Prassinos, and back in England I was writing on their work. I was particularly interested to see Lurçat's illustrations to a *Bestiaire Fabuleux* by the poet, Patrice de la Tour du Pin, having translated verse of his for my anthology, *Apollinaire to Aragon*, and was also eager to see how Lurçat had treated his edition of *Vingt Fables de La Fontaine* and the choice of fables he had made. Added to all this, I was Nancy Cunard's guest at Lamothe-Fénelon, not all that distant from Saint Céré and the Château Les Tours Saint-Laurent. Transport there was willingly provided by Pierre Vorms, the publisher of *The Raven* illustrated by Prassinos, which, thanks to my

* Tapestry is principally something architectural.

intervention, had been exhibited at the Hanover Gallery in London in 1951. Vorms lived in Belvès, lower down the Dordogne Valley.

Vorms intended the itinerary to be a royal progress. And it was. If I give a few details here it is because it embraced a visit to the Lascaux Caves and Les Eyzies, and was in the *maquis* region where in 1944 Lurçat had been active with the local Resistance movement. At great personal risk, he had manned a transmitting post at the Tours Saint-Laurent from which he broadcast messages and instructions every night at 10.10. His studio at Lanzac, with its priceless contents of tapestry cartoons, had been burnt down by the Germans. So I felt very conscious of the events of less than a decade before, as well as of the beautiful Dordogne Valley and Lot setting.

Nancy Cunard waved us off from her house at about 9 a.m. on the morning of April 17, 1952. The journey began with a passage through Carsac, where Pierre Vorms took me into the church to see a fine romanesque nave containing a painting on wood by Léon Zack. A few kilometres on and le Château de Montfort came into view, towering above us. On to Domme, which offered a splendid panorama from its terrace. Through La Roque Gageac to Beynac with its thirteenth-century château. Lunch at Cazenac (not gastronomic: we had other eggs to fry). A pause in the town of Sarlat to see the house of the sixteenth-century philosopher, La Boétie, with its fine renaissance skylight. When we passed near Boussac, I recalled that the château had possessed *La Dame à la Licorne* before its transference to the Cluny Museum.

Next, Montignac for the caves at Lascaux. They had been discovered by two boys looking for a lost ball. Fortunately a watchful eye was kept on the prehistoric wall paintings as — to their detriment — multitudes of tourists breathed on them and the caves had perforce to be closed for a time after protective measures had been applied to the murals and are now, of course, permanently closed. I was tremendously impressed by the paintings, the observations of movement in the *'bovidés'*, the generic term applied to bison, bulls, mammoths, reindeer, rhinoceros and other animals by the Abbé Breuil in his finely illustrated volume about Lascaux. Equally impressive were the figurations of animals economically incised on the cave walls of Les Eyzies and Combarelles. Enchanted but exhausted, I was glad to have supper with Pierre

Vorms and retire for the night in the house of his friend, Madame Palissier.

The second leg of the journey, if less exciting than the first, was through charming villages: Daglan to S. Margial, Pon Carral to Gourdon, Payrac, Creysac, Vayrac to a climax at Beaulieu-sur-Dordogne. The church there has wonderfully grotesque caryatids joined together, one with elongated forearms. The church itself is a fine example of twelfth-century romanesque and contains another curiosity, a silver reliquary of Virgin and Child (to be seen by permission).

Bretenoux, and one feels the vibrations of drawing close to Saint-Céré — now a Lurçat pilgrimage centre. The Tours Saint-Laurent, appears on the skyline. This twelfth-century fortress looks, though impressive, such a ruin, that I am surprised to find how well the interior has been restored. Fortunately the great hall has been left intact (no intervening ceiling). So I had an immediate view of Lurçat's vast tapestry *Europe*. It had been commissioned for the Council of Europe and was awaiting its imminent transference to Strasbourg. To meet its author below it was indeed a thrill. Lurçat of medium height, a face easily relaxing into a smile. No vanity but he had the self-assurance that confidence in his work and recognition gives — as it gave to Moore when I first visited him a decade earlier. Once again, I felt myself to be confronting genius, authority. But he put me at ease at once, as we had a brief chat, with his or Madame Lurçat's Afghan hounds spread decoratively about the room. The artist sat upon a canapé upholstered in Lurçat tapestry, woven at Beauvais.

First we talked about mutual friends in Paris. Mario Prassinos, a near neighbour in the Villa Seurat in Paris. Prassinos had designed his first tapestry, based on his wood-engravings for *The Raven* in 1951/2. He soon adopted the Lurçat system called '*numérotage*' (numbering the skeins of colour from the weaver's repertoire). Then lunch, eaten off the artist's own ceramics. He had started on ceramics not long before my visit and gave me photographs of his work — monumental dishes with surrealist designs.

Lurçat's versatility is typical of the French artists of the period. First working on individual lithographs and engravings, in 1938 he received a commission from Beauvais to design tapestry upholstery for a settee and four armchairs to accompany the first tapestry of his, executed by the Gobelins (the State workshops), *Les Illusions d'Icare.*

We wound up an excellent luncheon with a liqueur of his own recipe, and then dashed off to the *briquetterie* where he needed to see the craftsmen. Then over the boundary of Lot into Auvergne to buy plants at a market: he was a keen gardener. Then we began looking at his book-illustrations. They were set out in chronological order. He showed me and gave me trial proofs to keep and use to illustrate any article I wanted to write. The discussion was on his fondness for lithography — he loved colour. The *Bestiaire Fabuleux* started with the artist's gouaches: he presented me with one experimental gouache at the first idea stage, the fabulous *'Taurillon-Zèbre'.*

All the illustrations were in his own unmistakeable surrealist language. It takes various forms, from the large-format colour lithographs for *Vingt Fables de La Fontaine* to the miniature monochrome lithographs — small masterpieces — for his own prose poem, *Mes Domaines.* He explained how he had used lithography combined with collage for the *Fables*, an examination of which shows his lithograph superimposed on what may be a coloured map. Another example: *'Le Cerf blessé'*, with a large red tear welling from its eye, evocative of Shakespeare's image of the 'stricken deer'. My favourite is the lithograph of frogs boasting before the sun, *'Les Grenouilles et le Soleil'.*

The sun, an image that recurs in Lurçat's work, is associated in his imagination with life force; the cockerel symbolizes the dawn. No symbol could have been more daring, more appropriate, in the years of German Occupation: *'Coq chante ou non, viendra le jour'.** General de Gaulle was to make a gift to Churchill College, Cambridge, in memory of Churchill, of Lurçat's tapestry with the banneret quotation from Paul Eluard: *'Assieds toi et rend justice solaire...'*** And the *Trois Soleils* is there for all to see at Orly airport.

That day in 1952 I was impressed by Lurçat's own text and lithographs for his *Géographie Animale.* Here, as in the La Fontaine *Fables*, he evokes a philosophy from the fantasies of the animal kingdom. Creations such as *'La Chouette de la Bonne*

* 'Let the cock crow nor no, the day will come.'

** 'Sit down and dispense solar justice.'

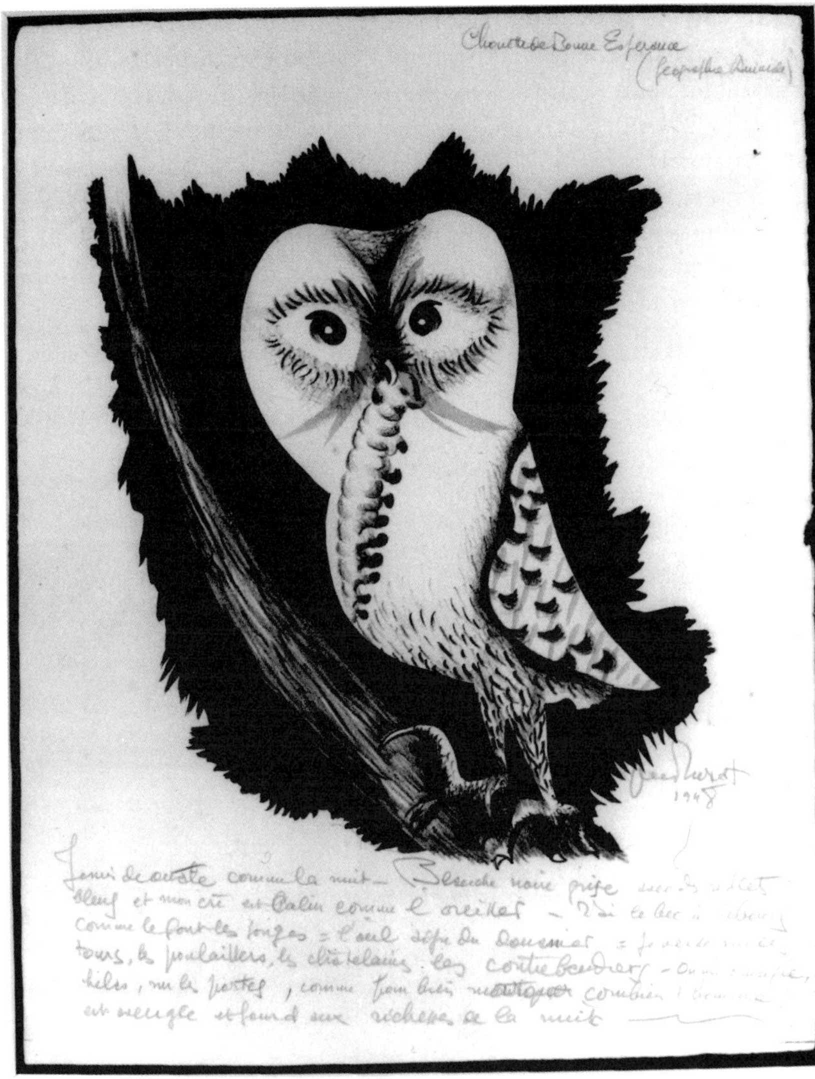

Espérance' ['The owl of good hope'] (of which he gave me an original print with the poem pencilled in his own hand) are a castigation of man's cruelties. In the accompanying prose poem in *Domaines*, Lurçat echoes the verses of Apollinaire which Dufy had illustrated with woodcuts. In the tear of *'Le Cerf Blessé'* he rises to the transcendental heights of that poet whom André Gide puts among the greatest: Aesop transfigured.

The next excitement that day came when we moved into the tapestry studios, the old *salle de garde* from which he had broadcast to the *maquis.* From the material surrounding us he picked out the stages in the preparation of a cartoon for tapestry. First the large-scale sketch drawings, quite detailed as in the case of *l'homme:* man depicted as poacher, fisherman, poet. There were various versions of the cock, and a photograph of this bird — (*'le plus impertinent des oiseaux'*)* who followed us into the *maquis* — landing on Lurçat's wrist. Then he produced the black-and-white cartoons, which looked like relief maps, their contours

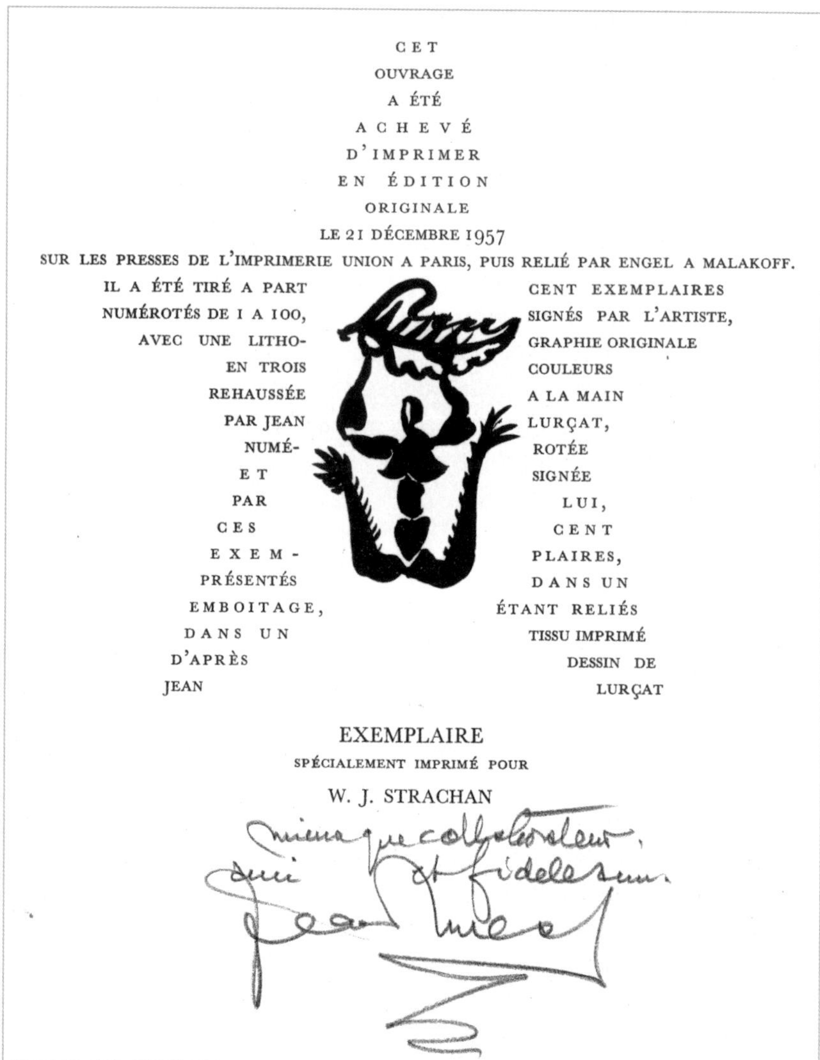

CET
OUVRAGE
A ÉTÉ
ACHEVÉ
D'IMPRIMER
EN ÉDITION
ORIGINALE
LE 21 DÉCEMBRE 1957
SUR LES PRESSES DE L'IMPRIMERIE UNION A PARIS, PUIS RELIÉ PAR ENGEL A MALAKOFF.
IL A ÉTÉ TIRÉ A PART CENT EXEMPLAIRES
NUMÉROTÉS DE I A 100, SIGNÉS PAR L'ARTISTE,
AVEC UNE LITHO- GRAPHIE ORIGINALE
EN TROIS COULEURS
REHAUSSÉE A LA MAIN
PAR JEAN LURÇAT,
NUMÉ- ROTÉE
ET SIGNÉE
PAR LUI,
CES CENT
EXEM- PLAIRES,
PRÉSENTÉS DANS UN
EMBOITAGE, ÉTANT RELIÉS
DANS UN TISSU IMPRIMÉ
D'APRÈS DESSIN DE
JEAN LURÇAT

EXEMPLAIRE
SPÉCIALEMENT IMPRIMÉ POUR
W. J. STRACHAN

* 'Most impertinent of all birds.'

numbered ready for the Tisserand craftsman weavers at Aubusson. We looked into drawers containing what he called *éléments*: constantly recurring motifs such as leaves, foliage, butterflies in innumerable variants. All part of an organized plan, Lurçat's system of *numérotage* greatly speeded production, enabling him to cope the more easily with commissions that came in from all over the world. His *Apocalypse* had been woven thus in 1950 for Notre Dame de Toute Grace at Assy, a modern church for which many great artists contributed, Rouault (stained glass) and Germaine Richier (sculpture) among them.

Lurçat never flagged under my persistent questioning. Nor did Pierre Vorms show impatience during the long day. (He had after all the prospect of publishing his fine book: *Tapisseries de Jean Lurçat* in the foreground of his mind). We had supper in a relaxed manner, and eventually took our leave near midnight, returning to Lamothe by a less circuitous route. When Pierre put me down there I could hear nightingales in a nearby wood celebrating my triumphal two days. Sandwiches and a bottle of vin de Cahors put out by the thoughtful Nancy, awaited me. It was 4 a.m. Rather than try to sleep, I went over the highlights of the two days.

There was a thrilling follow-up. I was asked to provide English captions for the scores of tapestries reproduced in the Vorms publication. The Avant-Propos was by 'Vercors' (the *nom de plume* or *de guerre* of the author of the war's best-seller, *Le Silence de la Mer*, which had given a boost to morale when the Narvik débacle had lowered it). Lurçat signed a specially printed copy of Vorms's *Tapisseries de Jean Lurçat.* The special *exemplaire* with a pencilled message for me on the colophon contained several drawings and original lithographs, vignettes, and an original pen drawing.

After that I wrote an article on 'Modern French and English Tapestry' (*Studio*, December 1955), naturally with emphasis on the French pioneer. My article on Lurçat's 'Book Illustrations' was published in *Motif* No. 1 (1957). The artist wrote to me with generous praise for my contribution to Pierre Vorms's volume. A bond had been established. I now included Modern French Tapestry in my lecture list for NADFAS (the National Association of Decorative and Fine Arts). My *Studio* article showed how much Lurçat's method of work and writings had influenced other *peintres-cartonniers*. Carried away, I went so far as to draw up a synopsis for a book on Lurçat and contemporary tapestry but no

English art publisher was interested. They pointed out that there were so very few examples in this country and that tapestry was not of interest here, except for the historic examples in country houses, Chatsworth etc. I was sure that there were enough francophiles and English visitors to France to justify such a work but '*en l'occurence*' I could not pursue the matter, despite the continuing encouragement of Madame Simone Lurçat after Jean Lurçat's death in 1966. (In November 1990 she paid me the compliment of leaving the Villa Seurat to come and hear my lecture on Lurçat at the Victoria and Albert Museum.)

Madame Lurçat was a great and generous helper, bringing me up to date on what was both spiritually and literally her husband's *magnum opus* (it occupies 347 square metres) *Le Chant du Monde*. Just as Rodin put everything into his Bronze Gate (*La Porte d'Enfer*) and Rembrandt into his final etchings, so Lurçat took all the themes that had initially been embraced under the title *Joie de Vivre* but some from his later sombre reflections — following Hiroshima and Auschwitz — on death and destruction. But man survives, in adventure, symbolized by *La Conquête de L'Espace* and, above all, in *La Poésie*. 'All that is worth remembering in life', wrote Coleridge 'is the poetry of it'. Lurçat's tapestry and his other work is the visual embodiment of this philosophy.

So the vast conception *Le Chant du Monde*, a sequence of ten great tapestries, was completed by the time of his death. The following year, thanks to Madame Lurçat's collaboration, it was acquired by the City of Angers, where it hangs in the former Hôpital Saint-Jean.

PART FOUR

THE ITALIAN DIMENSION AND THE SCULPTURE YEARS

1960 – 1984

BATTERSEA, 1948

To Henry Moore

Three chimneys soar against a violet haze,
A coil of smoke about each towering rim
Writhing and red caught in the sun's last rays,
The distant descant in this modern hymn
To harnessed power, served by its hidden team,
That governs indifferently the nights and days.

Three sculptured forms among the pillared trees,
Timelessly anxious in their prison of stone,
The heavy drapery about their knees
Echoing the burden kindred to each one
That each within herself must bear alone,
Since the uptilted heads spy no release.

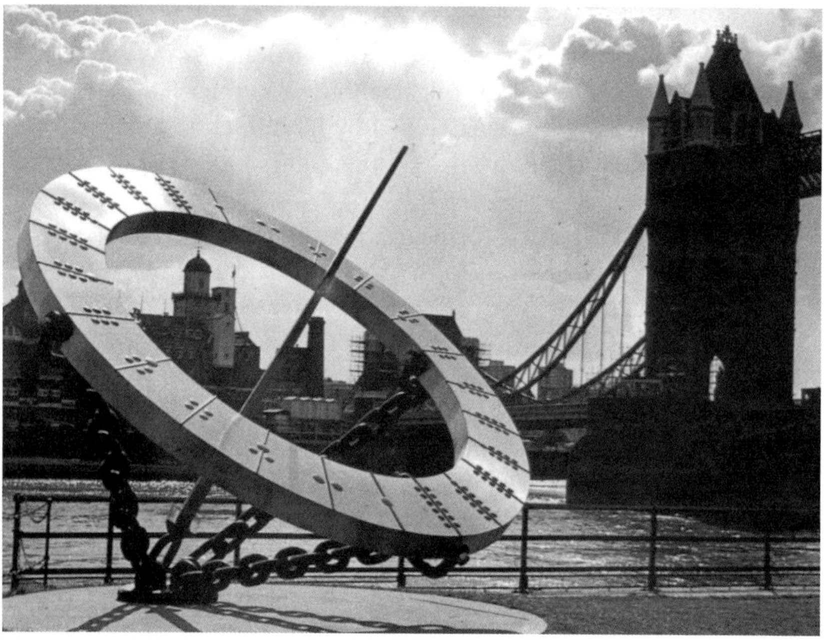

THE ITALIAN DIMENSION AND THE SCULPTURE YEARS

By the mid nineteen-fifties Walter Strachan had published translations of two art books and five novels from the French. He now began adding translations of Italian fiction to his prodigious output. This followed an energetic burst of language learning, using an Italian Linguaphone course as a springboard, and quickly plunging into wide reading among the works of modern Italian writers. Soon came the publication of a mixed volume of stories by twentieth-century writers and translations of novellas by Cesare Pavese and Vera Cacciatore. It also led to Strachan's first visit to Italy in 1955, which was followed by further visits in 1962, 1972 and 1978. He recorded the background to these visits in the chapter he calls his 'Italian Dimension'.

He made the first two visits armed with a sketchbook, eager, as he noted of his first visit to Venice in 1955, to pay as much attention to the outside of buildings and the atmosphere of places as to the content of museums. In 1962 the translation of Antonio Fogazzaro's novel *The Little World of the Past*, on which his work was almost completed (he was reading the proofs), led him to the village of San Mamete, on the borders of Italy and Switzerland, where the novel is set, to draw the look and soak up the feel of the place.

By the time of his third Italian visit, in 1972, this time to Rome and Florence, it was research for his book, *Towards Sculpture*, published in 1976, which drew him there. Strachan's period of translating Italian fiction had ended. His active interest in the French *livre d'artiste* was to continue throughout the last four decades of his life, but this had, to some extent, reached a climax with the publication of *The Artist and the Book in France* in 1969. During the seventies and early eighties much of his writing energy became focused on sculpture. *Towards Sculpture* was followed in 1983 by *Henry Moore: Animals* and in 1984 by *Open Air Sculpture in Britain*, the fruit both of several decades of passionate interest in the work of post-war sculptors, Moore in particular, and, in the run up to its completion, several years of intensive field research and correspondence with sculptors. (Much of the background documentation for this book, as a result of a bequest agreed with the Scottish National Gallery of Modern Art, is now held in Edinburgh.)

Strachan's interest in modern sculpture had been greatly stimulated by his first meeting with Henry Moore in 1942 shortly after Moore had left London and come to settle in Perry Green, a hamlet not far from Much Hadham and about five miles from Bishop's Stortford. Moore was always warmly hospitable to those who were interested in seeing his work and visiting his studio. He was welcoming both to Strachan, his pupils and his family and to the many artists and friends whom Strachan took there, over four decades.

During the fifties and sixties Strachan published a number of articles on Moore's sculpture, beginning with 'Henry Moore's Unesco Statue' in the December 1958 issue of *The Studio* as well as an account for *Image* of Moore's major contribution to the *livre d'artiste*, his lithographic illustrations for the Goethe/Gide *Prométhée* (1951), in the creation of which Strachan played a vital role as go-between and interpreter between the book's architect, the typographer, Henri Jonquières, and Moore himself.

But it was during the seventies and eighties that Strachan's focus in his writing and lecturing broadened to embrace the work of other contemporary sculptors, both British and European, and that of earlier generations too. In 1974 *The Connoisseur* published a series of articles by him on 'The Sculptor and his Drawings', featuring, among others, Bernard Meadows, Kenneth Armitage and F.E. McWilliam. In 1976 Thames & Hudson published his richly illustrated study: *Towards Sculpture: Drawings and Maquettes, from Rodin to Oldenburg*. By now he was attending sculpture exhibitions widely, collecting exhibition catalogues from all over Europe and beginning to correspond with and meet many sculptors, among them Barbara Hepworth, Elizabeth Frink, Lucille Passavant, Wendy Taylor, Kenneth Armitage, Reg Butler, Geoffrey Clarke, Peter Thursby, Roy Kitchin. As in the case of the creators of the *livre d'artiste*, he always regarded the sculptors themselves as the prime sources of information about their work and aims and many of the sculptors he met became firm friends.

Two sculpture-related enterprises which absorbed much of Strachan's energy in the seventies and early eighties should be mentioned. In 1977 the publishers Chadwyck-Healey of Cambridge had published his translation of a book by Jurgis Baltrusaitis, *Anamorphic Art*. This inspired Strachan to follow up with a study of his own for Chadwyck-Healey, which embraced both painting and sculpture, *Distortion and Obsession in Modern Art: Monet to the Present Day*. It was planned as a copiously illustrated book, as *Towards Sculpture* and *Anamorphic Art* had been, and needed the collaboration of an American co-publisher to share the production costs. Unfortunately none could be found and the book was never published. While striving to wait patiently as the search continued for a co-publisher, Strachan began planning his guide to modern sculpture in the open air.

Meanwhile in 1974 one of Strachan's former pupils at Bishop's Stortford College, Christopher Hewett, who had trained at the Ruskin School, Oxford, under Percy Horton and the Royal College of Art under

Hugh Casson and then spent some years in France and North Africa, returned to London and opened a small gallery and private press, Taranman. For some ten years Hewett presented a remarkable series of exhibitions, each accompanied by a catalogue designed and printed with elegance and restraint. Many of the sculptors and graphic artists whose work Hewett presented at Taranman, Geoffrey Clarke, Bernard Meadows, Kenneth Armitage, Raoul Ubac, Vincent Guiro, Charles Marq, Brigitte Simon and Ralph Brown, were artists known to Strachan, about whose work he had already written.

No doubt Strachan made a number of introductions and suggestions to Hewett, particularly in the early years and in a few cases he wrote introductions to some of the catalogues. But Hewett, whose early interests in poetry, architecture, art and typography Strachan had so fostered, as he did with countless pupils over the years, had grown up and made his way in the world and become a mature 'kindred spirit', whose tastes and style were his own. The fact that his own tastes now coincided so often with Strachan's was a source of delight and encouragement to the older man. They made several trips to France together and, as with so many of the artists whose work he admired, from Mario Prassinos and Abram Krol onwards, Strachan was delighted that exhibitions at Taranman, alongside the exhibitions of his own growing collection of *livre d'artiste* material which he was beginning to arrange, offered yet more ways of drawing public attention to fine modern work. The exhibition of Pierre Lecuire's *Livre des Livres* in 1975 (for which Strachan wrote the catalogue preface) and that of slate sculptures by Raoul Ubac in 1980 were probably two of the most important shows to be held at the gallery.

The element of collaboration on an artistic or literary project, so characteristic of many of Walter Strachan's relationships with his 'kindred spirit' friends, was extended further through Hewett's publication in 1976 of a volume of Strachan's poems, some reprinted from the earlier books, some new work, some translations. The volume (which is a signed, limited edition, very much in the private press tradition followed by Nancy Cunard at the Hours Press in the 1930s) contains two copper engravings by Charles Marq. This was followed by the publication of a collection of letters to Strachan, written between 1927 and 1977 by a wide range of English, French, Italian and German friends — poets, painters, sculptors, pupils and others. Called *The Living Curve*, a phrase taken from the poem 'August' by Louis MacNeice, the volume was originally planned for publication in 1983, the year of Strachan's eightieth birthday. As it turned out, the book was delayed, partly owing to the tragic and premature death in 1983 of Hewett himself. It finally appeared in the autumn of 1984 as part of a series of memorial tributes to the remarkable founder of Taranman, an enterprise that inevitably had to be wound up by his family and friends during the months that followed Hewett's death.

Meanwhile, on the sculpture and graphic art front, Strachan had been pleased to be invited in 1982 to write the text for an illustrated study of Henry Moore's sculptures, drawings and prints of animals, which would be compiled with Moore's full involvement and published by Aurum Press. Work on the volume involved a good many visits to Moore and conversations with him over a whole range of artistic topics, in addition to his own work. The selection of illustrations was discussed closely with Moore and the publisher. Once more Strachan was treating the artist himself as the prime source of information about his vision, technique and intentions and once more enjoying active collaboration on a creative enterprise with an artist he had known, liked and admired for some forty years. *Henry Moore: Animals* appeared in 1983.

The following year A. Zwemmer (the publishers of his very first translated art book, André Lhote's *Treatise on Landscape Painting*) published, in association with Tate Gallery Publications, Strachan's deceptively compact but in some ways monumental *Open Air Sculpture in Britain, a comprehensive guide*. This contained descriptions and photographs of 552 sculptures on public sites throughout the length and breadth of Britain. It was the fruit of several years of painstaking research and correspondence, involving the willing collaboration of almost two hundred sculptors and of scores of official and unofficial scouts and photographers, ex-pupils, friends, relations, enthusiasts. The book was eagerly snapped up but sadly (unlike *The Artist and the Book in France*) quickly went out of print.

Of it Peter Murray, Executive Director of the Yorkshire Sculpture Park wrote (shortly after Walter Strachan's death in 1994): 'In many ways one of his greatest contributions was his publication *Open Air Sculpture in Britain*. It is a publication that only Walter could have produced, as it balances research, intimate understanding of the subject, an eye for detail, a love and enthusiasm for sculpture and a touching respect for artists. In a sense the publication could be compared to a sculpture, as the final form masks the dogged determination, hard work and complex technical material at its core. Totally lacking in bias, the book provides a unique record of what was happening in Britain and the immense range of sculpture in public places. However, it is much more than a record, as it deals with many issues. He encourages us to make comparisons between different works by the same artist in different settings, emphasizing the importance of context. Above all, the book captures the flavour and mood of the times: the optimistic enthusiasm for projects concerned with sculpture in the open air from Yorkshire to Scotland and from Cumbria to Portland.

Walter Strachan was a good friend to the world of sculpture. He respected artists and their strange ways. He had an unshakeable belief in the power of art as an essential part of our society'.

Two years after the publication of *Open Air Sculpture in Britain*, which the Henry Moore Foundation had helped to fund and which Moore had praised on its publication, the sculptor and friend of over forty years died (in 1986).

This part of the book, which focuses particularly on the sixties, seventies and early eighties, contains four chapters. The first of these describes Strachan's interest in Italian literature and art, ancient and modern, refracted through his accounts of his four visits to Italy in 1955, 1962, 1972 and 1978.

The second of these chapters is a digression into the world of the Hatch Sisters, former child friends of Lewis Carroll, for whose writings Strachan had a lifelong passion, a connection which, obliquely, had led him to translate a novel by Enrico Emanuelli.

The third chapter in this part evokes the early years of Strachan's friendship and correspondence with Christopher Hewett, whose premature death in 1983 was a source of great sadness. The text is one he wrote for the catalogue of the memorial exhibition at Taranman in 1984.

The fourth chapter is an account of Strachan's friendship with Henry Moore over forty years, based on the long pamphlet he wrote and published in 1988. This goes right back to their first meetings in the forties, covers the articles Strachan wrote about Moore in the fifties and their collaboration over *Prométhée* in 1951. However, given that this chapter culminates with their collaboration on *Henry Moore: Animals*, and Strachan's account of his work on *Open Air Sculpture in Britain*, the whole text seems to belong chronologically at the conclusion of what I have partly characterized as 'The Sculpture Years'.

During the period covered by this section Walter Strachan retired from full time teaching at Bishop's Stortford College in 1968, the year in which the College celebrated its centenary. At a farewell dinner the then headmaster, Peter Rowe, himself a former pupil of Walter's, observed: 'Good schoolmasters... are divided into two sorts, pillars and lights. Walter I see more as a light... It has shone as a beacon in Stortford life for over forty years, lighting up for successive waves of the young a whole new world of experience, visual, imaginative, literary, which might so easily have gone unnoticed'.

To mark this moment, not mentioned in any of Strachan's four chapters, I have included, after the one about Lewis Carroll, a flyleaf drawing by Geoffrey Rhoades, one of many he sent in little books over the years to Walter, which seems to echo something of that chapter's spirit. Also included is a rhyme sheet, one of a folder of twenty, presented to

Strachan at that time by the boys of the most junior form he taught, lower five alpha, and images of the front covers of anthologies of the creative writing he helped to encourage: *First Offence* (1929), *Stortford Miscellany* (1961) and *New Wine* (1968).

9 Four Visits to Italy

1 1955: Milan, Venice, Florence

It was in the early fifties that I suddenly decided to work at my Italian. I won't go into the dull mechanics of how, but I was fascinated by the contemporary Italian stories that came my way. This led to a number of translations and, eventually, to four visits to Italy over a period of some twenty years.

Whereas the visits to Paris became an annual, and increasingly purposeful, spring event from 1949 onwards, Italy came into my life a few years later. When Nancy Cunard learnt that I 'had Italian too', she added her persuasions to my half-formed resolution that I should visit Italy forthwith. And in 1955 when my trip was decided and imminent, she listed the friends she had in various parts of Italy whom I must visit. Exciting names and, from my point of view, as a sketcher and gallery-haunter, in ideal locations: Freya Stark, the traveller, in Asolo, near Venice, where Peggy Guggenheim had her Gallery, Harold Acton in Florence.

My first stop would be Milan. From there I would have a look at Turin, a city associated with Cesare Pavese, perhaps the greatest contemporary Italian writer, two of whose novellas I had, by then, translated. Pavese had tragically committed suicide in 1950 after writing his masterpiece, *Il mestiere di vivere*. The publisher of many of my other translations, Peter Owen, had commissioned me to translate two of Pavese's novellas, *Il carcere* (*The Political Prisoner*, a book, based on his own experience, about a writer under house arrest) and *La bella estate* (*The Beautiful Summer*). They appeared in one volume in 1955. Now I was to visit the region where these stories were set. Even if I did not come across an Amelia (the working-class girl in *La bella estate*) or anyone who, like the hero of *Il carcere*, had spent years under house-arrest, I could stroll round a typically Northern Italian city, famous for its endless arcades.

My real love-affair with Italian — previously there had been brief flirtations — had come about through my discovery of excellent fiction and short stories by contemporary Italian authors, not just the internationally famous writers such as Pirandello, Moravia, Silone and Natalia Ginsberg, but authors little known outside Italy. I set about translating my favourites and had some success in placing them in periodicals, *Harpers*, for example. A story by Giovanni Papini, 'The day that was not restored' was broadcast by the BBC. Eyre and Spottiswoode agreed to publish my collection, *Modern Italian Stories*, which appeared in 1955. This happened to be a period when I was particularly caught up in the revival of Italic handwriting and typography. The publishers willingly adapted my calligraphic design for the jacket, using the names of the authors represented in the book. The collection was well received. The work of modern Italian writers, even those as celebrated as Moravia, was not well known in Britain. Pirandello was known only for his plays. Angus Wilson commented that most of the stories were 'quite excellent', (and indeed that the translation had 'the pleasant quality of reading like good English').

The publication of this collection was to lead to another volume, which Eyre and Spottiswoode published four years later. Marie Scott-James in a review in *The Observer* had picked out one story for special praise, 'The Auction', by a new author, Vera Cacciatore, whose animism I had myself found appealing. In writing to her, I suggested that I might devote a book wholly to stories by her. I felt confident that she would give her permission since she had already written to say the translation of 'The Auction' was *'molto bella'*. I had now learned that she was director of the Keats and Shelley Memorial House in Rome and this added to my interest. She expressed the hope that we should meet. In

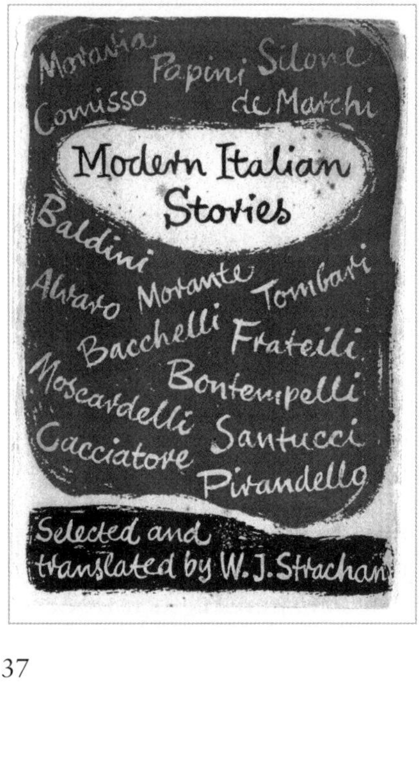

the event this only happened later, and in England. She and her husband, a well-known poet, Edoardo Cacciatore, paid us a visit in Bishop's Stortford. They were absolutely charming: Edoardo presented me with his latest poem, '*La restituzione*', a text of epic proportions and scope.

Following the *Modern Italian Stories* it was decided that I should translate three of Vera's novellas, using the title of one of them, *The Swing*, as the title of the book. As in the case of *Modern Italian Stories*, I had a hand in the cover design, which incorporated a delicate line-drawn portrait of her by de Chirico. The volume was published in 1959. The other stories, *The Bridge* and *Demitrio*, have transcendental overtones. The animism of the latter — a youth identifying himself with the instruments he is serving — is almost a reversal of the attitude that satirizes machines that have taken man over, as exemplified in Chaplin's film, *Modern Times*. Ignazio is obsessed by the idea of a bridge. He imagines the swirling river pursuing him. He will defeat the enemy by building a bridge that will serve the town. A charge is trumped up against this visionary and in an Ibsen-like situation he is shot as an enemy of the state. But the authorities are defeated: he has thought himself into the very Carrara marble in which the bridge — ultimately to bear his name — is constructed. 'The lively imagery and strength of her writing', wrote the *Sunday Times* reviewer, 'seems to have lost nothing in Mr W.J. Strachan's fresh and vital English translation'. Also published in 1959, my translation of Pavese's *The Comrade*, which portrays the world of political reality under Mussolini, could hardly have been more different in style and atmosphere.

Back in 1955 my first visit to Italy began with a cursory tour of Milan, a city I was to get to know better in 1972. I then entrained for Venice. I might have had more foreknowledge of Venice if my school prize had been the complete three volumes of Ruskin's *Stones of Venice*, instead of an economy remainder of volumes one and three only, a meanness I resented and which no wartime economy could justify. What I did have with me was an excellent pocket guide published by the unbelievable Krachmalnicoff of Milan. From a long list of pensions I chose the Casa Paganelli, on account of its position on the Riva degli Schiavoni, described as a 'wide and animated walk'. Out came my sketchbook as I tried to record familiar Venetian figures in their frock coats, staves and cocked hats.

As my stay was for some eight days, interrupted by Eastertide at Asolo, I had decided to limit myself mainly to outdoor 'sights' — sketching bridges and *palazzi* in watercolour. The highlight of this visit was the bronze horses of San Marco (not seen again until they were brought to be exhibited in London in 1983) and Santa Maria della Salute (I was familiar with John Singer Sargent's watercolour). I admired the Longhi in the Accademia delle Belle Arti. I made a special visit to the Palazzo Venier Galleria Peggy Guggenheim. I had Nancy Cunard's introduction to Peggy Guggenheim but, alas, she was temporarily absent, so I had to enjoy the mostly surrealist paintings without her comments. The Palazzo Venier has a formidable display of her choices of the chief Dadaists. It did not occur to me to inquire about the Venice Biennale, at which in 1948 Henry Moore had won the prize for sculpture. Ancient, or rather eighteenth-century, Venetian presence tends to exclude thoughts of contemporary art — and music — except seasonally. Instead, one bathes in images of Canaletto (better represented elsewhere), Guardi, Longhi, and the polyphonic music of Vivaldi. My pocket guide made no mention of the equestrian statue of Colleoni, Verrocchio's masterpiece, so I never saw it. I later greatly regretted having missed this fine work when I was writing about equestrian statues in *Towards Sculpture.*

It seemed a good idea to combine escaping the Easter crowds in Venice with making prearranged visits to Freya Stark and Alix Alfieri in Asolo. Asolo is a small town built on a hill among hills with olive-growing slopes. It is not more than two hours' coach drive in the direction of Treviso, with stops at Caerano and Montebelluna, yet it seemed completely rural and unbelievably bucolic — given its proximity to the Serenissima with its noisy vaporettos, its tourists and the flapping pigeons of Piazza di San Marco. The hotel where I stayed, the Albergo Al Sole, was quiet. The subdued atmosphere of the Roman Catholic Easter was being maintained. The bedrooms were lit with lamps that had had shades added for the Easter weekend. These gave off a smell of scorched paper and precluded reading in bed. The solemn procession on Good Friday, bearing the crucifix up the hill of the *borgo*, which would be its temporary resting-place, a procession in which all the inhabitants of the town seemed to take part, was made more impressive by the chanting that accompanied it. I, a non-Catholic, was deeply struck, moved.

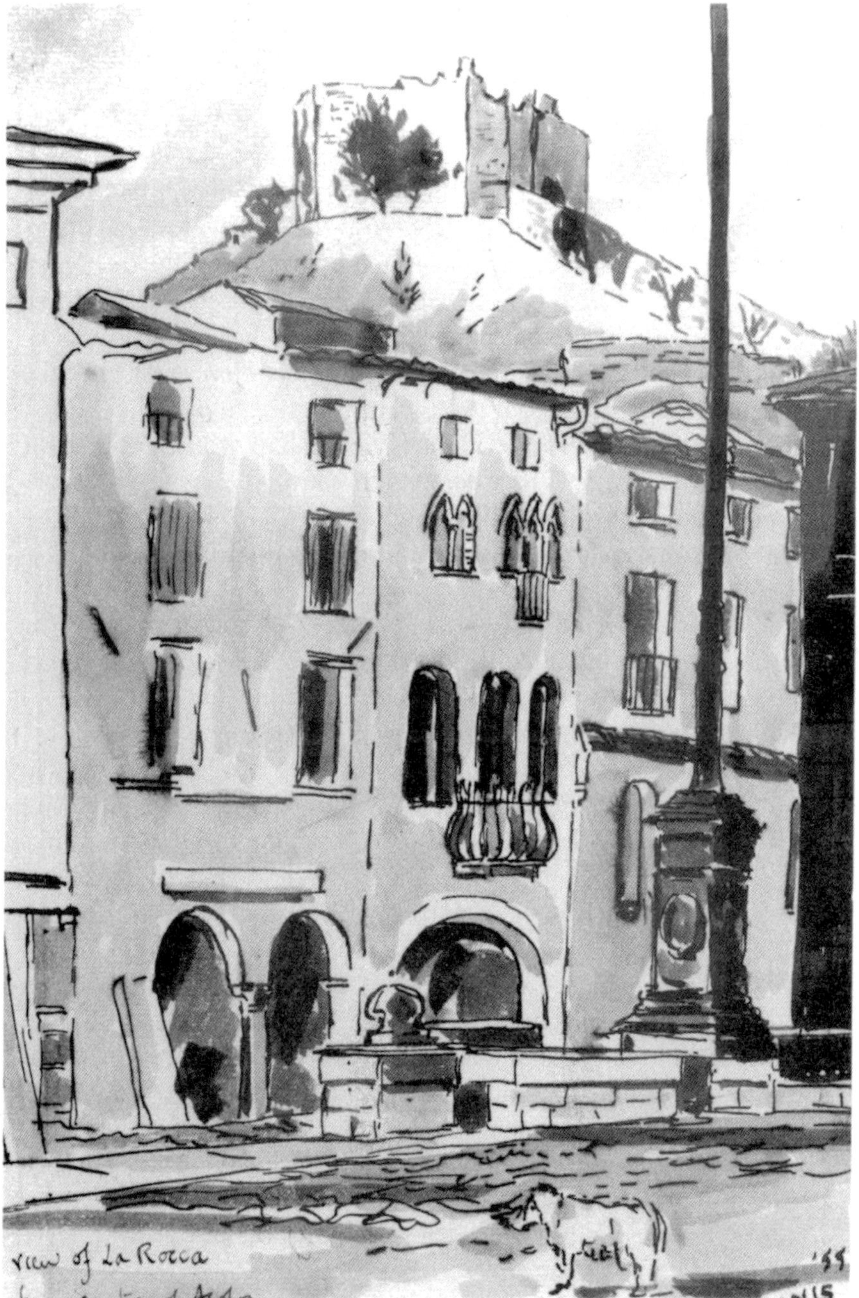
view of La Rocca
from centre of Asolo
'55
WJS

On Easter Saturday I decided to sketch the *borgo*, a picturesque crumbling mediaeval fortress. As I sat on the edge of the pavement my foot caught against my precious bottle of Winsor and Newton sepia ink. I wiped my ink-stained fingers and asked a passer-by — who happened to be English — where I might be able to buy *inchiostro nero*. He told me and left me to it. The *inchiostro nero* turned out to be *inchiostro verde*; a quite impossible green. I had to abandon drawing and do further subjects — I think to their gain — in watercolour.

On the Sunday I visited the grave of the famous dancer, Elenora Duse, in the Cimetero S. Anna. It seemed a good thing to do since, thanks to Nancy Cunard's contriving, I had been invited by a famous retired ballerina, Alix Alfieri, to a cocktail party at 'Sotto Castello' on Easter Monday. 'Have you met Lord Portsmouth?' my hostess asked me. 'Yes', the latter interpolated, 'I met him sketching. By the way, how did you get on with your *inchiostro nero?*' I apologised for the inky state he had found me in. Next introduction was to John Sparrow, the Fellow of All Souls. And next, a Mr Whitehead. 'The philosopher?' I inquired. 'No, the torpedo'. As it happened, I knew all about the Whitehead Torpedo. I had done sketches of it during the First World War for a hand-made magazine *Shell Splinters*, for which I was art editor and my schoolfriend, Tom Divine was editor. I have always collected things and at that time, at the age of thirteen, it had been war relics.

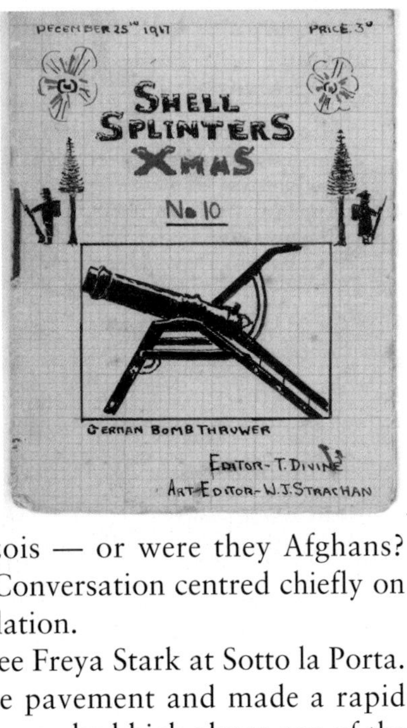

Our hostess, surrounded by borzois — or were they Afghans? exotic anyhow — exuded charm. Conversation centred chiefly on Nancy Cunard and poetry in translation.

Next day I went, as invited, to see Freya Stark at Sotto la Porta. Arriving a little early, I sat on the pavement and made a rapid sketch of the Villa Freya which was perched high above one of the town gateways. On the other side of the road was a picturesque section of the original town wall. However, no lyrical contemplation was possible since, as the traffic sped past, I was becoming covered with dust. Freya Stark, who had noticed me sketching, approved of my drawing and asked to see other sketches in the sketchbook. We had a simple lunch on her revolving table — so practical, she said, for moving any pile of material to where one is sitting. Everything in her workroom was obviously organised to make the best use of space, a vital consideration for a long-distance traveller, whose load must be reduced to a minimum.

Sketching in Asolo had been a very different experience from sketching in Venice, where small children gathered behind me with many an encouraging *'molto bello'*. The Piazza San Marco was crowded as one might expect at Easter, with all the vulgarity of the tourist trade, the litter, the pigeon-droppings. These had somehow to be ignored. I was fascinated by the two facing cafés, Florian's on the north side, Quadri's on the south. I was intrigued by the rows of identical chairs at the former. I have always been interested in chairs, and in my unpublished book on obsession and distortion in art I included a chapter on the treatment of chairs from Matisse to David Hockney, both chair-obsessed. When, years later, I met the Venetian painter, Ida Barbarigo, in Paris, I was fascinated to see the variations she had painted and drawn in Venice. Perhaps it was my own chair obsession that decided me to translate a story by Mario Soldati about an English woman who plotted to steal a chair from Florian's one moonless Venetian night.

I came away from Venice with more memories of 'the incidental things that pass', than of famous sights. Time spent sketching a corner of the Via Roberto Browning. An iced coffee at a café facing a house where Ruskin lived in 1877 with the plaque *'Sacerdoto dell'Arte nelle nostre pietre nel nostro S.Marco, quasi in ogni monumento d' Italia cerco insieme l'anima dell'artifice e l'anima del popolo'** — Ruskin's tribute to the part played in art by the ordinary man. The inscription continues in the same flattering terms. The plaque came from the Comune di Venezia and is dated xxvi gennaio MDCCCC. (January 26 1900) — I copied it down as I sipped my iced coffee.

* 'Devotee of the art of our stones in our San Marco, what I seek in almost every monument in Italy is both the soul of the craftsman and the soul of the people.'

Venice before Florence is the right order for a first visit. After the panache of Venice, the images we carry about with us of Turner's Venetian watercolours — our permanent luggage — you come to the quiet assurance of Florence, a city that half conceals its riches. You can wander about the place unconscious of the Uffizi. You need the guide book to tell you about the Bargello. Without previous knowledge (from a reading of Banister Fletcher) you might pass by the Palazzo Pitti, thinking it to be, perhaps, a prison. You halt at the Duomo; you cannot ignore the sculpture sheltering under the Loggia della Signoria. The Cellini Perseus carrying the head of the Gorgon will have no horror for the child of today. It is a refined work by a craft jeweller as well as sculptor.

I stayed at a good pensione (Morandi) in the Piazza Santissima Annunziata. Impersonal but correct. I made friends with a ninety-year-old Miss Howie. I regard her with respect. In her youth she followed the vagaries of the South African war. She was a link with a British Empire at the height of its pomp, of which I had witnessed only the last uniformed relics, the colours of full regimental parades to celebrate Empire Day, before the death knell of 1914 prophetically dressed the soldiery in the colour of Flanders mud. Miss Howie had a small footwarmer, a *scaldino*, which I made it my pleasure to place for her at mealtimes. Literally and metaphorically at her feet, in honour of the bent diminutive figure she had become. Never did the lines, which come to mind as I think about her, seem more appropriate: 'Ripeness is all / Her in her cooling planet revere / Do not presume to think her waste...'

Miss Howie was extremely knowledgeable about the Italian Renaissance and, when she realised I was seriously interested, arranged for me to make a visit to the gallery of a personal friend, Count Contini Bonacossi. There I saw many smaller paintings by famous Renaissance painters but came away with no special title to record. A very different matter in the Uffizi. It was hard to tear oneself away from the Botticelli 'Allegory of Spring' and 'The Birth of Venus'. The earlier Florentine master, Masaccio, had (on strict orders from Henry Moore) to be seen. In his large frescoes I found no difficulty in relating the bigness, the monumental treatment of the drapery, the gestures of arm and hand to Moore's drawings of his early period — grand matronly nudes.

Fiesole had a special attraction for me: frescoes by Fra Angelico in the church of San Dominico. On the grassy slope outside the monastery of that name I engaged in a long and fascinating conversation with a young Frenchman on the subject of Virginia Woolf. How it started I don't remember. I knew her novels were greatly admired in their French translations. We began the game of 'how many times...' He had read *Mrs Dalloway* fourteen times. I made a case for my own favourite — if I had to choose one — *To the Lighthouse.*

On my return to the pensione, I found a pencilled note from Harold Acton; it was an invitation to lunch at *La Pietra*, with instructions about which bus to take and which stop to use for *La Pietra* (anyone in Florence could have directed me there). I walked from the entrance grille towards the imposing mansion, sculpture in evidence on both sides of the drive. Two large limousines with national emblems informed me that the Danish diplomatic corps was represented. Fortunately Harold Acton knew about me from Nancy Cunard (who had kindly suggested I present him with one of my volumes of poems). He introduced me as a poet and translator of Italian stories. As I was probably the only guest to arrive in neither a limousine nor a taxi, a little literary cachet was useful. This opened up a conversation on trends in poetry and Acton's own book of poems, *This Chaos*, which Nancy Cunard had published at the Hours Press in 1930.

'Araldo', as Nancy called him, asked me to stay on, so that he could take me round the estate to see the remarkable collection of classical sculpture which his father, who had been British Ambassador in Rome, had built up. They were fine examples of the work of *classicisti* sculptors of the seventeenth and especially, the eighteenth century. When finally I left and made my way self-consciously back along the drive to the bus stop I felt like Charlie Chaplin walking off into the sunset. But I was glad to have met the author of *This Chaos* (of which I possessed a numbered and signed copy), as well as *Memoirs of an Aesthete*, now a freeman of Florence.

There were two pleasant letters about my visits from Nancy Cunard. 'How very glad I am that you enjoyed Italy so much. Both Freya and Alix wrote me enthusiastic notes about your visit. Isn't La Pietra incredible, with dear Araldo browsing among *tre-quattro-cinque-cento* and all the eighteenth century, *et tout, et tout...* I knew they would all love you because you are so appreciative'. Well, I hadn't, it seems, let her or myself down. So, off to

Paris from Florence for further research on the *livre d'artiste* and meetings with Krol, Gischia, Prassinos and Henri Michaux.

2 *1962: San Mamete*

My second visit to Italy was not until Spring 1962. After the publication of *Modern Italian Stories* and Pavese's *The Political Prisoner* a number of Italian translation commissions had followed. Peter Owen, publisher of *The Political Prisoner* asked me to do two more Pavese novellas, *The House on the Hill* and *The Comrade*, which were published successively in 1956 and 1959. All three were later published in paperback editions. It was a good period for more adventurous publishing.

Two further Italian translation projects came my way at the beginning of the sixties. It was the second of these that led to my second visit to Italy. The first came about because Enrico Emanuelli, the literary editor of the Milan newspaper *Corriere della Sera*, happened to see an article of mine in *The Times* in which I had referred to my interview with one of Lewis Carroll's former child-friends. A keen reader of Carroll, he asked me if I would interview the now ageing Ethel Hatch, the child in question, for the Sunday edition of his paper. I tell the story in a later chapter, but I mention it in the present context because Emanuelli, also a novelist, asked me to translate his most recent novel, *Uno di New York*. I liked its anti-hero theme — the story of great success effecting a moral revolution in the subject's life. Most Italian emigrants — whether successful or unsuccessful, contented or resigned — seem to remain in the country they have adopted. The hero of *Uno di New York*, Alessandro Enne, is a successful portrait-painter working in New York. Suddenly he feels nostalgia for Italy and takes a holiday there, visiting the friends and scenes of his childhood. This ends, not in revulsion against his successful career in New York but in disillusionment with what the people with whom he once associated have become, their morality no better than that of big-city life in America. It is a convincing portrayal of a personal situation, and won the author a prize, the coveted *Premio Bugatti* for 1959.

My translation was published in 1962. Emanuelli liked it and asked me whether I would translate his next novel, *Settimana nera*. I agreed but Emanuelli died suddenly and the project was not followed up. It was a sad end to a career full of promise and for me the loss of a respected and lovable friend who — a small indication of his nature — went out of his way to procure for me an Italian edition of Lewis Carroll's *Alice nel paese delle meraviglie.*

My second Italian visit in 1962 came as a sequel to two commissions received from the brilliant Italian scholar, now widely known for his masterly translation of Lampedusa's one and only novel, *Il gattopardo* (*The Leopard*), Archibald Colquhoun. Colquhoun edited the Oxford Library of Italian Classics series for the Oxford University Press. He was collecting material for a volume of Italian regional stories for the series and commissioned me to translate one involving conversations in dialect, 'The Phryne Case' by Edoardo Scarfoglio. Taking a calculated risk, I produced a version with dialogue in a kind of West Country speech, vaguely inspired by Hardy's peasant language. In the critics' views it came off, apparently, and John Bell of Oxford University Press sent his congratulations. The volume was published in 1961. My contribution gave Colquhoun enough confidence in my work for him to ask me to undertake the translation of Antonio Fogazzaro's classic novel *Piccolo Mondo Antico* (*The Little World of the Past*) for the Oxford Library of Italian Classics. This was a challenge. John Bell had doubts about the project because of its length (380 pages in the Italian edition). In addition there would be an introduction by Tommaso Gallarati Scotti.

I was very conscious of the distinction of being commissioned to translate an Italian prose work of this stature, considered by many to be in merit second only to Mazzoni's *I Promessi Sposi*, (*The Betrothed*). I had a preliminary discussion over lunch at the Travellers Club with Archibald Colquhoun, who then left me to it. The next communication from him came in a letter in March 1962: 'I saw Gallarati Scotti last night; he is doing his piece for *Piccolo Mondo*. Bell says the Introduction must be ready in English by the end of the month. I could do it myself but feel it would be much better if the complete job were yours'. By then I had decided to visit San Mamete, beside Lake Lugano, where the book is set, in April. Armed with a sketchbook, I would be able to record some of the places connected with the story. And I was going to be taking the proofs of the text with me.

It was one of my most exciting translation ventures. Looking through old letters, it seems that the idea of doing an up-to-date translation was mine (the previous one, in my opinion — and Colquhoun's — too Italianate, had been in 1907). Colquhoun approved with a clinching 'this seems a novel where *language-tone* is important'. When the question of a cover design arose, I was not so fortunate as with Eyre and Spottiswoode, in that the publishers preferred to use a still from the film version of the book made by the writer and film director Mario Soldati in 1940, rather than one of my sketches done *in situ*. In retrospect however, I am quite glad, since it became a talking-point with Soldati when I met him much later in Tellaro in 1978.

Piccolo Mondo Antico, which Fogazzaro regarded as his best and favourite work, won academic and public acclaim. Not for nothing had he spent a decade (August 1884 to August 1895) over its writing and revision. It was internationally recognised. The Academy of Science of Turin conferred on its author the prestigious *Premio Gautieri* 'for the best literary work of recent years'. The book has gone into its hundredth Italian edition.

The novel concerns domestic tragedy against a background of rebellion in the province of Valsolda, which is under Austrian domination. The first *Risorgimento* (rising) of 1848 and the second of 1859 had taken place during the author's childhood and youth. The hero, Franco, is a rebel suspect, having to avoid house arrest above all for the sake of his wife, Luisa, and the ill-fated child, Maria, who is drowned playing in a boathouse with her doll. The success of the book depended on a skilful combination of elements, not the least important of which is the climatic and topographic setting. Their importance is underlined in the opening chapter that takes place under a prevailing *breva*, a west wind laden with damp and fog. The tethered boats and gondolas rock in their moorings. Signor Pasotti ('Pin') the controller of customs, is proposing to take his wife and the parish priest to a party given by the domineering old Marchesa Orsola Maironi, but is not anxious to venture out onto the lake in their boat. The frightening *breva* abates; out come the Tarot cards, Pasotti's obsession. The author pauses and — himself a native of this region — reminisces: 'He sees once again the boat sailing between the reefs of San Mamete and Cressogno, he sees in memory dark houses reflecting their vulgar splendours in the lake waters... the ancient Oria mulberry tree, the old Madonnina beech...'.

After the storm the child's unconscious body is found floating

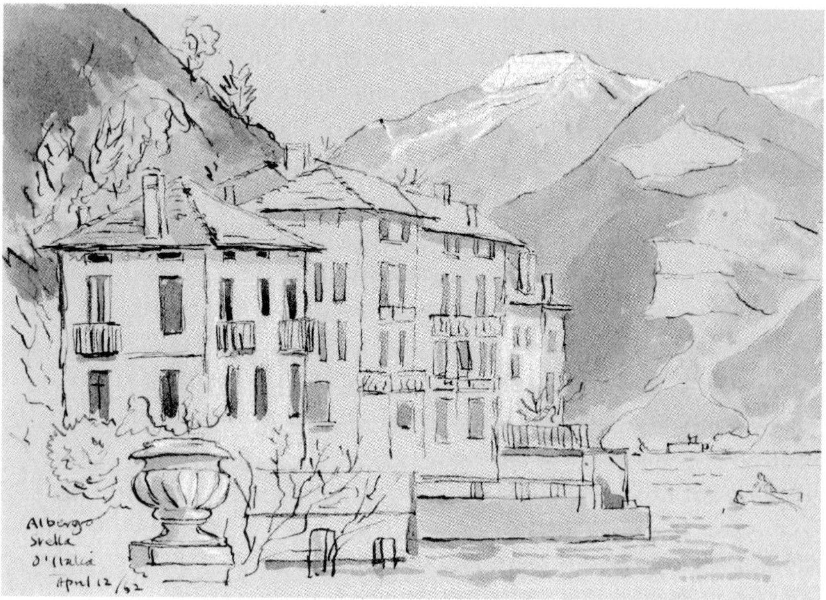

there in the water. This dramatic event is written with great poignancy. Fogazzaro had lost his only son in similar tragic circumstances. His own philosophical doubts are echoed in the disputes between Franco and his pious God-fearing wife, Luisa. The tragic side of the book is relieved by almost Shakespearean humour in the depiction of local characters. The dinner-party, with steaming *risotto* and fragrant truffles, introduces humour in the very first chapter, overshadowed as it is by potentially perilous storms.

My visit in April 1962 to San Mamete, which lies on the frontier between Italy and Switzerland, could not have been more different from those to Venice and Florence seven years earlier. There the only rural part of my stay had been the journeys to and from Venice to Asolo and my walks in the hills above — rich, warm, fertile land. I arrived at San Mamete by the Porlezzo ferry (*traghetto*) from a landing-stage in Lugano, a pleasant trip right up to the landing-stage of the Hotel Stella. My first westward view took in the mountain, San Salvatore, against which some of the most dramatic scenes in *Piccolo Mondo Antico* are set. At the hotel, where I had a room with a balcony overlooking the lake. I was plunged straight into the atmosphere of the novel. The daughter of the Hotel, Signorina Liliana Ortello, knew the book and we talked about it. I inquired whether there was perhaps a local schoolteacher who could coach me in oral Italian; my vocabulary was adequate but the speed of Italian, unless rather academic, I sometimes found tricky. No such coach was found but our sessions after breakfast on the balcony in the cool of the morning gave me a wonderful start to the day. Liliana was as generous as she was beautiful. She firmly refused any payment. 'If you want to see me again, come before October. I am marrying an officer in the Bersagliere regiment'. I felt a pang of jealousy.

The first day I walked eastwards from the village up the steep hills that turned into mountainsides. Some of the spring mountain flowers were out. During my stay I located and made sketches in some of the *paesini* (hamlets) that occur in the Fogazzaro novel. I found the Maironi family's house, visited the church of San Sebastiano near the house of Franco and Luisa. I took a ride to the region of Isola Bella on Lake Maggiore, ventured up some of the *sentieri* (footpaths) which traverse the Vasolda region. To have the page proofs of my translation with me to correct *in situ* was an added excitement. Nor had I ever enjoyed more the sketching of evocative subjects. What pleased me most in the response to the book's publication the following November was personal messages from Nancy Cunard as well as from Vera Cacciatore (who had given me valuable advice on a number of textual points).

When the Italian connection in my life was beginning to turn away from literature and towards sculpture, one last novella by Cesare Pavese, one of his best, *La spiaggia* (*The Beach*) landed on my desk. This was to be paired in the same volume (which appeared in 1963) with *Fuoco grande* (*A Great Fire*), a novella written by Pavese in collaboration with Bianca Garufi, in which chapters giving Giovanni's version of his relationship with Silvia, written by Pavese, alternate with chapters giving Silvia's version, written by Garufi. As in *The Beach*, the interest lies in the probing of ambiguous male-female relationships in the setting of the Riviera di Ponente, the coast which faces onto the Ligurian Sea, near Genoa. In *The Beach* the strained relationship between Doro and his wife Clelia is related by Doro's friend. We are dealing with characters several notches higher in the social scale than those in Pavese's other novellas. There is a comparable atmosphere of purposelessness but the author presents the characters around the beach party with objective acuity. *The Beach* has rightly been compared to Antonioni's film *Le Amiche*, in which characters wander in and out of frame with a minimum of explanation. In *The Beach*, for example, Doro paints, a former pupil turns up, one of the girls breaks a collarbone. What are they there for? But, wrote the critic Robert Taubman in the *New Statesman*: 'There's a striking energy in Pavese. He conveys more about the beach party than meets the eye or than they know themselves'.

3 *1972: Florence, Rome, Milan*

My visit to Florence in 1972 was in aid of research on Renaissance sculpture for the opening chapter of my book, *Towards Sculpture*. I was interested in exploring the influence of Renaissance sculpture on — and also noting contrasts in the approaches to — the treatment of similar themes in later periods. One theme was bronze reliefs, and it was while I was inspecting Ghiberti's panels on the Baptistery doors that I had my encounter with Mrs Hazel B. Sobernheimer of San Marino, California, which led to a continuing correspondence and friendship.

The assignment of authorship to the various bronze panels is quite complicated, for example, Andrea Pisano, who was responsible for the mediaeval panels, was unrelated to the better known Nicola Pisano and his son, Giovanni who did the fine reliefs on the pulpit at Pisa. The commission to do all twenty-four panels of the Baptistery bronze door in Florence had been won by Lorenzo Ghiberti on the strength of his high-relief panel 'Isaac'. I was inspecting this and other Biblical themes when a lady with a guide book and, as it turned out, more knowledge of the scriptures than I had, asked if I needed help with the identification of the subjects. She quietly answered my questions and asked what particular interest I had in the Porta del Paradiso. I told her about the book I was preparing and the object of my present study. She accompanied me for the rest of the day, and we have occasionally met in London since and correspond fairly regularly.

From Florence I travelled on to Rome, my purpose being to follow up the Renaissance sculpture in Florence: under the Loggia dei Lanzi: 'Rape of the Sabines' (Giambologna), the Canova 'Venere Italica' — of special interest since it was presented by Napoleon in exchange for the famous Medici Venus. I mentioned earlier the private collection in Florence of the Conte Contini Bonacossi, a nephew of the elderly Miss Howie's. There, thanks to a grace and favour visit, I saw memorable works: a Goya sketch for his 'Duchess of Alba', 'The Homage of Velasquez to Titian', the former's 'The Water-Carrier'.

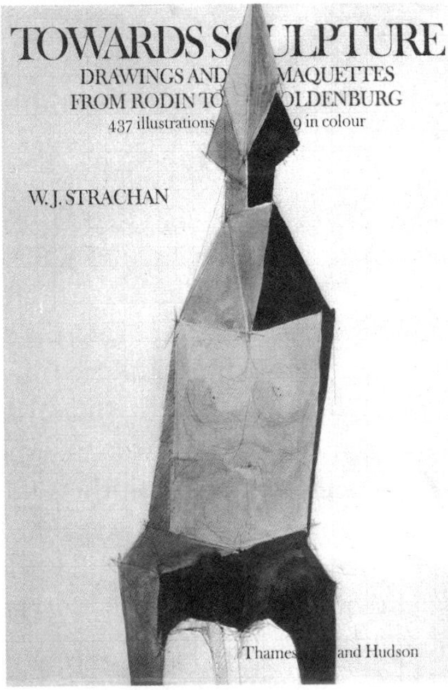

In Rome I had two rather jarring encounters. On arrival there I presented myself at the desk of the one hotel where I had got an agency to book a room. No record of the booking. Furthermore no room. It was 8.30pm, no chance elsewhere, and pouring with rain. As I turned away despondently, I heard a cry — there was a cancellation — room on the top (eighth or tenth) floor. A wonderful meal, and later the best bath I've ever had. When you turned on the tap of the huge bath it was as if the Tiber were pouring in. Hotel Moderno: bless its name and situation, near every bus station.

So, in the morning, off to the Forum: as impressive as I had expected. The impassioned evocation of Rome in Corneille's *Horace* passed through my mind, along with earlier remembrances of classroom Julius Caesar. A strong atmosphere of place. On to St Peter's, and there I questioned a priest. Where were Manzù's reliefs on *La Porta della Morte?* He affected ignorance and stalked off into the Duomo. There had been, I believe, some criticism of Pope John XXIII's approval of the general theme for this gate: various forms of death, with Christ's as the climax. I was already familiar with Manzù's treatment; he had sent me very fine photographs of the preparatory drawings he had made and of the final panels (and some of these were reproduced in my book when it appeared four years later). There were touches that might not have pleased Pope John's predecessor, Pius XII, who was suspected of turning a deaf ear to stories of the Nazi death camps. Manzù shows Death with a Nazi helmet. *The Gate of Death* had not originally been commissioned under this title. The work in its final form bears only a distant relation to the original subject stipulated: *The Triumph of Saints and Martyrs*. Controversy, aesthetic and religious, surrounded the changes introduced by the sculptor and, to judge from the attitude I encountered, had not yet ceased. In 'Death on Earth' Cardinal Testa had objected to the positioning of the child's face, looking in through a window at the form of its mother, collapsed on a chair. He wanted the child removed to a conventional place beside the mother's skirts. But in this, as throughout, Pope John had staunchly supported the sculptor's own judgements, with regard to both themes and treatment. It was therefore fitting that on Pope John's death in June 1963, a year before the *Gate of Death* was completed, Manzù should have replaced the proposed 'Death by Drowning' with the subject of 'Pope John in Prayer'; an aesthetic improvement also, since the panel balanced the seated figure of Pope Gregory on the other wing. The whole treatment compared well with the existing relief in St Peter's by Filarete, executed in the mid fifteenth century.

My next assignment was to see some of Canova's sculpture-carving: which, in its classical idealism, is the sculptural counterpart of the paintings of David and Ingres. The carving I most enjoyed was the portrait of Paolina Bonaparte in the Borghese. It is Canova's masterpiece. I had hoped to visit Vera Cacciatore in the Casa Keats/Shelley by the Spanish Steps. Unfortunately she was away but the journey was not wasted since I was near the church of S. Andrea della Valle, an important objective for the marvellous Bernini sculpture of an angel holding out a scroll, carved in white marble. Its tall plinth is in red and green marble. What a man, Bernini! As if architecture wasn't enough! It is hard to leave Rome without mentioning other works of his. 'Daphne', the charming 'Boy with a Duck', the later (1652) 'Verità'. But the fountains allow another opportunity of seeing his genius: the Fontana del Tritone in the Piazza Barberini. Fountains are to Rome what the fountains by Coyszevox are to Louis XIV's Versailles. The Italians inherited the Romans' love of water — baths becoming fountains.

I arrived at Milan railway station in pouring rain after a long journey. I made my way to my hotel, the Argentina, too late to expect dinner, and settled for quick sandwiches in the bar. I was especially eager to view the first episode on television of a much advertised serial of the children's book by Collodi, *Pinocchio*, better known in Walt Disney's film version. I had the job of persuading other customers at the bar to switch from a Sunday sports programme. They were prepared to give Collodi's masterpiece a trial — there were famous actors in it — and in the event admitted to enjoying it. What reminded me of this episode recently was re-reading *Curiosità della Lingua Italiana* by Dino Provenzal and learning that the use of *'la lingua di Pinocchio'* in schools was such as to affect substantially the speech and writing of pupils. Indeed it had helped to fix the Tuscan dialect (or language) as standard Italian where local dialects still predominated. *Bravo*, or rather *Bravissimo* for Collodi!

4 1978: Tellaro

A sequel to my visit to Italy in 1972 came six years later. An encounter I had with a young medical student, Camillo Binda, who was visiting a church with his mother in Milan in 1972 when he was still a schoolboy — though a precocious one — proved to be the start of a continuing friendship. I remember his enthusiasm for the small portrait sculptures (clay modelling) by Marino Marini in the Centro Studio Piero della Francesca. One was a portrait of Henry Moore. It was not very good, but it stimulated Camillo to want to learn more about the sculptor, and the chance presented itself with the open-air exhibition of work by Moore in Florence in 1972. So when Camillo came to stay with us in Bishop's Stortford, I was able to take him over to Henry Moore's studios.

My fourth visit to Italy was to the villa of Camillo's parents in Tellaro in Liguria. Camillo was now a medical student. The villa, at Via D.H. Lawrence 1, was a reminder of the English author's period in nearby Fiascherino (also visited by Shelley and Byron) and these places facing the Ligurian Sea are within the ambit of Genoa where parts of *The Beach* have their setting. And it was at a villa in the same Via D.H. Lawrence, that I had my encounter with Mario Soldati, the writer and film director, in a riot of 'only connect's. Soldati had directed the film based on Fogazzaro's novel *The Little World of the Past* but we talked more about his interest in Robert Louis Stevenson and Henry James, whose works were fully represented in his library, than about Fogazzaro. The latter now seemed distant news to one preoccupied with his own novellas. He presented two volumes of these to me.

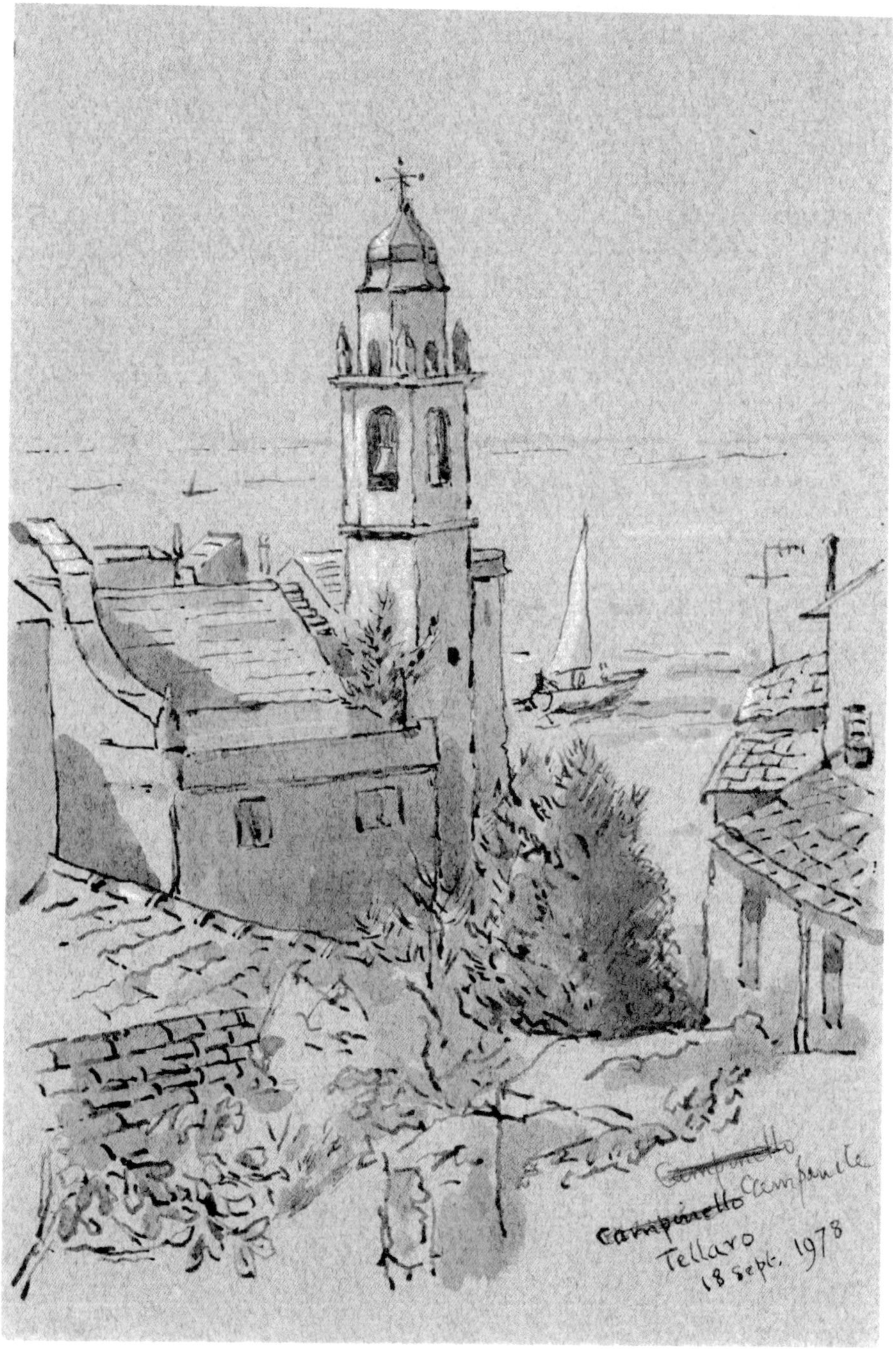
Campanile
Tellaro
18 sept. 1978

Another connecting link was the Moore villa and studio at nearby Forte dei Marmi. Moore's earlier exhortation had been that I must see Michelangelo's last *'Pietà'* at the Castello Sforzesco in Milan. Now his message in 1978 was that the carvings on the pulpit in the Baptistery at Pisa by Nicola and Giovanni Pisano, father and son, must on no account be missed. Nor should I neglect Giovanni's carvings on the façade of the Cathedral at Siena, work considered so favourably by contemporary authorities that, for these and his work as architect, he was exempted all taxes. How much more practical than our honours system! During that same holiday, Camillo drove me over to Forte de Marmi in mid-September. He showed me the Carrara quarries where Michelangelo, Moore's hero, had preceded him by five hundred years. Michelangelo was very much in my mind at that time, as I proposed to show his final *'Pietà'* in my book on obsession and distortion in art. Moore was very co-operative about my using several of his works to illustrate my thesis. I chose his Upright Motive No. 8 — echoing the Michelangelo in its crucifix. I planned to include his 'Rocking Chair bronze' in a chapter on 'The Chair Obsession' and ear-marked his Green Marble Mask carving of 1924 for a sub-section of the chapter on heads. The chapter which I felt was most important was on 'Art from Art' — transcriptions by one artist of a predecessor's work. This was a kind of homage — as in the case of Francis Bacon's to Van Gogh's 'Painter on the way to work' or Picasso's fragmentation of Delacroix's 'Les Femmes d'Alger' or a redrawing as a form of exploration. Moore's transformation of Dürer's 'Portrait of Konrad Verkell' was one example. He has seen the prominent nose as a mountain in the landscape. However, in his version of Bellini's 'Mary Magdalene and the Dead Christ', Moore emphasised the tenderness of the original by raising the position of Mary's hand from the wound in Christ's body to just below his head...

10 The Hatch Sisters and Lewis Carroll

Lewis Carroll, the Reverend Charles Lutwidge Dodgson, had a lifelong relationship with the Hatch family of Oxford. Its head, the Reverend Edwin Hatch, had a Canadian-born wife and three daughters: Beatrice, born in 1866, Ethel in 1869, and Evelyn in 1871. There were also two sons, of whom Wilfred ('Wilfie') appears in a photograph of Dodgson's as 'Cupid'. Dodgson's friendships with children were an all-important emotional outlet for an affectionate and lonely cleric. They took the form of entertaining a succession of the children of Oxford middle-class families. Some of the mothers insisted, especially if a photographic session was proposed, on the presence of a chaperone. His entertaining took many forms: playing games (card and board) of his own invention with them, reading to them from his books. But the most exciting game, as both Evelyn and Ethel emphasised in my interviews with them in 1944 and 1963, was dressing up. They were let loose on his huge trunk of disguises, from rags to exotic costumes, and were often photographed in the costume of their choice.

It is doubtful if his friendships with children, and women as they grew into maturity, would have been documented but for the Alice books. There is a succinct entry in his diary for 4 July 18: 'Up the river [to Godstow]. I told them the fairy tale'. 'Them' were the three Liddell sisters. It seems that the story flowed uninterruptedly as he wrote it down afterwards. It is as miraculous as Coleridge's transcription of 'Kubla Khan'. Dodgson's personality, charming and affectionate, imprinted itself so strongly on some of his child-friends as to become an omnipresent background in their subsequent years. This is especially true of the Hatch sisters. Significantly none of them married.

My initial contact with Evelyn was fortuitous. I had contributed to *The English Weekly* an article entitled 'Lewis Carroll Revisited' which had been inspired by my reading *Lewis Carroll's Letters to His Child-friends*, edited and introduced by Evelyn Hatch. The book is long since out of print. Two passages illustrate contrasting aspects of Dodgson's character. The first, from a letter to Agnes Hughes, daughter of the painter Arthur Hughes, is unbridled in its hilarity but too undisciplined for the Alice books. The whole letter is a pretext for a cat extravaganza. 'About the cats you know... I lent them a portfolio for a bed — they wouldn't have been comfortable in a real bed, you know; they were too thin — but they were *quite* happy between the sheets of blotting-paper — and each of them had a pen-wiper for pillow...'.

The second is not intended to hide Dodgson's deep disappointment over the failure of his correspondent, Agnes Hull to keep a rendezvous. 'I have succeeded in forgetting you. It's been a very hard job, but I took lessons in forgetting at half-a-crown a lesson. After three lessons I forgot my own name and forgot to go for the next lesson. So the professor said I was getting on very well. "But", he said, "I hope you won't forget to pay for the lessons"'. It reveals the melancholy side of the bachelor who lavished all his affection on these young friends and who, in consequence, became vulnerable to any neglect.

I questioned Evelyn Hatch on this side of her hero's personality. 'Too much', she countered, 'has been said about Mr Dodgson's melancholy. He was never sad with us; he was always gay and full of life, though it is true that he never indulged in romping games with his child-friends. Nor is it true that he was shy and taciturn in grown-up company. He was, on the contrary, the life and soul of the party — as we knew from the direct evidence of our parents and friends'. I came away from Evelyn in 52 Sheffield Terrace that April day excited by the experience of feeling close to one of my literary heroes, the Prince of Nonsense.

My invitation to visit Ethel Hatch came as a surprise. The article I had contributed to *The Times* (2 January 1963) 'What happened to Nonsense?' had been sparked off by what I considered a stupid French translation of 'The Hunting of the Snark', translated word for word by the poet, Louis Aragon. The result literally made no sense. All the humour and wit were lost. Of course I took the point: he was treating the poem as a masterpiece of surrealism! I went on to consider the problem facing any would-be translator of Carroll or Lear and mentioned Evelyn Hatch in the context of her book, *Lewis Carroll's Letters to His Child-Friends*, with its hilariously surrealist passages.

Her sister Ethel wrote to me, intriguingly, 'I can give a first-hand account of Mr Dodgson' — she usually referred to him thus — 'instead of all the foolish things that were said about him'. As if I needed any further inducements to visit her, she threw out two more baits. 'I came to live at 12 Earl's Terrace in 1945 — not knowing at that time that Mr Dodgson had often visited this house when the George Madconalds lived here, and later Walter Pater. I was only a child when he knew my parents in Oxford'.

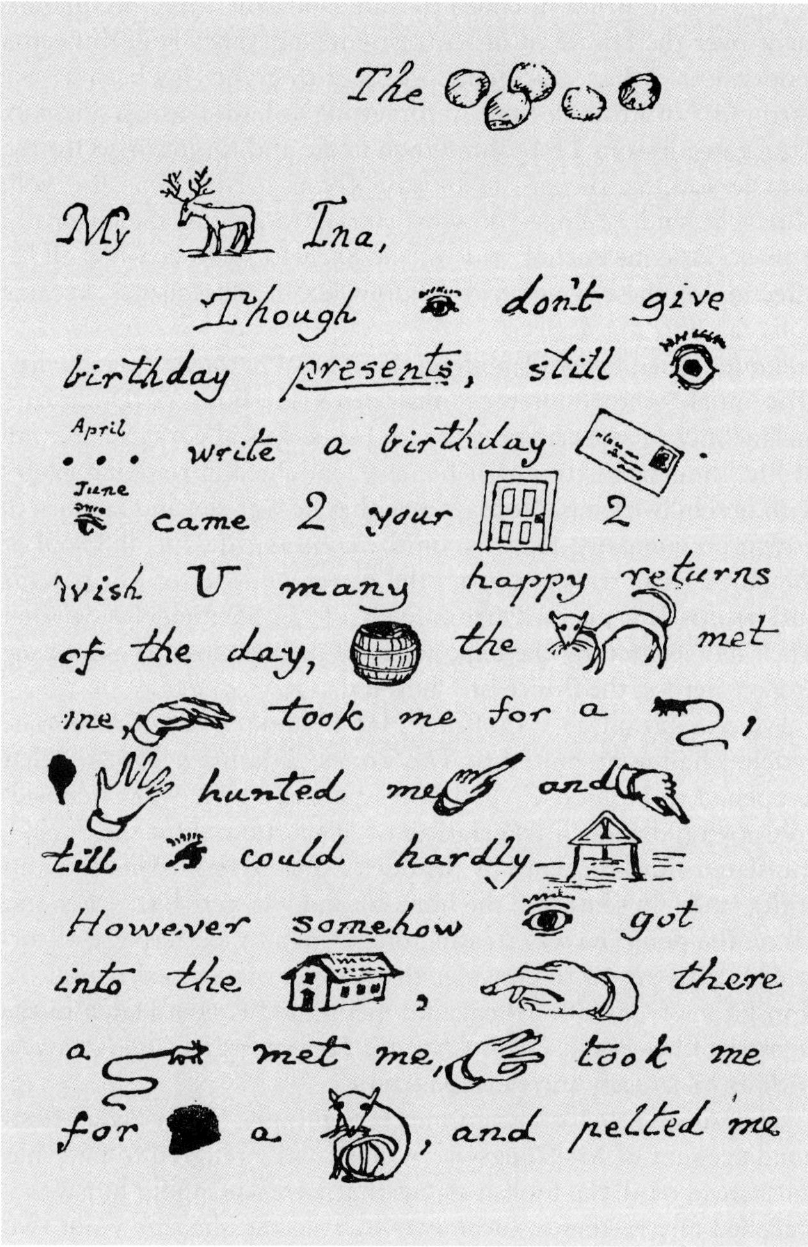

The

My Ina,

Though don't give
birthday presents, still
April
... write a birthday .
June
came 2 your 2
wish U many happy returns
of the day, the met
me, took me for a ,
hunted me and
till could hardly
However somehow got
into the , there
a met me, took me
for a , and pelted me

When the visit could be arranged Ethel Hatch was able to show me the square notepaper on which Dodgson wrote his invitations in purple ink and several albums of photographs. She remembered a special wind-up black furry bear which ambled along, growling and recalled looking at his collection of fourteen musical boxes (she counted them) when a cupboard door was open. She told me how exciting it had been to rummage in Dodgson's great basket of disguises, but she had not enjoyed the posing: she had felt cold and uncomfortable in undress. Eyebrows had sometimes been raised over resulting photographs, not so much of the 'undress' as of the nightgowned figures: these he favoured as a contrast to the raga-muffins.

Ethel had gone on to study at St Hugh's College, for a certificate in modern history: no degrees for women yet. Dodgson protested to the Principal when a chaperone was required to accompany her with him to his rooms in Christ Church. Although he wrote for approval to Mrs Hatch about Ethel taking the train from Goring to Paddington unaccompanied, he felt no qualms about having her to stay as his guest for a week at Eastbourne. There would, he assured her, be a landlady and her maid at 7 Lushington Road. The frequent invitations to all the Hatch sisters to stay at Eastbourne — but strictly one at a time — gives us the measure of Dodgson's deep friendship for them: a platonic friendship, quite different from the almost passionate love he expresses for his favourite child-friends. Touchingly — after the death of Edwin Hatch, which distressed Ethel to the point of illness — Dodgson pressed her to come and recuperate at 7 Lushington Road. There were visits from there to the local theatre, one to a triple bill with Martin Harvey playing the lead in each. 'All three pieces were good', Dodgson reports to Mrs Martin Harvey.

Dodgson had a particularly soft spot for child-actresses and took an active part in their promotion. Of the Hatch sisters, it was Beatrice who had the talent for elocution, and it was she whom Dodgson chose to declaim *The Prologues* which he had written for one of Mrs Hatch's drawing-room entertainments. He fostered her talent and took a delight in taking her to see *Much Ado About Nothing* when his great friend Ellen Terry was playing the part of Beatrice. The actress knew that Beatrice was present, and after the performance sent her a photograph of herself as Beatrice, inscribed 'From Beatrice to Beatrice', with her words to Don Pedro, 'There was a star danced, and under that was I born'.

Dodgson, who was passionately interested in the theatre, made sure that his child and girl friends should share the pleasure he gained from playgoing. It was a period of great actors: Henry Irving, Herbert Beerbohm Tree, Martin Harvey, George Alexander: striking, charismatic figures, idolized by the public, all four of them knighted. He took the Hatch sisters, singly or in pairs, to shows as different as fairy plays like *The Rose and the Ring*, historical drama like Bulwer-Lytton's *Richelieu*, and the entertainments of John Lawrence Toole ('I always find Toole amusing' he wrote to Coventry Patmore). And, of course, to the stage version of *Alice: Alice, a Dream Play in Two Acts*, first performed in 1886 and revived in 1888 at the Globe Theatre when Dodgson had the thrill of seeing one of his protégées, Isa Bowman, a great favourite of his, as Alice while one of Isa's sisters, Empsie, played the Dormouse.

Dodgson's relationships with the special favourites — not all to do with the stage — bring us back again to the question of the nature of these child-friendships which I discussed with Ethel Hatch. His friendship with all three Hatch sisters was purely platonic and for life since, in each case, it was based on shared interests. But 'My own darling Isa', 'Your loving (putative) uncle', betrays a lover's love. I didn't go into details over tea with Ethel Hatch, but I had in mind a passage Dodgson wrote about the general run of his child-friends. 'Usually the child becomes an entirely different being as she grows into a woman, [so] that our friendship has to change, too, and that is usually done by sliding down... from a loving intimacy into an acquaintance'. This feeling may account for the fits of depression and melancholy which — *pace* Ethel's testimony above — we saw in his letter to Agnes Hull.

None of the Hatch sisters were as close to Dodgson as Agnes Hull or Enid Stevens (to Mrs Stevens: 'I have lost a considerable fraction (say 2/5) of my heart to your little daughter'). But he was an affectionate man and demonstrative to his young friends. We get a hint of it in a letter to the Reverend Edwin Hatch (26 December 1887, when Ethel would have been 24): '... love to your girls (it is as well, perhaps, that they have left Oxford just now, as I should be much puzzled to know on what terms to meet Ethel! We were on kissing terms last time we met...)'.

Most of the special child-friends got married and, as Ethel admitted, Dodgson tended to lose interest in girl friends once they married. Can it be that the Hatch sisters remained single because Dodgson was too dominant an influence in their lives? Above all, he wanted children to be happy and to enjoy themselves — with no reservations. To a Mother Superior who wished to know what the religion was in the *Alice* books, he replied: 'The *Alice* books do not teach any religion; in fact they don't teach anything at all'. This absence of any didactic purpose (in contrast with such books as Kingsley's *The Water Babies*) shows his complete understanding of children. He even mocks at the Victorian concern for moral lessons in the Duchess's 'and the moral of that is...'.

Dodgson, the amateur artist himself and a frequent visitor to Royal Academy exhibitions, did all he could to help Ethel gain entry to an art school. When she failed to be accepted by the Herkomer School of Art at Bushey under its formidable Principal, Sir Herbert von Herkomer R.A., he sent her a comforting letter which encouraged her to try her luck with the Royal Academy Schools, where she got in. I noticed incidentally that some of her

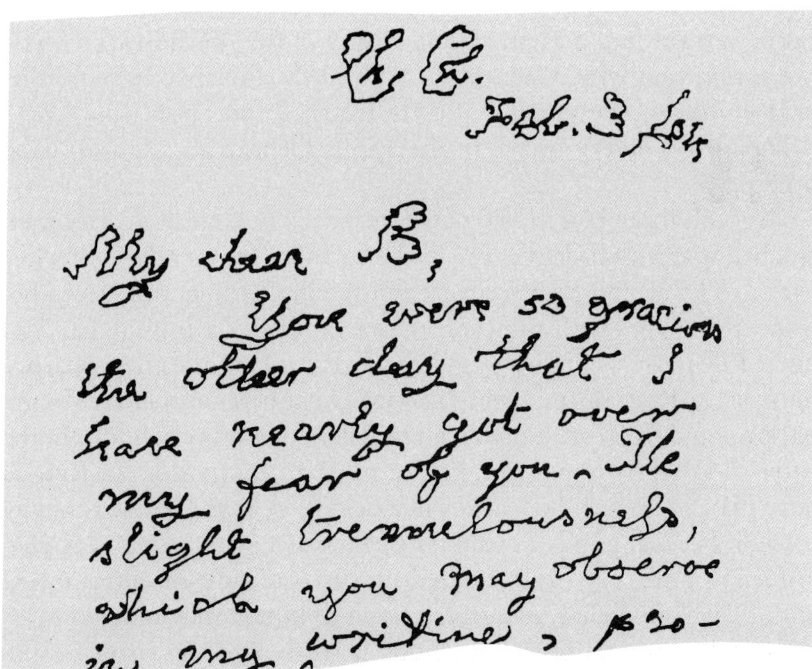
Ch. Ch.
Feb. 3, /95

My dear B,
You were so gracious the other day that I have nearly got over my fear of you. The slight tremulousness, which you may observe in my writing, is so-

charming watercolours were hung in the room in which we were talking. Dodgson came to her rescue when she was working on a commission to do portrait drawings in chalk line, a medium, with which she was unfamiliar. Remembering that Beatrice had some work of this kind by Gertrude Thomson, he got her to send some examples to Ethel.

Ethel, the intellectual of the sisters, was able to follow the intricacies of Dodgson's lectures on logic, which she attended at St Hugh's and at Eastbourne. She was a student during the regime of Miss Moberley, the first Principal of St Hugh's and, oddly, author of a ghost story, *An Adventure*, her account of an experience on a visit to Versailles of seeing the ghost of Marie Antoinette. Were people more liable to see ghosts at that time? Ethel Hatch told me, in all seriousness, that 'a woman living here temporarily saw on at least one occasion a silent, smiling "presence" in a chair opposite the one in which you are now sitting'. The woman's description of the 'presence' fitted perfectly the late Walter Pater, whom Ethel had known from his visits to her parents at Oxford. 'Doesn't living in a haunted room disturb you?' I asked. 'Not in the slightest. I would welcome a visit from Walter Pater, the gentlest of men'.

If any room in a London house should invite haunting, 12 Earl's Terrace had a good claim. 'It was in the room in which you are sitting that Mrs Macdonald, wife of the novelist, egged on by her children, persuaded Lewis Carroll to publish *Alice's Adventures Underground*. In the 1860s George du Maurier lived here'.

With all three Hatch sisters the influence of Charles L. Dodgson reached a spiritual depth. He wrote to them frequently — his last letters to Ethel and Beatrice were written in October and December respectively of 1897, the year before he died. In July of 1897 he invited Beatrice to dinner to meet an artist. One notes that Beatrice must leave Eastbourne where she was his guest on Sunday 'to get back to my boys' (presumably a reference to Sunday School). In the letter to Ethel he hopes to take Bee to *The Children of the King*, a fairy play, for which he has got five tickets so as to be able to invite three of her girl pupils as well. His generosity with guests was phenomenal, and the sisters carried on his tradition of entertaining with their young charges in the schools in which they taught.

I was conscious of the mystique surrounding the sisters, especially in the case of Ethel in 1963, the last living link with Lewis

Carroll. I felt moved by the experience. It was strangely extended. Some years later an artist pupil of mine, John Frye Bourne, was living quite close to where Ethel Hatch had retired to in Devon. The artist, Joan Hassall (Sir Sydney Cockerell's favourite engraver) effected their introduction, or rather re-introduction, since Bourne had known Ethel in her years at the Royal Academy Schools. In March 1985, I had a letter from Bourne. 'Only the other day, I was reminded of Ethel Hatch. I found two of her Christmas cards sent to us after she visited us here and we returned the visit at Earl's Terrace. The drawings (watercolours) are from a sketch pad. I was going to throw them away'. In fact he sent them to me, two charming works, and of course I had a special reason for cherishing them: a tangible reminder of the last living child-friend, only one remove from Lewis Carroll himself.

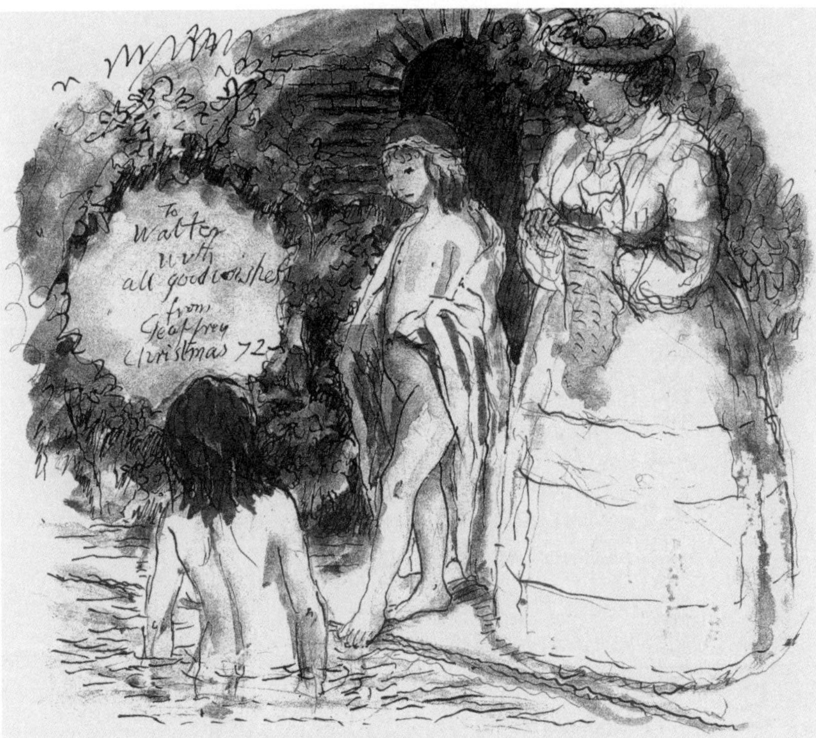

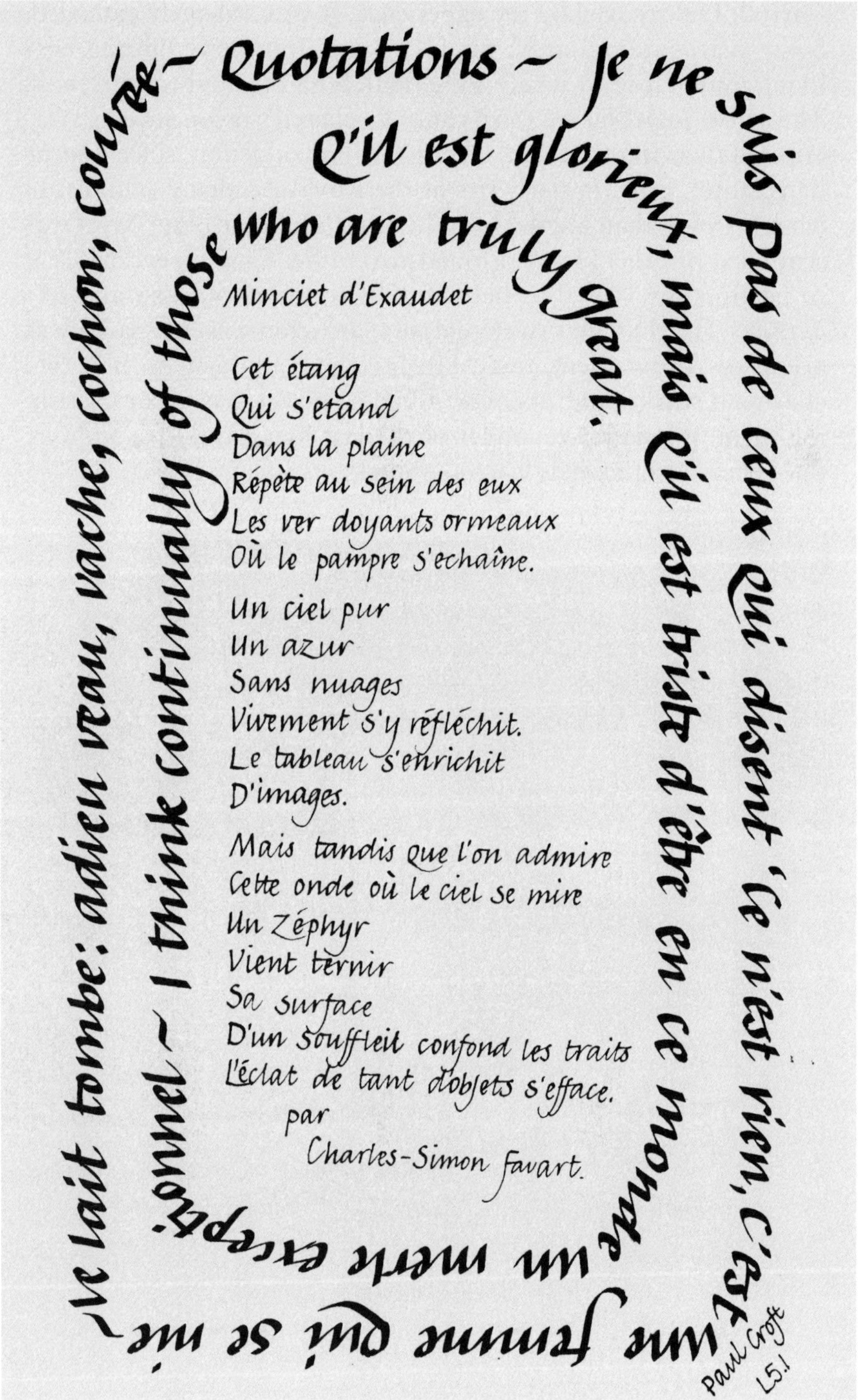
Quotations ~ Je ne suis pas de ceux qui disent 'ce n'est rien, c'est une femme qui se nie ~ le lait tombe; adieu veau, vache, cochon, couvée ~
Q'il est glorieux, mais Q'il est triste d'être en ce monde un merle exceptionnel ~ I think continually of those who are truly great.
Minciet d'Exaudet
Cet étang
Qui s'etand
Dans la plaine
Répète au sein des eux
Les ver doyants ormeaux
Où le pampre s'echaîne.
Un ciel pur
Un azur
Sans nuages
Vivement s'y réflechit.
Le tableau s'enrichit
D'images.
Mais tandis que l'on admire
Cette onde où le ciel se mire
Un Zéphyr
Vient ternir
Sa surface
D'un souffleit confond les traits
L'éclat de tant d'objets s'efface.
par
Charles-Simon Favart.
Paul Croft
L5.1

Walter Strachan at Bishop's Stortford College: 1928-1968

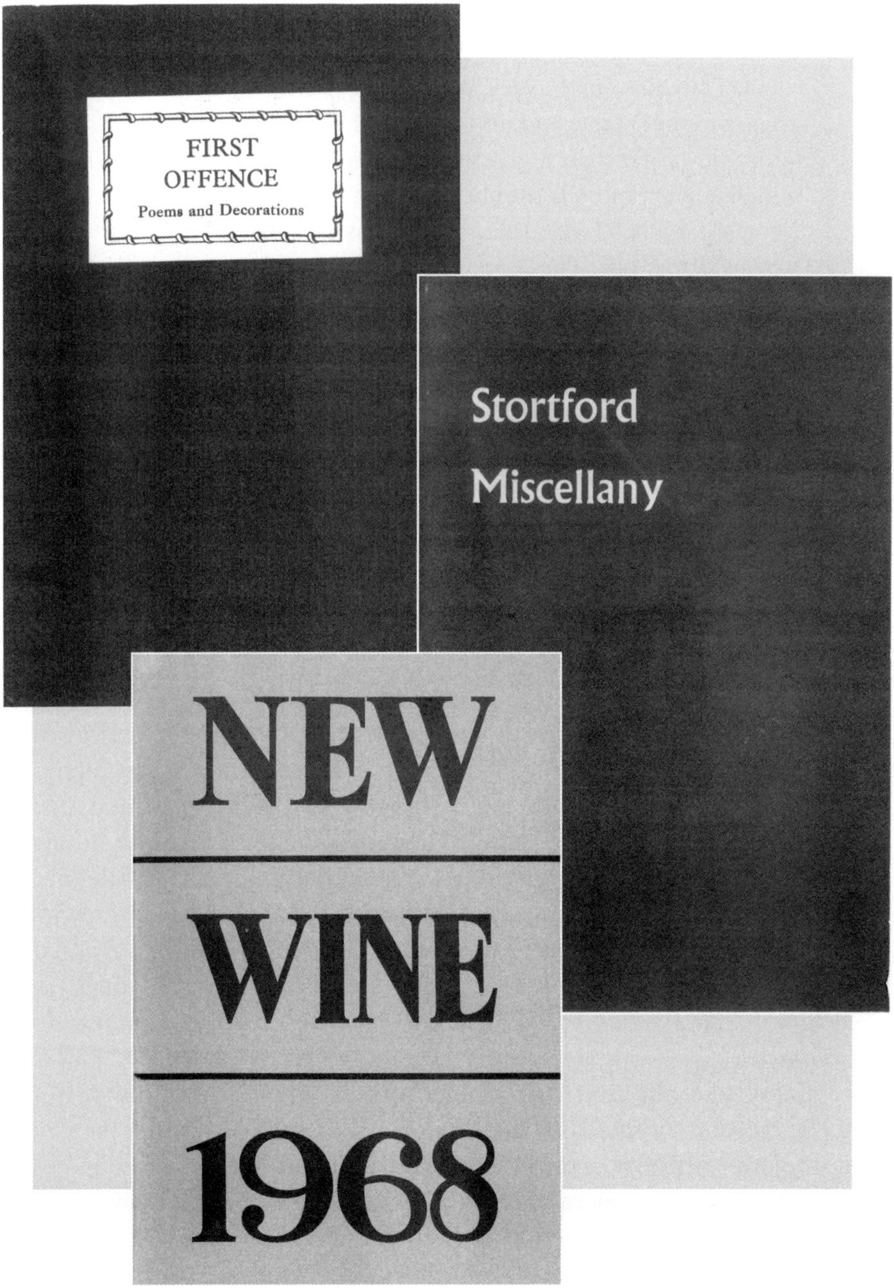

11 Christopher Hewett and Taranman

> 'An interest in the French Nineteenth Century first led me in October, 1974 to Taranman and an exhibition of etchings by Alphonse Legros. However, it was a little later, in the following year, with *Pierre Lecuire and Le Livre des Livres* that I became fully aware of the exceptional refinement of Christopher's taste and his integrity of character. The gallery was no larger than a good-sized drawing-room, but a very high ceiling and Christopher's skill in hanging contrived to suggest a much larger space which was capable of surprising transformations. The contents were the round wooden table and two high-backed chairs in the centre with, in the far left corner, as one entered, Christopher's desk, typewriter and bookshelves. There were no partners, assistants or secretaries. Christopher did absolutely everything himself and, not content with all that involved, would simultaneously be preparing his next publication for the press. In one other important respect it was unlike any other gallery: its matchless catalogues. They were not priced but given away with reckless liberality to anyone at all interested'. COLIN CLARK (*in 'Christopher Hewett 1938-1983', the last Taranman catalogue 1984*)

Other friends and admirers have recorded their appreciation of Christopher in his Gallery years, years when he more than repaid my affection and confidence in his work. I have confined this account to the formative years. We witness a life of promise, finely balanced between the wish to achieve something worthwhile and the life of the imagination, summed up for him in C. Day Lewis's poem 'O Dreams, O Destinations' which he declared (2 August 1956) 'the greatest revelation of my life' and later, in Cyprus, in Proust's *A la Recherche du Temps Perdu — 'l'édifice immense du souvenir'*.

Every schoolmaster experiences a thrill when a pupil he senses to be 'special' comes into his life, someone with whom he feels in complete rapport. It is especially exciting when, as in Christopher's case, it extends beyond the classroom framework to a shared enthusiasm — indeed, there were several across the years.

The first was his love-affair with church architecture. I remember him as a younger member of the Bishop's Stortford College Architectural Society, chatting knowledgeably on the subject as we cycled along to local churches and sketching features that caught his eye — a practice he continued into the school holidays. On a postcard from Tewkesbury (1953) he writes: 'One of the towns in the course of a fifty-mile ride. I was very impressed by the nave — long columns. Coming to a little village called Asleworth (15th century tithe-barn) I was ferried across the Severn by a grizzled boatman'.

The following year I introduced him to Sir Sydney Cockerell, then a bedridden but alert octogenarian who had been director of the Fitzwilliam Museum and one-time secretary to William Morris and a friend of John Ruskin. 'Dear Mr Strachan, yes, I sent a thank you letter to Sir Sydney Cockerell soon after the visit... I also visited the famous or infamous All Saints Margaret Street by Butterfield; I sat down and had a good laugh. Actually Mr Pevsner has led me into trouble upon several occasions; the vicars like to know if the church is mentioned,* and one particular incumbent got the shock of his life when he found the building called "grim" and instructed me to write to the man to tell him to the contrary...'.

Attuning to the introduction of the italic hand into the College, Christopher wrote to me (14 September 1954), in as solemn terms as those of Charles Wesley resolving in his diary never to laugh

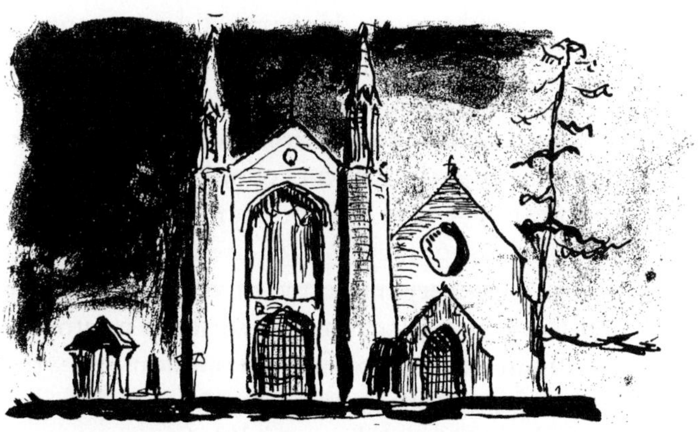

* Reference to The Buildings of England, edited by Nikolaus, later Sir Nikolaus Pevsner

again, 'I have decided to reform my handwriting... everyone should have beautiful writing... I have just finished reading *The Pre-Raphaelite Dream* by [William] Gaunt — I enjoyed it so much but I really should not have read it; Rossetti's death moved me to tears, and poor Millais!...'

On 9th January 1955, he sent me the news that he had won an RIBA prize for his essay on the chapel of St Edmund's College, Ware. He was to have a more significant architectural success later but meantime poetry was becoming the handmaiden of his calligraphic and typographical interest. From this time on, he began to transcribe — and sometimes decorate — in a calligraphy which was becoming exquisite — English and French poems that impressed him, including Lamartine's 'Le Lac', from which he astounded the whole class by declaiming not 'any twenty-four lines' (as set) but the whole poem of sixty-four lines. He never lost his love for the French 'romantics'.

Sketching was going strong. He wrote (11 August 1955) after his holiday in Normandy, 'I returned from France well satisfied with some forty places visited and thirty-one drawings made. I saw such wonderful churches and passed through such attractive country — in the fields ... people rested from harvesting... and started at the mad English boy who floated by, reciting 'O Dreams, O Destinations' out loud...'

Appreciation arrived from Sir Sydney Cockerell (27 April 1956). 'I was very pleased to see Christopher Hewett and his admirable drawings of East Anglian churches. I still feel he should try to do figures from memory. Hogarth did a memory drawing every day of his life. What a nice fellow Christopher is, and how beautifully he writes'.

Christopher took such exhortations to heart, as later he did urgings to paint boldly at the Ruskin School of Drawing in Oxford whereas his natural bent was for line and subdued tones. S.C.C. (as he was known) had great confidence in Christopher's future (17 August 1956) 'I am very interested in your brilliant pupil who seems destined for a high place in the world'. Christopher was a stern self-critic: 'I am flattered by S.C.C's opinion', he wrote to me (5 September 1956). 'Naturally in my eyes it is not true. Nevertheless I feel a responsibility to fulfil. I can never overstress the importance of C. Day Lewis's poetry... I wish very much to recapture the archaic dawn wherein I started. Let me take the plunge. I must go to the Oxford (Ruskin) School of Drawing'.

First, however, National Service. Eagerly he snatched the opportunity, inspired by his reading of *Le Grand Meaulnes*, to cycle in the intervening months to the Cher to discover what he could about Alain-Fournier from the inhabitants of La Chapelle-d'Angillon. He interviewed the Mayor and a sympathetic Madame Rocher as they sat talking on wicker chairs outside her cottage and made sketches of the famous Château of the story.

Many years later, in 1978, we followed the same trail to the 'lost domain' together in Christopher's Fiat, visiting Bourges and chatting about Frantz de Galais as we sat on a park bench that the thoughtful Stendhal had presented in memory of the park seats he had admired in London. Marvellous hours of picnics, sketching together near Montrésor before a thunderstorm interrupted us ('Glad to have sat under thunder and rain with you' quoted Christopher, recalling the experience). During a lyrically happy Lakeland holiday in 1974 the aura surrounding Ruskin's house at Brantwood seemed to inhibit Christopher's drawing. He was content to observe.

But to go back to his army days. No conscript can have made a more profitable use of spare hours, determined to make the best of the alien world in which he found himself. 21st October 1956, he writes from Catterick camp 'My time is my own today and I want to do justice to your letters... At Richmond yesterday at dusk I climbed away up to rolling grassland and a wood clinging to the steep slopes which rushed to meet the river... and a remnant of my former self whispers "Ruskin School" and remembers sunset over Firle and two figures eating bacon and egg over an oil lamp — pattering down through the dusk beneath majestic Downs by the light of the moon — "So, we'll go no more a'roving", Goodbye for now, Yours ever, Christopher'.

A friend of Cockerell's, Charles Bramley, invited him out when the Signallers moved to Leicestershire. He had already made a drawing of Moore's 'Northampton Madonna' and several village churches. At Bramley's house he was fascinated to see 'letters from Ruskin, some Joan Hassall woodcuts, Charles Keene engravings... I have written in gratitude to S.C.C. It has been a vision. What a triumph over the army!' and in a typically irrelevant postscript

2 Squadron 2 Wrls Regt.
Famagusta.

14th April.

Dear Walter,

What did I write to you this time last year? I suppose I mentioned Cyprus. The end of it seems now to be just within reach. The second notebook is complete and I am pleased to be on friendly terms with the 'Griggs'.

I shall write to 10 Pleasant Road if this letter fails to reach you in time. Thank you in advance for 'Moments of Time' and the translation. How kind and consistent you have always been. That is what I shall remember among other things.

I would like to have done so much – now with May on the doorstep, and one very lonely and unhappy year spent. I have paper for your rhyme sheet, and will send it in an oversize cardboard roll if only I can be given peace and the tent to myself.

Sometimes when I think of the Ruskin School as I first thought of it as the 'vista drowned in gold-dust haze', an impossible goal, I sense the old anticipatory thrill. Disability has swamped much of this – I note it carefully, an entry in the broad margin of my six-hourly log.

The Early Release has been denied me. I'm bound to have difficulty finding lodgings in Oxford. Have you any idea what steps I ought to be taking?

Why shouldn't OS subscribe – well many won't of course. I'd borrow a sum from my father. It would bring such prestige for the school. May you have every success because you deserve it.

Apologies for two things: Writing and this paper.

Yours, Christopher.

'Yes, I keep thinking of Mme Renal waving a white handkerchief on a sunlit staircase "*le grand air me fait bien*"'.

Next, Cyprus — *'Beau chevalier qui partez pour la guerre, / Qu'allez-vous faire / Si loin d'ici?'* — one of the many quotations from poems, English and French, exquisitely calligraphed and interleaved with drawings of local flora, rocks etc in the notebooks he kept in the Ruskin tradition. Even in Cyprus he was pursued by S.C.C. 'Are you doing some drawing from memory and getting to be at home with moving figures?'; echoed in Christopher's letter (16 August 1957), 'I am tormented at the moment by figure drawing...' Nostalgia alternates with observation. 'Your voice distantly calls', he writes (22 July). '"I have torn off the whole of May and June and twenty days of July", says Susan in *The Waves*... I shall write out MacNeice's "August" for you soon... Sketching enlivens me, but are they (sketches) good enough?' Perfectionist, he was to write — on a sketching holiday — from Abbeville, 'I am ill-equipped compared with Ruskin'.

Books and nature meant everything to Christopher in curfew-bound Cyprus. '*Père Goriot* has been completed. I want to make notes on Mme Nucingen, sketch like Guys (Constantin). I must re-read *Le Grand Meaulnes*; *Swann's Way* half done. I like best the first months, the moment of seeing Gilberte — pink hawthorn — Northern France all through...' (1957). Later (7 August) — no one *lived* his books more than Christopher — 'Soon after writing to you I was plunged into despair on completing *Le Grand Meaulnes* — the nobility, the steadfastness of youth'. Then a

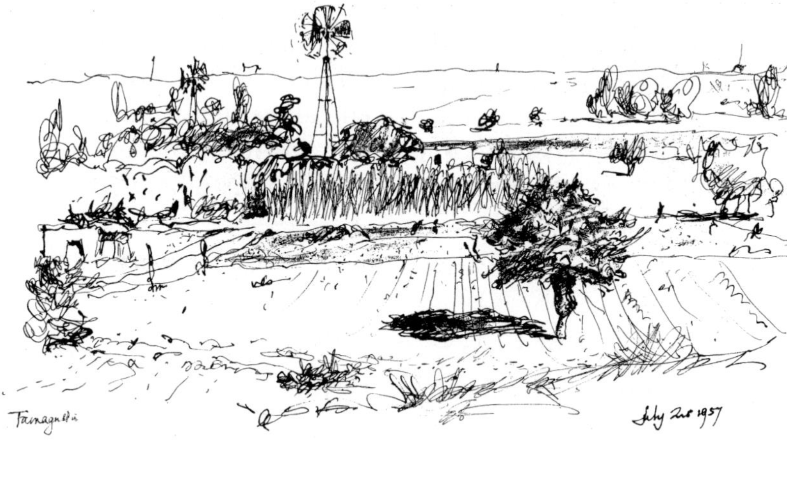

happier note (the following Spring), 'Heavenly day, Spring and I had been reading James Joyce, laid down the book as the small, sand-coloured combat truck nosed its way up the hill…'.

The Oxford years (1958-60) provided a discipline of drawing, but Christopher found the atmosphere at the Ruskin too relaxed. However, his charm and purposefulness impressed, as ever, his seniors — the Ruskin Master, Percy Horton, and the don, Neville Coghill, who commissioned him to do topographical drawings in the city. Oxford was important for 'the incidental things that pass' (1959). 'Walter, a very fortuitous meeting I had yesterday. Mounting the steps of the Ashmolean, I happened upon the tall, bespectacled figure with an unmistakeable air of greatness which I recognised instantly as Pevsner. He remembered me after three years…'. It had, in fact, been Pevsner's interest aroused by the illustrated piece by Christopher — then sixteen — published in the *Architectural Review*, that had brought him over to Bishop's Stortford College to see the work of the Architectural Hobby. Moments of 'dazzle' and we bathed in the effulgence.

Not so the interview for the Royal College of Art entrance, as reported by Christopher (21 February 1960). 'Did I know what I wanted to be? Had I private means? I was not a graphic artist or designer?… It was with some relief that I saw and liked immediately Casson, who admired my photographs of Stortford oasthouses and some of my Avignon thumbnails. He said I was the joker out of the twelve candidates…'.

A quarter of a century later, by tragic irony, it was on Sir Hugh Casson's highly successful exhibition that at the Taranman Gallery the final curtain fell. Here, for an unforgettable ten years, Christopher had given generous encouragement to English and French artists, dispensed hospitality to his Anglo-French clientèle. He had created not just a commercial gallery but a cultural centre where he could make the longed-for 'gestures of permanence' which long years of preparation, allied to his innate sensitivity, had enabled him to make.

(1984)

LA CHAPELLE D'ANGILLON

Lost in a maze of minor roads
Each like the last, bordered with brackish pond

And grey scrub —
We stopped at an ambiguous crossroad —
A bunch of cowslips had caught our eye,
A golden beacon of hope.

The gatherer, artless, smiling, helpful.
Yes, she could show the way —
First this, then that, then the other turn.
We listened, nodded, thanked, took nothing in —
The flowers so lush and she so beautiful,
What was the hurry?

Later, sketching the village church
Where Alain-Fournier's name is recorded,
I thought of him who was truly lost,
And how the heart can stir
At fifty years' remove.

12 Sculpture should be permanent: meetings with Henry Moore

My first meeting with Henry Moore, on 20 September 1942, was at his house, 'Hoglands', at Perry Green, a hamlet near Much Hadham. It was a twin cottage but, after a short time living in one half, Moore and his wife, Irina, were able to acquire the whole. In the remote past it had been part of a mediaeval 'hall-house' of which the buttressed chimney-stack was the chief remaining feature. I was struck by the intense blue of the sculptor's eyes, so often echoed by the blue tie and shirt he favoured, and surprised by the smallness of the hand I shook. But not, since I too hailed from Yorkshire, by the gravelly voice and accent, which became less noticeable as the years passed. In the kitchen, I noticed an oil painting of a matriarchal woman with an impressively determined expression. It was the sculptor's mother, painted by Moore's friend, Raymond Coxon.

We began by talking about Yorkshire. Moore admitted that he missed the Yorkshire countryside — the outcrops of rock around his native Castleford. He also missed the Kentish coast and, in particular, the beaches around Broadstairs. However, he was happy to be settled in what Charles Lamb had, in his memories of childhood days, called 'sweet Hertfordshire'.

Moore brought out his *Shelter Sketch Book* — the original — which his great friend and ally, 'K' Clark, as he called him, had had specially bound for him. I was struck by the texture he obtained by his use of a watercolour wash over lithographic crayon, combined with drawing in pen and ink. With a smile, he told me he had been introduced to the chinagraph medium by a young visitor whom he was entertaining by drawing with the 'Woolworth' crayon the child had brought. It sounded as fortuitous as Michelangelo's exploitation of the stain.

With his early struggles evidently in mind, Moore went on to talk about schemes for encouraging the arts. He told me he was on a committee as the referee for appointing four people to represent art, music, sculpture and architecture. Those selected would spend six months a year for two years, in the Leeds district (that of his own art school) at the benefactor's expense. This benefactor was the well-known collector of modern art (especially Moore's), Eric ('Peter') C. Gregory, then Chairman of Lund Humphries. Herbert Read was the key member of the committee. I was later to meet 'Peter' Gregory at many tea-parties at the Moores'.

In the cosy atmosphere of the small parlour — which the Moores continued to use for informal occasions even when 'the new room' was built on — and with Moore's drawings around us, we had tea, chairs pulled up to the table, Yorkshire fashion, with his wife Irina (who never totally lost her Russian accent, any more than Henry his Yorkshire 'I knaw') presiding. This was the normal routine whoever the visiting VIPs happened to be — from Sir Philip Hendy, of the Leeds City Art Gallery, in the early years, to Lauren Bacall in more recent times. As I was admiring the primitive artefacts in the showcase let into the foot-thick wall, Irina remarked, 'I do all the collecting, not Henry'. She invited me to inspect a thirteenth-century English vase, much better, she said, than one of the same period in the British Museum.

We talked about H.S. Williamson, the principal of Chelsea School of Art, where Moore had taught up to 1939, following his time at the Royal College of Art. Williamson had been the part-time art master in my first year (1924) at Stortford. This tall, remote figure failed to impress the younger boys, who wilfully allowed their open-air sketches to float off into the wind so that they could chase after them. Percy Horton, who took Williamson's place, was an exact contemporary of Moore's at the RCA. His power to communicate on the subject of his favourite painters — Rubens, Delacroix, Cézanne — was as valuable as his capacity to teach drawing. My friendship with Horton had for many years been one of the most important of my life: it was strengthened by our common link with Moore.

Moore then spoke, with contained excitement, about the fact that some of his sculptures were about to be flown by Flying Clipper to the US. I thought it was a considerable risk at the height of the war but important in view of the prestige it would bring to this country when American support was so vital. (Moore was in fact an official war-artist and, at Herbert Read's prompting, had been doing drawings down the Yorkshire coal-mines which his father had managed). No romanticizing here.

As I left, Moore invited me to come again and bring a few boys from the school. I drove back, pondering on the quiet authority that a belief in his work gave this small, unassuming, friendly sculptor. I thought about his explanation of his 'reclining figure' theme and why he had chosen it: 'it is free and stable, can recline on any surface and fits in with my belief that sculpture should be permanent and should last to eternity'. A poem by his friend in Chelsea days, Stephen Spender, came back to me: 'I think continually of those who are truly great...' and I wondered if — even already at that date — he had felt that applied to Moore.

I took Moore at his word. Exactly a fortnight later (4 October 1942) I was back, this time with six boys. As we stood in the studio, he explained how he gave his bronze figures structural emphasis at certain areas — such as at the elbow and knees where the (surrogate) flesh was taut over the bone. He clenched his fist to show the 'focus of thrust' at the knuckles. On this second visit to the studio, Moore, at my request, again produced the original *Shelter Sketch Book*. This time, he gave a practical demonstration of how the watercolour wash 'took' only on parts of the paper where he had not drawn with a greasy chalk (lithograph crayon). He then added a few lines in pen and ink. The result was the familiar 'speckly' texture, characteristic of his shelter drawings and others.

The visit, as did all such subsequent visits with other boys, made a great impact on them. Those who went on those early visits sometimes write to me about having seen Moore bronzes, which I had seen only temporarily sited in his grounds, now on sites in the Near or Far East. Moore was right in saying to me that people like myself were creating his future public and a public not only for his own work. Having seen his sculptures, the boys became eager — as at the Battersea Park exhibitions (triennial from 1948) — to extend their interest to the work of other sculptors, such as McWilliam, not easily accepted by the public. Moore's policy of allowing access to his studios was in marked contrast with that of Picasso, a direct reflection on the two men's personalities.

My third visit (6 February 1944) was one of the most exciting and memorable. Moore was putting the finishing touches to the 'Madonna and Child' destined for St. Matthew's Church, Northampton. It had been commissioned by the rector, Walter Hussey. The Hornton-stone carving was one of the sculptor's rare 'frontal' pieces. He gave me a set of photographs of the carving at progressive stages, to which I was later able to add the final one taken *in situ*. He hoped the sculpture would not offend any religious susceptibilities — he thought of the Christ Child as a kind of boy genius. He need not have felt anxious. It is the most naturalistic of Moore's sculptures and was found acceptable by the general public. Who, at that time, could have prophesised that, four decades later, a variation on the same theme — 'Mother and Child; Hood' — would find a home in St. Paul's Cathedral? Though not without some ecclesiastical protest at the language of symbolic form.

1944 was a year rich in meetings with Moore. On one occasion my old dentist friend, Newman Catchpole, who later acquired a maquette for the 'King and Queen' bronze, the bronze 'hands' of the Queen, went over to Moore's with me. Moore showed us the original drawings which were to be reproduced in an edition of Edward Sackville-West's Trojan war text *The Rescue*. I found myself increasingly caught up in Moore's work and, as at that time I was writing and translating verse, poetry was the vehicle that came naturally to me to express my feelings about, for example, his drawing 'The Grey Sleepers'. I showed him the poem in typescript, for his approval, when he made his first visit to our house on 10 August 1944. (It was published first in *Tribune* — in October — and then in *Moments of Time*.)

THE GREY SLEEPERS OF THE SHELTERS

Anonymous grey sleepers line the shelter,
The underground necropolis of the time,
Faintly to infinity receding,
Sunk in eternal attitudes of sleep
Beneath the blankets' heavy, draping folds;
War-torn bodies dumped — so many bundles
Dragged from gashed home, rubble or plaster-heap,
Carelessly stretched or curled on hasty bedding.
Closer look reveals their ashen faces,
Eyes deep in socket (image of sightless statues
Irrelevant athwart a thoroughfare lying)
Identity erased by desolation
From each anaesthetised expression,
From parted lips emitting stertorous sigh;
Yet arms and hands in restful pattern fallen
In poses only desperate sleepers find,
Adopting like a child's the easy curve,
The unconscious grace when the sudden sea
Of irresistible sleep overwhelms them...

And here and there, like craven figures brooding,
Composed and timeless spirits, waiting, waiting,
The proud ones drowse or slumber, still erect,
To circumstances only half-surrendered,
Their knitting-needles clenched in bony fingers,
Each row of stitches contact with the world above;
And lift a drooping eyelid as the first
Electric-train, vault-echoing, tells night ended...

Now sleep-numbed limbs will stir and saunter forth
Into the changed but never-changing London,
Synthetic ozone left for the chill dawn
Each countenance identity resuming,
Restored to sullen hate or resignation,
As each woman with her precious burden
Makes her deliberate way across the traffic
Eastward or North to cracked, windowless hovel
Which was and was to be, she hoped, a home.

Moore's own interest in poetry is symbolised in the 'Lyre Bird' cover design he did for Tambimuttu's *Poetry London*, Number 7, 1942. He admired equally — but for different reasons — the poems of Auden (which he was to illustrate decades later) and Dylan Thomas — to whose widow, Caitlin, he gave moral support in the period immediately following Dylan's tragic death. He could also enjoy poems of more modest pretensions. He liked my poem 'Battersea 1948', inspired by the 'Three Standing Figures' and accepted the dedication to him. It was only much later that I learned the story of Moore's battle to meet the deadline for the completion of the sculpture. I had had this hint in a letter from Moore, dated 25 January 1948. 'Do come and see us some day when you've got the time to spare. I am working hard on the outdoor group of three figures but it is very slow work'. The 'Three Standing Figures' had to meet the deadline for the opening of the first-ever open-air exhibition of sculpture in Battersea Park. The carving in Darley Dale sandstone of three seven-foot high figures was a tremendous undertaking. In the final stages, he called in willing help from Reg Butler and Shelley Faussett, who tell of working in the dark with the aid of arc lamps. Re-reading a letter from Moore written later in the year, in August 1948, I sense the mood of relief. He was having a 'spell of drawing' for inclusion in an exhibition at Roland, Browse and Delbanco's.

The next note I had from him was about my 'Battersea 1948' poem. 'I am pleased to see in print your poem inscribed to me [it had appeared in *Poetry Quarterly*] and I like very much "Perfection's Image"'. Then there was a reference to our recent visit. ' We enjoyed very much you and Margaret coming to see us...' That had been a very special and exciting occasion for my wife and myself. We were offered first choice from a batch of drawings. The drawing we chose in a medium of chalk, watercolour, pen and ink was related, spiritually, to the 'Three Standing Figures' but not in style. The figures represented 'The Three Fates' of classical legend, suitably impersonal, but I always see a slight likeness to Irina in one of the figures and to Sybil Thorndyke — in tragic mood — in the central figure, 'Atropos'. The drawing was not complete when we saw it but Moore said that of course, we were not obliged to like it when he had finished it. For me, at that time, it meant two months' salary. But my wife and I realized how lucky we were to have had the chance of acquiring it and there was the prospect of so much pleasure ahead.

Before going to Paris in 1949, for my first visit there since before World War II, I consulted Moore about which of the younger artists were likely to have done book illustrations. Although I found no books illustrated by two of the artists he named, Edouard Pignon and Fourgeron, I later discovered a work illustrated by number three on his list, Maurice Estève. Moore's interest in French book illustrations was very important to me. When I returned from that initial foray, I showed him the proof-material and original *'bonnes feuilles'* I had brought back. After that I repeated this procedure — also with complete books — annually. His involvement became direct in the very next year when the French typographer, Henri Jonquières, enlisted my help to persuade Moore to make a set of colour lithographs for the text of *Prométhée*, Goethe's dramatic fragment, translated into French by André Gide.

Moore was very preoccupied at the time with sculpture projects since, following his award of the International Sculpture Prize at the 24th Venice Biennale, his work was in great demand. Yet he was eager to make a contribution to the *'livre d'artiste'*, and took the necessary steps very seriously. At Jonquières' request — he was the *maître d'oeuvre* and initiator of the production — I acted as the intermediary, interpreting Jonquières' instructions and comments as the various proofs arrived from Mourlot's lithographic workshop in Paris. Moore, of course, paid a visit to Mourlot's at certain stages to check everything was as he wished. I, too, went there and met the young expert, Henri Deschamps, who was working on the lithographic stones for *Prométhée*. Over the months the operation involved cycling the five miles from Stortford to Perry Green — as I had no car in commission at the time — ferrying precious proofs and corrections.

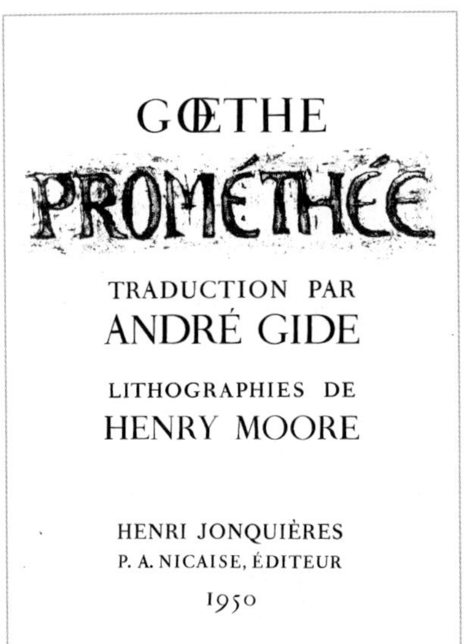
GŒTHE
PROMÉTHÉE
TRADUCTION PAR
ANDRÉ GIDE
LITHOGRAPHIES DE
HENRY MOORE
HENRI JONQUIÈRES
P. A. NICAISE, ÉDITEUR
1950

'Operation *Prométhée*' had begun in earnest when I received a card from Moore (dated 11 December 1950). 'Could you please telephone me. This letter has just arrived from Jonquières and I am not sure I completely understand it'. On one occasion, I was caught in a violent thunderstorm and had to sacrifice keeping my clothes dry to the more imperative need to protect my vulnerable cargo. Irina Moore insisted I should get my wet clothes off and produced a pair of Henry's trousers. The fact that I am one of the few people, possibly the only one, to have worn the great sculptor's trousers is an intimate detail that naturally did not appear in the article 'The

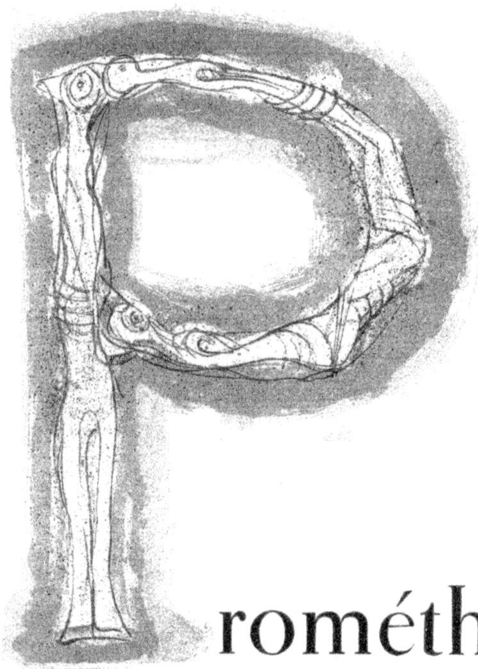

rométhée

Non. Je ne consens pas : va le leur dire.
En tout, pour tout, je ne veux pas.
Leur volonté contre la mienne.
Ceci contre cela
Je crois bien que ça se balance.

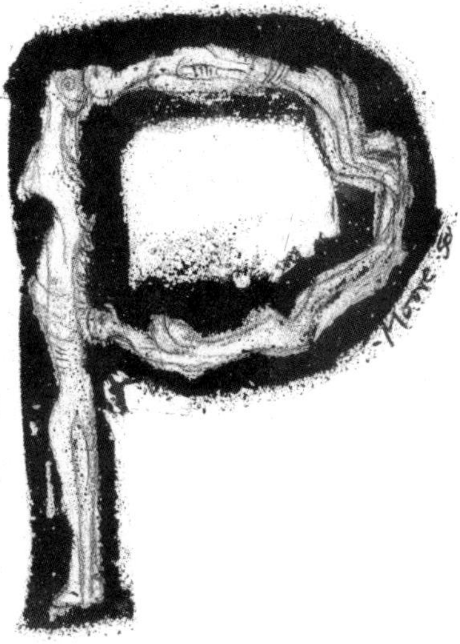

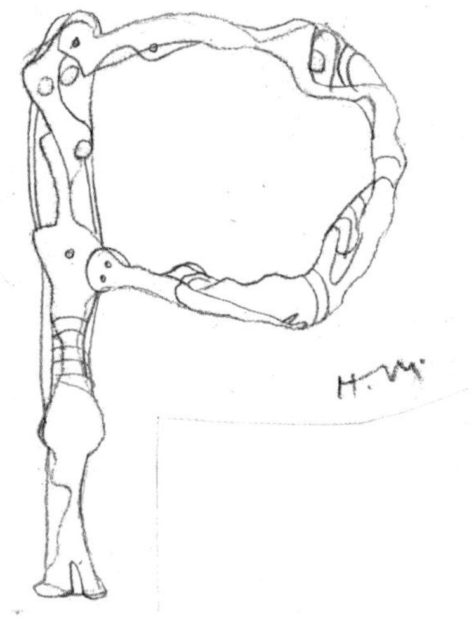

Evolution of *Prométhée*' which I wrote for *Image 8*. Moore had been encouraging when I proposed the idea: 'I should be very pleased indeed for you to do an article (with reproductions in colour) on the evolution of the book... I cannot think of anyone more suitable, especially as you have been in on it since the start... It would seem a good idea to have it in *Image*, for which you have written already in a similar vein on French artists and the standard

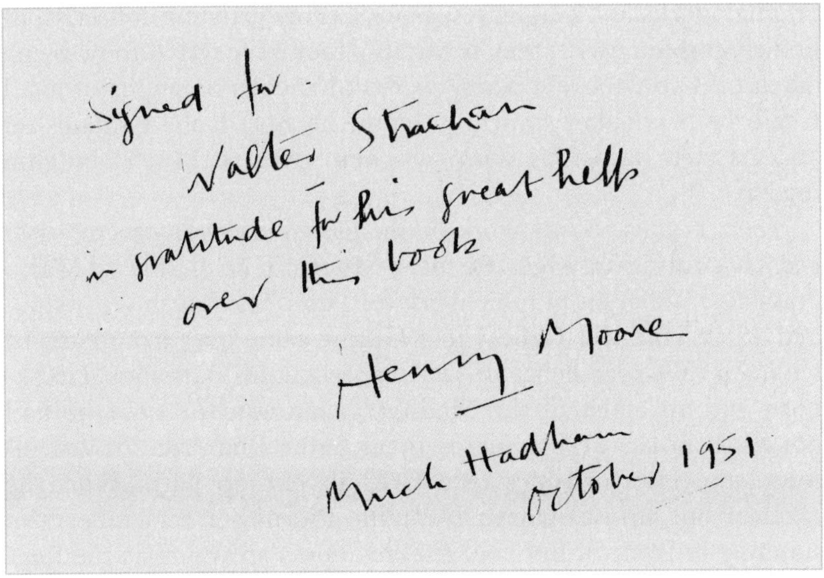
Signed for
Walter Strachan
in gratitude for his great help
over this book
Henry Moore
Much Hadham
October 1951

of reproduction is very good from what I have seen of it…'. (letter dated 10 January 1951). By this time, I had received my *'exemplaire nominatif'* of the book inscribed with a note of thanks from Moore.

In the mid 'forties and early 'fifties, Moore was less beset than he was to become later with constant requests for visits (which he rarely turned down). Dealers, 'gallery folk' (his term), various VIPs to be shown round the studios. There were, however, delightful diversions, especially at the tea-table — as when — in the midst of a serious discussion with Philip Hendy on some aspect of the Renaissance — Moore would signal for silence so that we could listen to his newly acquired 'budgie' reciting 'Little Boy Blue'!

Naturally, I got to know Moore's assistants. In the early days they included names — like those of Oliffe Richmond and Anthony Caro — which were to become well-known in the sculpture world. The assistants he engaged later were less absorbed in their own work and three, in particular, became permanent staff but with long week-ends free to do their own work, often for exhibitions. Moore won the devotion of his assistants and his other ever-increasing staff. His warm manner with everybody, regardless of social distinction, created an atmosphere of friendliness and also of efficiency. I rarely had a letter from any artist or sculptor who knew him that did not reflect this. When other British artists and sculptors visited our house (I had by then a few original works and maquettes, as well as my growing collection of French graphic owls), they invariably looked forward to be being taken over to Moore's. Many were old friends or pupils of his. I recall the particularly warm welcome he gave Robert Adams on at least two occasions when we went over to Much Hadham together.

Then, because of my work on the *livre d'artiste*, — there was a French contingent eager to meet Moore. The first was Mario Prassinos. When his graphic work for Poe's *The Raven* was exhibited at the Hanover Gallery in 1952, he came over from Paris to see it. In that year February was bitterly cold: Prassinos, Greek-born and an artist of the Mediterranean sun (in 1951 he had bought a house at Eygalières [near Saint Rémy de Provence]) found the Hertfordshire cold hard to put up with. When he reached our house, frozen from the journey, I remember him standing in front of our coal fire, his boots steaming as the fragments of snow thawed off. He said it was the first time he'd been warm since coming to England.

There was rarely a time, in all the forty-four years of my meetings with Moore, when something important was not happening in his career. Nevertheless, he himself considered certain events as particular watersheds in the public recognition of his work. Appropriately, given his Yorkshire origins, Leeds was the first university to confer an honorary doctorate on him in 1945. The following year brought an invitation for a one-man retrospective at the Museum of Modern Art, New York. On the domestic front, the great event of 1946 was the birth of a daughter, Mary, the more welcome for coming late in Irina's and Henry's lives. The foreseeable result was a spate of drawings recording Mary's babyhood: Mary being bathed, Mary on her mother's knee, and so on, sometimes featuring the familiar 'Rocking Chair' of the bronze series.

The immediate effect on Moore's work of Mary's infancy and childhood was a new emphasis on the mother and child theme with the incorporation of the father figure — rare in the sculptor's oeuvre, symbolizing the family. Hence the two major 'Family Groups', that at the Barclay School, Hertfordshire, and the Harlow 'Family Group' in Hadene stone, which was unveiled by Sir Kenneth Clark in 1954. Moore seems, in fact, to have anticipated a family. The 'Family Groups' go back to 1944, as does a maquette on which the Harlow carving was based. The latter, Moore told me, evokes the notion of neighbourhood and was therefore appropriate to a New Town where many young families settled.

The Harlow 'Family Group' has twice been re-sited, in the first instance it was moved from the original site to a less vulnerable one after a child had thrown a missile at the male head and chipped the nose, which needed a repair job. I recall asking Moore at that time if such incidents worried him. His reply was one I have vainly tried to introduce into my own philosophy. 'Yes, I feel worried for perhaps half an hour, then I dismiss the matter until something can be done about it'. Moore reserved his indignation for public causes and violations of principle.

In 1956 came an important European commission. He was to produce a sculpture for the UNESCO headquarters complex in

Paris. Whatever Moore made, whether bronze or carving, would be viewed alongside the work of the world's greatest contemporary artists who represented their respective countries. Picasso was responsible for two vast fresco panels (845 feet square): Miró, in collaboration with the ceramist Artigan, made an extensive mural. The other sculptors invited to produce work were Noguchi (Japan), Hans Arp and Alexander Calder.

I was privileged to watch and record each stage of Moore's projects for this commission. He finally decided on the present large-scale 'Reclining Figure', carved in Travertine marble. The proposed site meant that the sculpture would be viewed against the screen-wall of the light-toned granite building — eight feet high with a dark void above. Any large bronze — for Moore had first thought in terms of that medium — would have had its lower half showing up strongly, whereas the upper section would have been lost in the background blackness. Moore, therefore, devised a bronze screen against which he would set his composition. The idea was not new to him. In the year he received the commission he had already made his first bronze with a figure and screen 'Seated Figure against Carved Wall' (very reminiscent of one of his illustrations to the Sackville-West book). So although he ultimately decided in favour of a stone carving, there were the usual spin-offs of initial ideas, worked out and cast in bronze.

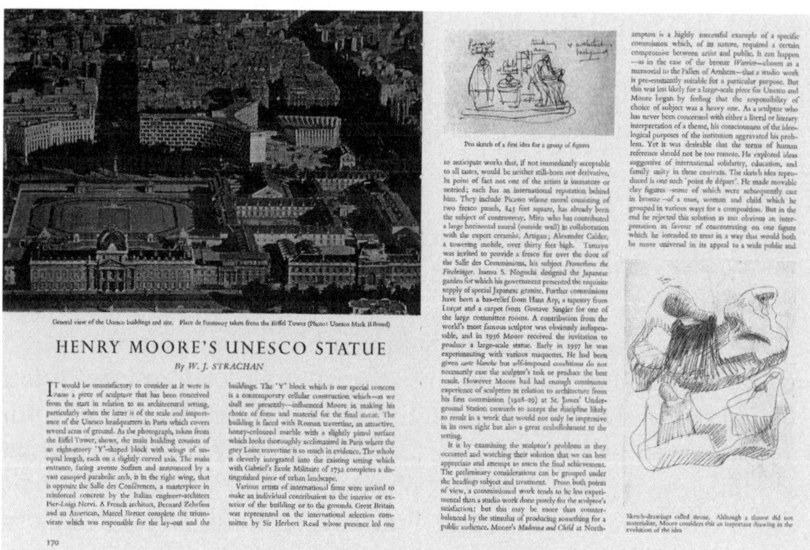

General view of the Unesco buildings and site. Place de Fontenoy taken from the Eiffel Tower (Photo: Unesco Mark Riboud)

HENRY MOORE'S UNESCO STATUE

By W. J. STRACHAN

IT would be unsatisfactory to consider as it were *in vacuo* a piece of sculpture that has been conceived from the start in relation to an architectural setting, particularly when the latter is of the scale and importance of the Unesco headquarters in Paris which covers several acres of ground. As the photograph, taken from the Eiffel Tower, shows, the main building consists of an eight-storey 'Y'-shaped block with wings of unequal length, each on a slightly curved axis. The main entrance, facing avenue Suffren and announced by a vast canopied parabolic arch, is in the right wing, that is opposite the Salle des Conférences, a masterpiece in reinforced concrete by the Italian engineer-architect Pier-Luigi Nervi. A French architect, Bernard Zehrfuss and an American, Marcel Breuer complete the triumvirate which was responsible for the lay-out and the buildings. The 'Y' block which is our special concern is a contemporary cellular construction which—as we shall see presently—influenced Moore in making his choice of form and material for the final statue. The building is faced with Roman travertine, an attractive, honey-coloured marble with a slightly pitted surface which looks thoroughly acclimatized in Paris where the grey Loire travertine is so much in evidence. The whole is cleverly integrated into the existing setting which with Gabriel's Ecole Militaire of 1752 completes a distinguished piece of urban landscape.

Various artists of international fame were invited to make an individual contribution to the interior or exterior of the building or to the grounds. Great Britain was represented on the international selection committee by Sir Herbert Read whose presence led one to anticipate works that, if not immediately acceptable to all tastes, would be neither still-born nor derivative. In point of fact not one of the artists is immature or untried; each has an international reputation behind him. They include Picasso whose mural consisting of two fresco panels, 845 feet square, has already been the subject of controversy, Miro who has contributed a large horizontal mural (outside wall) in collaboration with the expert ceramist, Artigan; Alexander Calder, a towering mobile, over thirty feet high. Tamayo was invited to provide a fresco for over the door of the Salle des Commissions, his subject *Prometheus the Firebringer*. Isamu S. Noguchi designed the Japanese garden for which his government presented the requisite supply of special Japanese granite. Further commissions have been a bas-relief from Hans Arp, a tapestry from Lurçat and a carpet from Gustave Singier for one of the large committee rooms. A contribution from the world's most famous sculptor was obviously indispensable, and in 1956 Moore received the invitation to produce a large-scale statue. Early in 1957 he was experimenting with various maquettes. He had been given *carte blanche* but self-imposed conditions do not necessarily ease the sculptor's task or produce the best result. However Moore had had enough continuous experience of sculpture in relation to architecture from his first commission (1928–29) at St. James' Underground Station onwards to accept the discipline likely to result in a work that would not only be impressive in its own right but also a great embellishment to the setting.

It is by examining the sculptor's problems as they occurred and watching their solution that we can best appreciate and attempt to assess the final achievement. The preliminary considerations can be grouped under the headings subject and treatment. From both points of view, a commissioned work tends to be less experimental than a studio work done purely for the sculptor's satisfaction; but this *may* be more than counterbalanced by the stimulus of producing something for a public audience. Moore's *Madonna and Child* at Northampton is a highly successful example of a specific commission which, of its nature, required a certain compromise between artist and public. It can happen—as in the case of the bronze *Warrior*—chosen as a memorial to the Fallen of Arnhem—that a studio work is pre-eminently suitable for a particular purpose. But this was less likely for a large-scale piece for Unesco and Moore began by feeling that the responsibility of choice of subject was a heavy one. As a sculptor who has never been concerned with either a literal or literary interpretation of a theme, his consciousness of the ideological purposes of the institution aggravated his problem. Yet it was desirable that the terms of human reference should not be too remote. He explored ideas suggestive of international solidarity, education, and family unity in these contexts. The sketch idea reproduced is one such 'point de départ'. He made movable clay figures—some of which were subsequently cast in bronze—of a man, woman and child which he grouped in various ways for a composition. But in the end he rejected this solution as too obvious an interpretation in favour of concentrating on one figure which he intended to treat in a way that would both be more universal in its appeal to a wide public and

Pen sketch of a first idea for a group of figures

Sketch-drawings called *throne*. Although a throne did not materialize, Moore considers this an important drawing in the evolution of the idea

170

The additional factor that made him decide on a carving was the opportunity of working on the grand scale with the Travertine marble he loved in its country of origin, Italy. He would carve it at the quarry at Querceta near Carrara. The half-size bronze working model duly arrived at a temporary studio. I happened to be travelling in his company in the boat-train when he was taking the plaster model of the head of the 'Reclining Figure'. The case containing it lolled on the luggage-rack and I jokingly whispered my thought: 'what if the plaster head were to roll out of its case'. (There had been a recent murder and dismemberment.)

As far as his personal life was concerned, Moore saw the advantages of an annual period of carving where the marble quarries are sited. It would afford him opportunities to work in his favourite medium. He remembered this when an opportunity came along for summer stays at Forte dei Marmi, adjacent to the Querceta quarries. Such breaks would be a way of combining some work with a family holiday. I have a card from him dated September 1962 showing the pulpit at Pisa, with the message: 'We're halfway through our holiday here and are loving the continuous sunshine and warm bathing. Yesterday we went to Pisa and tomorrow go to Florence, but we're mostly on the beach...' Implicit in the visit to Pisa, and the choice of the card, is Moore's admiration for Giovanni Pisano, who executed the pulpit carving.

The great news in 1962 was the commission to contribute a large sculpture for the Lincoln Centre, New York. The 'Two-Piece Reclining Figure' was to be on a far larger scale than any previous Moore bronze. It took a great deal of thought to plan and see through to the final result. The first impact on me was the materialisation of a small bathing-pool at 'Hoglands'. In theory Mary could use it, though the water looked cold and uninviting. But the pool served its purpose of providing the reflection-effects for a maquette. The bronze, eighteen feet high by twenty-eight feet long, was not finished and sited until 1965.

Already a Companion of Honour (1955), in 1963 Moore was appointed a member of the Order of Merit. He enjoyed meeting people and, after the years when his work was often received with coolness, if not misunderstanding, he must have found some satisfaction in this sudden flood of recognition. As he often said to me, it was marvellous to be doing what you liked and at the same time earning a living at it. It was almost as though it was still a surprise.

Despite absences for special occasions, he had his studio-work so well organized that no time was ever lost. He never missed important exhibitions, but sturdily turned down all the flattering invitations to make public addresses or prize-day speeches. He excelled at organizing his work and managing his staff — coping with bronze-casting firms; transport of the huge works abroad for exhibitions; supervising the scaling-up from his maquettes; the patination for individual bronzes; correspondence; filing; catalogue preparation, most of it delegated but superbly managed. Undoubtedly, the annual two-month semi-holiday in Italy provided periods of relaxation that made such a work programme possible.

The summers of 1969 and 1970 brought me the usual welcome view-cards. The first of these, undated, but some time in July, recorded 'thunderstorms and torrential rain'. Latterly, I noticed that he recorded the memory of this freak weather in a combined etching and lithograph entitled 'Storm at Forte dei Marmi' — no experience ever being wasted on Moore.

The 1969 stay at Forte dei Marmi was one of terrific carving activity. The sculptures included 'Large Animal Form', carved in one of his favourite stones — Travertine marble. It was later reproduced in my book, *Henry Moore: Animals* in 1983. This nine-foot-long sculpture, the climax of Moore's carvings executed between 1964 and 1973, is now sited outside the Museum of Modern Art, New York.

Italy was always Moore's favourite country. Here he found the classical Renaissance sculpture which he had neglected in his early visits and, although he preferred to get back to the primitives such as Mexican carvings and Cycladic figures, it was marvellous to return to. So, Florence for Michelangelo's 'Bozzi' and Ghiberti's 'Porta del Paradiso'; Pisa for the pulpits by the Pisanos. In 1972, when I was undertaking research for my book *Towards Sculpture* my first journey to Milan was to see Michelangelo's final 'Pietà' in the *Castello Sforzesco* — the reductive transformation of his original version — his great masterpiece. It was Moore who insisted on my making its acquaintance before I looked at the contemporary work by Manzù, Emilio Greco, Gio Pomodoro and Marino Marini.

In 1972, Richard Arend, a former pupil of mine, tackled me about the possibility of persuading Moore to let the Bank of

Switzerland, in which he was an employee, have a bronze — on favourable terms — for their new training centre at Ermatingen, some sixty kilometres from Zurich. It was a modern building, designed for courses not only on banking but on cultural subjects for their employees from various branches. With the aid of site-photographs, blue-prints and other documents, I was able to engage Moore's interest. Of course he would have to inspect the site. In due course, the principal, Herr Muhleman — who would be in charge of the Centre — came over from Switzerland and, with Moore, we discussed the project in more detail at a local hotel. Encouraged by Moore's reactions, the chief director, Herr Guyer, joined us at a second lunch which brought the realisation of the scheme a step nearer. Unfortunately, ankle trouble prevented Moore going over to the site for some time.

Meanwhile, however, he was able to move around enough on home ground to deal with a purely local matter in which I played a minor part. It was to try and save the Bishop's Stortford Corn Exchange from falling into such a state of dilapidation that those not interested in the building's preservation would have a case for its demolition. Built in 1828, it is a good example of the architect, Lewis Vulliamy's work. A local builder, Maurice Elliott, Henry Moore, a local official and myself met to discuss the question in the nearby George Hotel, so that Moore could make an inspection and suggestions regarding modification of the building for present use. Moore always did his shopping in the town on Saturday mornings but the crowded market interfered with a detailed view of the building which he very much liked. The outcome of our meeting was a scheme for repair and restoration that included a successful conversion of the neo-Greek styled building into shops and offices. A newly revealed feature was the row of Tuscan iron columns, formerly inside the building. The conversion received an accolade from Sir Nikolaus Pevsner in a new edition (1977) of his *Hertfordshire* in the 'Buildings of England' series.

In 1968, a *livre d'artiste*, *La Belle Inconnue*, by Alphonse Allais, (with original etchings by Michel Potier) had been published by a celebrated bibliophile society, *Les Impénitents*, which has the enlightened custom of commissioning a well-known older artist to provide a frontispiece to each book they publish annually for their hundred members. Among the artists who had made this contribution were Max Ernst, Edouard Goerg and Dali. I had persuaded Moore to let the Society have one of his etchings for the title mentioned. It was evidence to me and to the French of his continuing interest in the genre.

I note in a diary that in April 1974 I went to an exhibition in the British Museum of 'Recent Moore prints and illustrations to Auden's Poems'. Moore had known Auden in early days and had visited him more recently, in Auden's summer home in Austria. He thought he seemed in not very good shape (there is a portrait-sketch he did of the poet at that time). The outcome was that, from existing lithographs, Moore found ones that reflected the mood of the individual poems. Moore wrote: 'I had known Auden since the 1930s and had always greatly admired his poetry but it was some months before I felt I could get going. I began with the most obvious poem — "Lullaby" ("Lay your sleeping head, my love") to me a very beautiful and touching one — in a straightforward way as if I was translating *Alice in Wonderland*. But, after reading some of the other poems, I realised that it would be impossible to treat them in the same way...'.

In the general introduction to the catalogue, Moore referred to the etching-techniques of Hercules Seghers. As it happened, this provided a lead-in for me when I wanted to engage his interest, a short time later, in a *livre d'artiste* project around a still-life engraving by Hercules Seghers, an artist greatly admired by Rembrandt. The poet/typographer, Pierre Lecuire, had the idea of asking a number of artists and sculptors to do a variation on the subject, 'Three Books' — one of the only three still-lifes by Seghers. Naturally, he hoped for etchings, drypoints or aquatints on the said theme. In the event, Moore contributed two of the best etchings in the book — a straight etching and a drypoint combined with soft-ground etching.

When my former pupil, Christopher Hewett, opened his 'Taranman' gallery with an exhibition of etchings for the most part by Alphonse Legros in 1974 and followed this with drawings and etchings by F.L. Griggs, I remember receiving a letter from him, dated '12 IX 74'. He wrote that Henry Moore's visit to the gallery had been a memorable occasion and a source of encouragement. He had 'come in talking of Ruskin, "our greatest art critic", and left having spent over £500'. During the next month, I took Pierre Lecuire to meet Moore and to present him with two '*exemplaires de Collaborateur*' of the newly published *Le Livre des*

Livres. The text of the book, a poem by Lecuire, is accompanied by contributions from fifteen well-known artists. Moore was delighted with the production and was particularly interested in the variations on the theme shown in the engravings by three sculptors, César, Ubac and Etienne Martin. It must be added that his own work was an enrichment to the book with its total of twenty-two engravings, which was exhibited at Taranman in 1975.

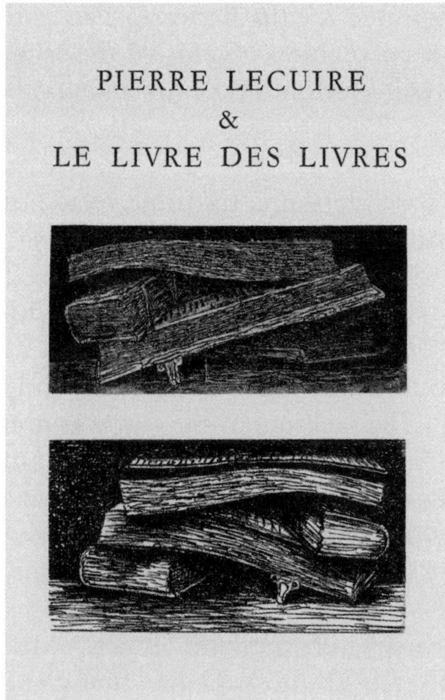

The year, 1975, was that of the sheep. Moore's admitted obsession with sheep — his favourite farm animal — was infectious as one got to see them through his eyes, in his drawings and etchings. Even if the farmer had not grazed them on his studio estate, Moore said he would have kept sheep for the pleasure he gained from observing them. He had gained the animals' confidence. Hidden from view in a small hut in his grounds, he had watched and drawn them as, sensing a human presence, they nosed around. He exploited this curiosity to get the close views he wanted. The results are now familiar to everyone who has looked at Moore's *Sheep Sketchbook* — the drawings and etchings are admired by an extensive public, including many unable to appreciate his sculpture.

Moore readily co-operated with me when I proposed to do an article for the Spring 1975 issue of *The Countryman* 'Sheep in Sketch and Sculpture'. He liked the Samuel Palmer etchings I used, particularly that of the sheep-head, and he thoroughly approved of the 'Sheep-Shearer' bronze by Ralph Brown, reproduced, along with the climax to the article — Moore's 'Sheep-Piece' — the monumental bronze photographed on an artificial mound Moore had had made to raise it against the sky-line. This is an ideal setting for a sculpture, as exemplified at Stonehenge, and the mound was repeated for the Battersea Park siting in 1979. At home, we have an agreeable souvenir of the 'sheep period' in one of the sheep etchings Moore gave my wife, on her birthday.

Three years after the project had been mooted in the spring of 1975, there had been progress on the siting of the 'Four-Piece Reclining Figure' in Switzerland. Moore's ankle had recovered sufficiently for him to have inspected the site with the lake behind, at Wolfsberg (Arenenberg), and everything was ready for the celebration of the official viewing in May, to which I was invited.

The pleasure of the trip was greatly enhanced for me by travelling with Henry and Irina to our destination. Moore was, by nature, a very relaxed person, but I noted that for the moment he was extremely put out when it was reported that no meal would be served on our flight from Heathrow. There had in fact been a misunderstanding, however, and we received full VIP treatment — whisky, champagne, lunch. Moore was looking forward to meeting the hosts he had first met at Hadham and to photographing his bronze *in situ.* As we drove through the Swiss countryside, poetic with pinewood and its meadows, where charolais cattle were browsing, I remarked on the frequent appearance of fair-haired girls in white stockings and nearly all wearing red or white blouses. They were everywhere, in the villages; cycling on the highway. Moore began to tease me about my obsession and kept remarking at the appropriate moment, 'Look Walter' — lapsing into Yorkshire — 'another fur-erd girl'. It was a delightful journey through the picturesque villages of Frauenfeld and Muhlheim, with their painted houses and picturesque hanging signs, to Wolfsberg.

We were able to enjoy our first viewing of the 'Four-Piece' bronze gleaming in the evening sun. We were taken on a tour of the management training centre. New functional timber buildings were equipped with a vast indoor swimming pool for the benefit of the course participants. Adjacent to this modern setting was the old Schloss Wolfsberg which had once housed Louis Napoleon and the Empress Eugénie and was now used for lodging visitors like ourselves.

After a session when the sculpture was photographed by the professionals, we went indoors for a cocktail and an informal dinner. There were fourteen of us at table. I had a long chat with Dr Baumann, the director of the Kunsthaus we were to visit the next day, who was interested to hear about my preparatory work for *Towards Sculpture*. Apart from including a good deal of Moore's drawings of sculpture, this would include Marino Marini, whose amazing 'Horse' sculpture I was to see on its site outside the Kunsthaus. After most of the guests had left, the party resolved itself into lively discussions with Moore as the centre of interest. He described his early days as a teacher at the Royal College of Art, when he had heard a potential sculptor say: 'Don't do sculpture. It's under Henry Moore and he's mad!' and how, at one point, he was asked by the students to resign. But, fortunately, thanks to the support of the Principal, Sir William Rothenstein, his services were retained. He recalled that at an early exhibition, he had realized £90 for a picture; framing it had cost him £100.

Conversation turned to middlebrow art which, oddly, Moore defended. I had made uncomplimentary criticisms of Russell Flint's smoothly erotic watercolours. Moore defended him on purely technical grounds, even though the subject might be considered trivial. I was also surprised that, on this occasion, he put music first, literature second and art in third place. However, his reservations made it clear that his criterion was based on which

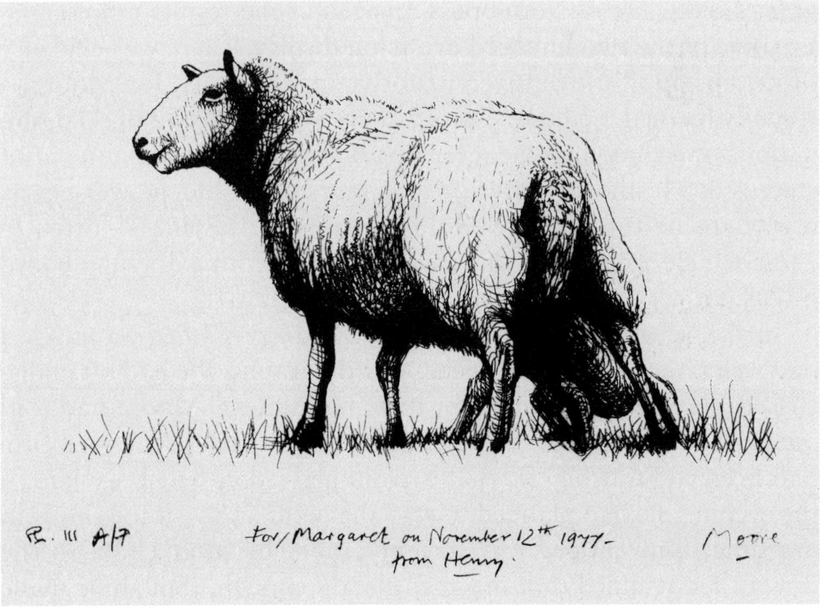

gave the greatest pleasure to the greatest number. On the other hand — even in terms of absolutes — he claimed the first place in civilisation for art over science. He illustrated his point, as I heard later on a TV programme, by saying: 'If there had been no Rembrandt, no one could fill the gap his work represented but if, say, Einstein had not discovered the principles of relativity, sooner or later they would have been discovered by someone else'.

Moore was very pleased with the trip. The weather had been perfect for viewing his bronze and he felt sure there would be some good photographs as a result. There were. And I have a good collection of them, as a reminder of the occasion. I note that Alan Bowness lists the 'Four-Piece Reclining Figure' among Moore's most memorable bronzes of that decade.

My annual visit to Paris in 1977, was particularly enjoyable, since it gave me the chance to see the exhibition of Moore sculpture in the Orangerie and that of his drawings and graphic work in the Bibliothèque Nationale. I was struck by the way Moore's wartime mining drawings were displayed — subdued lighting echoed the dark tones of the drawings he had done of miners and mines. I went to the Bibliothèque Nationale in the company of Charles Russell. We met Jacques Frélaut, whom I had seen at the Lacourière workshop in Paris and again at Much Hadham, when he was giving Moore technical help on etching, on which he is a great expert. He was doubtless amazed at the results represented by some of the two hundred prints on display. There was evidence of his apt pupil's inventive virtuosity in what was, for Moore, a recently learned medium. There always seemed to be novel combinations of techniques whenever I paid a visit to Moore in the print studios. Up to the last three or four years of his life, he was nearly always to be found there in the mornings, drawing — often in charcoal. He would sit in his chair for hours with a drawing-board on his lap.

In the Spring of 1977 *The Countryman* published an article I had written on Moore's Stonehenge lithographs. We had often discussed Europe's greatest prehistoric monument. Moore had told me how, when he was a student in London, his first expedition had been to Stonehenge. As his train arrived at Salisbury late in the evening, he had planned to stay the night and visit the site next morning. But, enticed by a bright moon, he took a taxi to the downs. He retained that memory clearly enough, though he made repeated visits to Stonehenge, to capture it in one of the series of lithographs — sixteen in all — he called 'Moon Lightfall'. He made etchings as well — the first two in 1972 — but lithography was the better medium for drawing the textures of the vast, rough-hewn stone columns and architraves. Moore drew with his mind as well as his eye — allowing his imagination to evoke strange images. These were reflected in the titles he chose — 'Fallen Giant', 'Cyclops'. Neither Constable nor Turner captured the timelessness of Stonehenge. I think the literary equivalent of Moore's lithographs of the site is Thomas Hardy's evocation of the ancient monument in *The Return of the Native*, looking at it with the same probing eye.

During 1978 the Much Hadham studios were busy with the various Henry Moore exhibitions to celebrate his eightieth birthday. London was full of Moore exhibitions — at the Tate and the Serpentine Gallery (indoors and outside). When I first set eyes on 'Hill Arches', even for Moore an amazing departure in the style of the integrated forms, I thought of Diaghilev's remark to Jean Cocteau 'astonish me!' I had seen most of Moore's carvings in his studios but, assembled in the Serpentine Gallery, they were a revelation of Moore as stone-carver. For the most part, I had seen him at work on his elmwood carvings, many of which are now in the Moore Centre, Leeds.

On August 11 1981, I paid my first visit to the new Henry Moore Foundation (the Foundation, at Dane Tree House, Perry Green, had been started in 1977). I had watched the transformation of the existing building and seen the extensions being built. But the interior was unbelievable: strong-room, sculpture studio, offices and storage space, meticulously organized. Then there was the conservatory: lofty, extensive, with glazed panels of the *Time Life* 'Reclining Figure' (plaster model). It became the place where Moore met his visitors; often potential purchasers of prints and drawings or students from abroad (especially the US) who, having come such distances, were never turned away.

Nevertheless, it marked an inevitable change of attitude from the simpler and more intimate setting of Hoglands — even with the large 'new room' extension. Before being told to go over to Hoglands, past the 'log-pile' (of etchings), even we lucky ones first reported our arrival to the studio's faithful secretary, Mrs Betty Tinsley. She herself, as she confided to me, felt a nostalgic longing for the small room near the original farmhouse front door which led into the office-studio (full of books and records but alive with continually changing pictures). After an invariably warm welcome, it would be 'I'll tell Mr Moore you're here, Mr Strachan'. Often he was in the adjoining parlour or she would send me to one of the studios, generally the 'maquette' studio. She herself retained the same friendly approach but the routine later involved a telephone call to the house or one of the studios.

The informal atmosphere remained with 'the boys' — as Moore always referred to his assistants, Malcolm Woodward and Michael Muller. 'John' was John Farnham, the patination expert. People wandered in and out. Visitors arrived by car or taxi. The routine break for morning coffee at the large table (it can seat fourteen and not infrequently did) allowed staff and visitors to meet and chat. There would be a similar tea-break routine in the afternoon — yet the work was done. The sculpture assistants were free from Friday to Monday to do their own work. They still are free to do so, in fact, John Farnham, for example, has his own sculpture studio and house in the nearby village of Braughing. All three had — and continue to have — personal exhibitions.

When Moore had important exhibitions abroad — however far afield — one or more of the assistants, with David Mitchinson or Moore's niece, Ann Garrould, in charge of organisation, would set up the display — whether in Spain, Japan, Korea or in the Yorkshire Sculpture Park. There can have been no parallel operations on the same scale. No exhibitions in the history of sculpture have been carried out with such efficiency and devotion. It all emanates from Moore's skill at organizing, evident from his earliest days, and a way of getting things done in the most effective manner.

There was always a lighter side. I remember the invitations to join a game of table-tennis — at which Moore excelled. He had been a good gymnast and he was a PT instructor in the army during the First World War — after he had been gassed at the Front and declared unfit for field service. He was a sergeant in the Home Guard in World War II. His great relaxation, all his life, was watching sport. The Wimbledon weeks became sacrosanct. No interruptions were welcomed by either himself or Irina. You just watched the 'box' with them. I forget which year but I happened to be at the Studios on the day of the Grand National when there was great excitement, all the staff taking part in a sweepstake in which I, too, was invited to join.

In my lectures to NADFAS branches over the country, I had often talked about Moore's sculpture and drawings. Sometimes I linked his work with Barbara Hepworth's — as a contrasting approach. Then I extended my repertoire (as I had done in monographs in *The Connoisseur*) to sculptors of the younger generation, making the point that Moore's work and international success had acted as a catalyst to British sculpture — a stimulus to its practice, beginning with Meadows, Armitage, Butler, Lynn Chadwick, Robert Adams... Moore's recognition of this fact would only come up incidentally, when we were talking about the sculpture scene in this country. He would remind his listeners — individuals or an audience — that when he started there were only Epstein, Frank Dobson and Underwood on the English scene.

One of the youngest of the new generation, David Nash, I first met at an exhibition of British sculpture sponsored by the US Government at the Royal Academy. I was particularly interested in one of his many wood sculptures (created with saw and adze rather than chisel). I very much liked the maquette for one of his pieces. After the exhibition was over, he brought it to our house in Bishop's Stortford. Like the other sculptors who have visited us, he welcomed the opportunity of being introduced to Moore. Moore quizzed him about his wood sculptures in the open-air parks, such as Grizedale in the Lake District and commented that they wouldn't stand up to the weather. Even indoors, his own elmwood pieces could develop cracks. Unabashed, Nash said, 'If my pieces last fifteen years I will be satisfied'.

In the summer of 1980 a Summer Holiday School was started at Bishop's Stortford College. I was invited to run a three-day course I called 'Looking at Modern Sculpture'. The much appreciated climax was a visit to Henry Moore's studios. It happened to be 30 July, Moore's eighty-second birthday, and our group presented him with a calligraphed greeting which he was very nice about. Later that year, I received an invitation to attend the unveiling of his 'Arch'. It was in October, in Kensington Gardens by the Serpentine. It was a sunny day and the 'Arch' of Roman Travertine marble looked glorious against the green background and early autumn leaves. Michael Heseltine's tall figure dwarfed Henry Moore as the latter leaned on his stick beside the soaring 'Arch', his gift to the Department of the Environment.

At this period, I seemed to be living and breathing sculpture. It had featured in *Towards Sculpture*, published in 1976. I was also lecturing widely on the subject (the Wirral, Welshpool, Lymington, York, Harrogate) and I was now planning a guide to modern open-air sculpture in Britain. This was inspired by an excellent little illustrated guide to sculpture in Harlow, Essex, written by Lady Gibberd, whose husband, Sir Frederick Gibberd had been the New Town's architect. I began my research, modestly enough, with the sculpture in my own area of East Anglia but, as I explored further afield, I decided to extend the range and embrace the whole of Great Britain. It seemed increasingly necessary, with the proliferation of sculpture parks: Grizedale Forest and the Yorkshire Sculpture Park in 1977, the Highland Sculpture Park, followed by South Hill Rufford and Portland Clifftop, all in 1983. Another factor in my decision to cover the whole of the country was the opportunity it offered of listing, with photographs, all the sculptures of Henry Moore on open air sites on permanent or long-term loan — not listed elsewhere. At that time there turned out to be no fewer than fifty-four.

Moore took a great personal interest in the book, which needed backing from the Moore Foundation to make it a viable proposition. The sculptor himself intervened to make this possible. It was finally published in 1984 with an introduction by Lady Gibberd. Moore was delighted to see how well his 'Arch' — in John Donat's colour photograph — had come out on the front cover. Indeed he liked the whole book. His 'jolly good, Walter, nothing like this has been done before' made up for the critics' neglect (the exception being an enthusiastic comment from Marina Vaizey).

Meanwhile, in September 1982 Moore, through David Mitchinson, had sprung a lovely surprise on me. He thought I would be the right person to write a book about his animal sculptures, drawings and graphic work. Of course, I was delighted to be entrusted with an aspect of Moore's work that had never been treated. We had an initial discussion that month and the book came out in the November of the following year.

Once I had collected all the photographs of relevant sculptures and drawings, I produced a plan. We decided to follow animals (using the term in the general sense) more or less in their evolutionary order. It happened to fit in with their materialisation in his work, since some of the earliest sculptures and sketch-book drawings had been of reptiles and birds — the 'Snake' (a small marble carving of 1924) and a bronze bird of 1927, 'Bird-form' in the Notebook of 1922/24 had been inspired by an Inca vase — one sheet of them had 'heads of animals — grotesque' written on it. It was a hint of the role imagination was to play throughout Moore's career. Among the bird drawings was a pencil sketch of 'Three Crows' c.1950 which I had always admired. It certainly gave the lie to those who had thought Moore incapable of a figurative drawing. Long before the 'sheep' period, it confirmed the fact that he could draw animals with the virtuosity of a Stubbs.

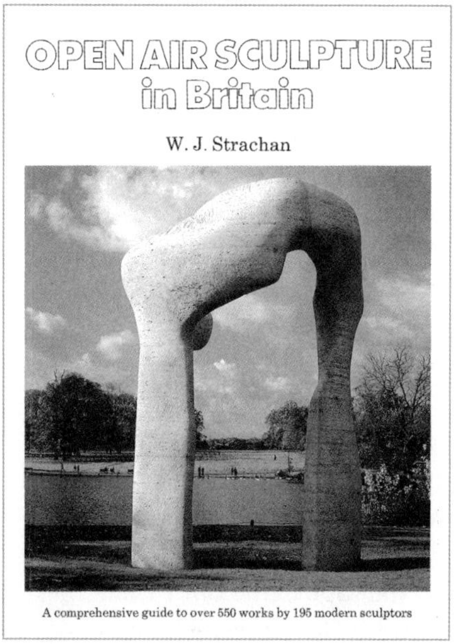

Next to his portrayals of the female form, Moore's finest drawings are undoubtedly of animals or animal-forms, bones, skulls etc. I placed his elephant lithograph facing Rembrandt's drawing; the highest compliment one could pay to a worshipper of the Dutch master. Rembrandt was Moore's favourite painter and etcher. We had spent many hours together poring over the complete volumes of Rembrandt etchings — studying all the 'states' and effects as he took up the medium.

In the chapter on 'Wild Animals' I included two drawings of bison executed by Moore for the gallery, Il Bisonte in Florence, which mounted an exhibition, *'Sculpture — Disegni — Grafica'* in 1980.

We had many sessions over the various sections. Angela Dyer, the editor from Aurum Press, the publishers, joined in. I had to persuade them both that the book would be of greater interest if we included works by other artists related to the sculptor's own; either to show influence or to make comparisons. I had in mind the prehistoric and exotic artefacts that Moore admired in, for example, the British Museum (which Moore was wont to refer to as his 'university' and more of an influence than any art college training). The sessions spent looking through and discussing material sitting side by side at the long table, were relaxed and enjoyable. I persuaded Moore to include relevant grotesques such as mediaeval bench-ends and some drawings — even a tapestry — by contemporary artists. 'Agreed', said Moore. 'Provided it is only the best art'.

I decided it would be useful to have a permanent record of Moore's views on animal themes. Recording was no novelty at the Foundation. Moore's voice on the tape came out rather cloudily at times. He was far from well. But there are parts that made the operation worthwhile and I naturally treasure the statements he made. The collaboration took me back thirty years, to the time when we were dealing with *Prométhée*. Moore inscribed my copy of the book 'To Walter with gratitude for having made such a good book, 18th October, 1983'.

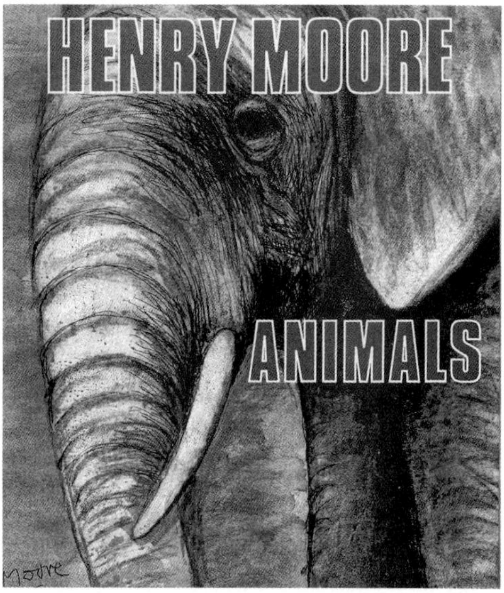

Following a serious operation, Moore was obliged to reduce his activities and by the year 1985, his work routine was limited to being driven to the sculpture studios and doing some — chiefly charcoal — drawing. In the afternoons he would be driven out into the surrounding country 'to stretch his eye', he would say. Sometimes he stopped to feed a donkey he liked. Moore would talk to me about his early days when he could not afford to buy stone to carve. He resorted to using stray pieces from builders' yards but he was glad, for example, to have specimens of various stones which were being cleared out of the South Kensington Museum — they included blocks of Hornton (brown), a stone that had not been used by sculptors in living memory. He found it workable and used it for many carvings; on a large scale for the 'Northampton Madonna'. He told me that the first piece of stone he bought with a specific carving in mind was the block of Hornton from which he carved the 'Mother and Child' (1924) acquired by the Manchester Art Gallery. Chat on this theme often led Moore on to the whole subject of carving; how he and Epstein were the first English sculptors since the Middle Ages to do 'direct' carving — as opposed to the practice favoured by academicians of scaling up from a clay or plaster maquette by the use of a 'pointing machine'. The foreign pioneers of direct carving, whom he greatly admired, were Brancusi — he had visited him in his Paris studio — and Gaudier-Brzeska, an exile in England.

Moore, who had many decades earlier said to me, 'Irina is the collector' had, in the last twenty years, acquired a remarkable variety of prints, drawings and paintings by great modern masters. I remembered best the two Courbet oils and the large Degas drawing of dancers; a charming Vuillard; a 'romantic' Odilon Redon and two charcoal (or conté) drawings by one of his favourite draughtsmen, Seurat. I noticed new arrivals — an early Vuillard and three Daumier drawings. But two or three works rarely moved out of the lounge — the ivory carving (Egyptian) of a lynx and a Rembrandt etching of Saskia, dated 1636, hung side by side with a drawing of 'Mary doing her homework'. The most recent acquisition was a Manet.

If, as in the case of most old people, Moore's memory became hazy about the present, it remained undimmed about the past and anything concerning the arts. It was typical, therefore, that when I took over to Hoglands a copy of the Waddington Galleries exhibition catalogue of Moore graphics (September 11 1985), he should recall the time (in 1950-1951) when we were working together on the various stages of *Prométhée*. We remembered Jonquière's panic when he received a message from Gide, threatening to take his text away unless the work was out by a certain date — a message I had to transmit to Moore as tactfully as possible! I remembered that he possessed the large Rodin maquette of *'l'Homme qui marche'*, exhibited in the first Hayward Gallery Rodin Exhibition of 1970. I talked to him about the forthcoming exhibition, in the summer of 1986 — which he was destined not to see — in the context of two newly published French volumes on Rodin, which I had taken to show him. I sat on the bed and turned over the pages of the books which he supported on his knees.

My very last visit to Hoglands, as it turned out, was when I arrived with a copy of the book, *Irina's Garden*, with a text by Stephen Spender. In this Spender said many of the things about Henry, the Moore household and its unaffected lifestyle, which only a few months later, after Moore's death, he would echo in an address at a service of Thanksgiving in Westminster Abbey. On this occasion it was typical of Irina's modesty that she seemed surprised I had bought a copy and not picked one up at the studio. This time I was asking *her* to inscribe a book. Moore was not in good health but, as ever, welcomed me warmly. However, there was a lively flash when he asked me if I could identify the new skull that was on a table in the lounge. They were amused at my guesses. 'It wasn't an animal'. In fact, it was — but I would never have recognised it. It was the skull of a dolphin. It was a good moment to treasure — Moore's lifelong preoccupation with bone structure. His wonder at the miracles of nature — no less than of rocks and of human form. Nothing in nature was alien to him — from a living tiger to a dead tree-trunk.

I always liked to hear Moore repeat his statement about sculpture in this country: 'When I began, there was Epstein, Hepworth, myself and one or two others. Now, I could name literally more than a hundred sculptors in this country who have achieved some recognition'. He did not point to himself as the main cause and he acknowledged his debt to the modern pioneers. 'When I was a student, direct carving was simply unheard of in academic circles, though Brancusi and Epstein and Modigliani had used it...' Typical of his generosity was his tribute to Epstein who, he said, made things easier for his successor, because he had 'taken all the knocks'. Epstein appealed to him not only as a sculptor (essentially a modeller, not a carver) but as 'an intensely warm man'. The persecution that Epstein had to put up with distressed Moore, whose own special characteristic was his outgoing humanity.

Artists are, almost by definition, introspective and self-orientated. They have to be. Whether they are poets, novelists, painters or sculptors, their inward life and its realisation comes through the work they create and that is their primary concern. Smaller personalities are largely concerned with their public image, their popular success, rather than with their work. The 'truly great' draw inspiration from particular 'heroic' figures — with whose merits they would not venture to compare their own. For Rodin it was Dante; for Bourdelle — Beethoven. It does not have to be the same walk of life. For Moore — much though he admired Michelangelo and Rembrandt — the debt was less direct. It was linked with his philosophy of life which had been expressed as early as 1935: 'I personally believe that all life is a conflict; that's something you have to know. And you have to die too — which is the opposite of living. One must try to find a synthesis, to come to terms with opposite qualities. Art and life are made up of conflicts. Really I think that in great art this conflict is hidden, it is unsolved'.

This is consistent with what Moore had said when asked whether he was satisfied with a work on its completion. 'No', he said firmly, 'there's always something'. And Moore had been drawn to art that showed some element of struggle or disturbance — primitive or sometimes classical; the cruelty in Mexican art, the panic in the heads of Lorenzo Ghiberti's horses on the bronze Baptistry gates — 'La Porta del Paradiso'; the self-agonising in Rembrandt's late self-portraits.

The painter Moore most admired was Cézanne. He was proud to have one of the studies for the *Grandes Baigneuses* on his walls. Like Rembrandt, he said, Cézanne, too, wanted to do the impossible. His art was always disturbing. One of his last works *'La Vieille au chapelet'* was 'almost a Rembrandt'. Moore even made a small scale sculptural version of 'Three Bathers', after Cézanne's, to show that Cézanne's vision could be directly translated into this medium, so strong is the element of construction in his painting. Although Moore voiced his thoughts only occasionally, I think these feelings about art and life need to be remembered when one looks at the more difficult or mysterious of his works. For the 'King and Queen' for example, he gave his own analysis. For 'Warrior with Shield' he gave an explanation. Others he left to be judged by their qualities of form — but by the mind as well as the eye.

For me there are still lectures to be added to the many I have given on Moore. There are others planned for the future. It means the continuation of the pleasure of sharing an enthusiasm; never without thoughts of a warm, long and unforgettable friendship — and the leafy, winding lane to Perry Green, Much Hadham.

(1988)

PART FIVE

A LIFE IN LETTERS

1984–1994

ETRETAT

Wave-hollowed arches
stride into the sea,
embrace a pointed figure,
seated hieratic
like a cardinal.

Landmarks to fishermen
long before Isabey discovered them
or Delacroix revealed the honeycomb cliff
where clean-edged chalk meets clay.

Myriad curved layers
that Courbet fashioned with palette-knife,
that Monet saw in the vibrant light
of dancing ripples,
that Seurat synthesized
and Moore modelled — distantly — in bronze.

But, for the late scatter of children
who with spidery arms and legs
now animate the pebbled foreshore,
the challenge is an invented game
played with the sea.

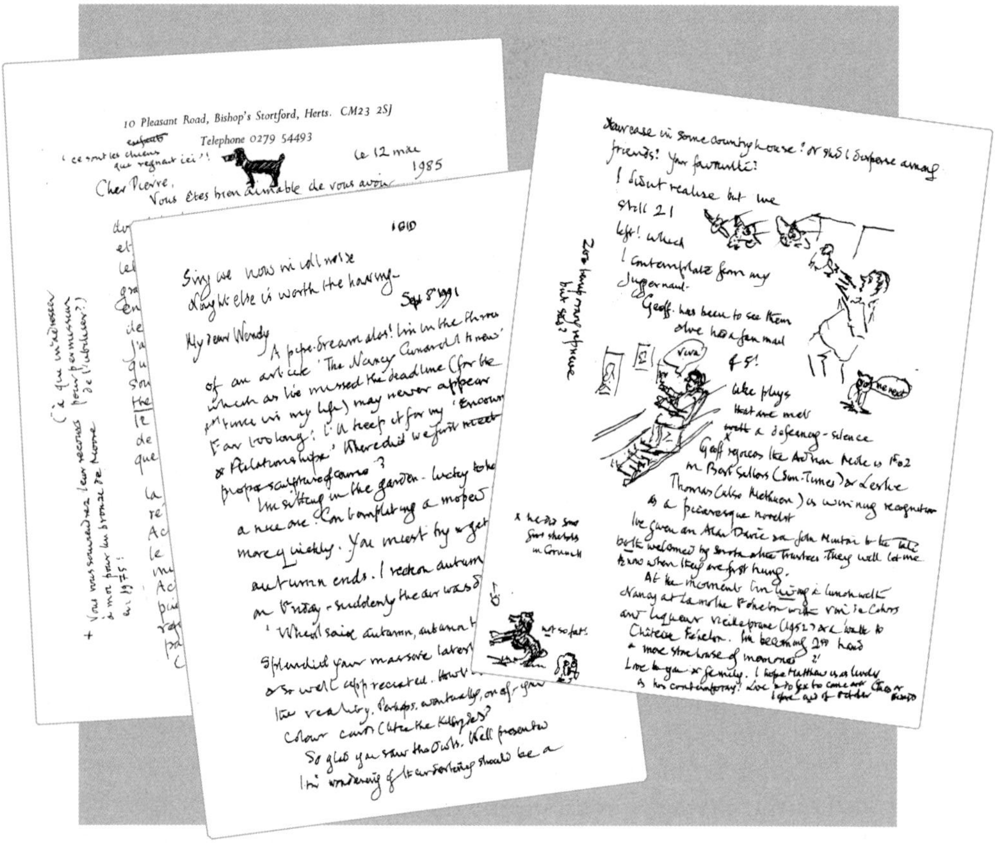
10 Pleasant Road, Bishop's Stortford, Herts. CM23 2SJ
Telephone 0279 54493
le 12 mai 1985
Cher Pierre,
Sept 8th 1991
My dear Wendy

A LIFE IN LETTERS

During the last decade of Walter Strachan's life a line from Edward Bond's play about Shakespeare in old age, *Bingo*, became one of his watchwords: 'Was anything done?'

If one looks at the number of books he had written, translated and edited for publication during each of the previous three decades, it could be said that during the last ten years he had rested on his oars a little. But for a man progressing from the age of eighty-one to that of ninety-one his output was still considerable.

Following the publication of *Open Air Sculpture in Britain* in 1984 he had hoped that a second edition might be published to include public sculptures either missed in the first or sited since its publication. He collected much fresh material. But there was a change of ownership at Zwemmers and no green light came for a new edition to be published, although the archive at the Scottish National Gallery of Modern Art was in due course to benefit from this late addition to the mass of photographs, written documentation and catalogues bequeathed to it that were the fruit of all his researches on sculpture.

His translation of Alain-Fournier's letters from London, *Towards the Lost Domain*, appeared in 1986. His publications in the late eighties also included a newly revised edition of *La Peste*, the text with which he had founded the Methuen Twentieth Century Texts series in 1959, and the extended memoir of Henry Moore which he was later to draw on for the chapter in this volume. 1987 saw the publication of *Le Livre d'Artiste*, the handsome, detailed and lengthy catalogue of his collection, as given to the Taylor Institution in that year, combining a new introduction to the subject and a major updating of his 1969 *magnum opus*, with the vivid account of his thirty-five-year love affair with the genre quoted earlier in these pages. The exhibition at the Ashmolean Museum which marked the donation was the culmination of a series of exhibitions drawn from the ever-growing collection.

His enthusiastic efforts to encourage successive headmasters of Bishop's Stortford College to continue acquiring works of art for the school collection, to which he contributed generously himself, led to its embodiment in the Walter Strachan Gallery, formally opened in November 1990. Another late loan exhibition was 'A Parliament of Owls' at the Victoria and Albert in 1991, a selection of some two dozen from the collection of prints and drawings that hung on his staircase. The very last small exhibition he arranged, presenting work by three masters of copper engraving, Vieillard, Flocon and Krol, was to open, also at the

Victoria and Albert, on March 16 1994, two days after Strachan's death.

Between 1984 and 1990 he had continued lecturing widely, at museums in London and Edinburgh and at many different locations around the country under the aegis of NADFAS. His subjects ranged from modern sculpture and the *livre d'artiste* to modern tapestry. In his chosen fields, as he somewhat bemusedly remarked, he was clearly regarded as 'a kind of *eminence grise*', contributing, on occasion, an introduction to a retrospective sculpture exhibition catalogue or a preface to one volume of an artist's catalogue raisonné. He wrote many articles: on literary, social and artistic topics for *Contemporary Review* and *London Magazine;* on the *livre d'artiste* and sculpture for *The Private Library*, *Modern Painters* and *Art Quarterly;* on rural (and artistic) topics for *The Countryman*. His last article for *The Private Library* would appear in autumn 1994. His substantial article on the *livre d'artiste* appeared in the thirty-four volume Macmillan *Dictionary of Art* in 1996.

Strachan continued to visit exhibitions eagerly, whether in London museums and galleries or in sculpture parks around the country, for as long as he could but as the decade progressed he was becoming less mobile. His talk on Jean Lurçat at the V and A in November 1990 was his last public lecture and by August 1991 a visit to a London exhibition was a rare occurrence.

My father's situation was painfully exacerbated from the late 1980s onwards not only by his own relative physical frailty but also by the increasing ill health of Margaret, who had given him her devoted care and staunch support, indeed had literally made all his work possible, for over sixty years. As it became clear that she was afflicted with Alzheimer's disease that grew gradually more severe, he was obliged to take over more and more of the running of the household. Eventually, in 1992, he had to see her into a small private home some twenty miles from Bishop's Stortford, where she was well cared for and could be fairly regularly visited by the family (as well as some local friends).

Just as the fact that Walter Strachan was blessed with good friends, able and willing to take him by car to sculpture sites, galleries and, occasionally, the venues for lectures, had become an increasingly crucial factor in his still active life in the eighties, so the wonderful neighbours the two of them were blessed with played a vital role in enabling Walter and Margaret — and eventually just Walter himself — to continue living at 10 Pleasant Road in the house and garden which, in the last years (as he wrote), had to be his gallery, his library, his landscape.

Throughout his adult life correspondence had been a vital means for him of establishing and maintaining contact, as well as exchanging ideas, with kindred spirits who shared his interests in the fields of art and literature. His generous schoolteacher friend Madeleine Pont, who plied him with books (and records of French chansons) for over forty years, was a shining example of this. Now, more than ever, writing and receiving letters was crucial to him. The other literary activity that occupied his time and energy was the compilation of draft chapters for his memoirs. Some were partly incorporated into published articles. Others remained in draft, incomplete.

I have therefore been fortunate, in seeking to round out Strachan's accounts of some of his literary and artistic friendships during the latter part of his life, in being given access to his letters to two people whose work he admired greatly and with whom he corresponded regularly during those years, the poet-typographer and creator of *livres d'artiste*, Pierre Lecuire, whose work had thrilled him and whom he had first met in Paris in 1960, as he embarked on his second decade of research and writing about the French illustrated book, and Wendy Taylor, the sculptor, whose work he had come to know and admire in the early eighties, when undertaking research for his book on open air sculpture. Born in 1945 and attending St Martin's School of Art in the early sixties, by 1984 Taylor had more public sculptures featured in Strachan's book (15) than any other sculptor except Moore, Hepworth, Geoffrey Clarke and Elizabeth Frink — all of them of much older generations.

As so often in Walter Strachan's life, meetings in connection with his writings on an artist's work (inspired by a passionate desire to tell the world about it) led to regular correspondence and friendship. He was able to write about Lecuire's majestic creations in his articles and books on the *livre d'artiste* and thereby to assist in the process of getting them better known in Britain. In Taylor's case he was able to list and illustrate her public sculptures in his book and feature one on the cover, for he quickly saw her as a pre-eminent sculptor of her generation, though circumstances did not allow him, as he would have liked, to devote a full-length monograph to her work.

Both the French poet and the English sculptor became faithful friends and confidants, supportive to him as he was to them. The extracts I have selected, and in the first case translated, from his copious letters to Lecuire and Taylor, evoke portraits of the two recipients, as seen through his eyes, as well as of Strachan himself in these years. These quoted letters must stand in here for countless others, written to so many other friends and kindred spirits throughout seven decades, including this last one. Strachan enjoyed receiving letters but was equally generous sending them. To call him a prolific letter writer is to risk understatement. He would share news with his correspondents of his passions, triumphs and achievements, on the one hand, and his problems, setbacks and disappointments, on the other, from time to time issuing proud bulletins about the doings of his family. In keeping with the themes of this book, I have here focused particularly on passages that show his response to his friends' work, and allude to his own activities and preoccupations, along with the occasional news flash about what he has just seen or been reading. These observations often echo his enthusiastic reports on such matters in his letters to Percy Horton and Tom Jason Wood fifty years earlier. For Walter Strachan a pleasure shared was ever a pleasure multiplied.

As in other parts of the book, I have taken some liberties with the chronology of this section, in that, to introduce passages commenting on the events of his life from 1984 onwards, I have selected a few from Strachan's early exchanges, with Lecuire from 1962, with Taylor from 1982. Even after 1984 there are, in any case, quite a number of references backward in time in these letters, inevitable and often enriching and poignant in the writings of a man who had lived a life characterized by such long-term commitment to certain ruling passions.

Late in 1993 Walter Strachan was writing the catalogue for his last exhibition of work by three artists he had first met and befriended in the 1950s. Now Roger Vieillard was dead but he was still corresponding with Albert Flocon and Abram Krol, as these letters show. When the exhibition opened in March 1994 the catalogue was prefaced by an appreciation from the Director of the Victoria and Albert Museum, Elizabeth Esteve-Coll. Her words, though they focus on only one of the fields to which Strachan had devoted such energy and passion over so many decades, carry a resonance that applies to all those other areas of his life, where he was determined to the very last, not just to enjoy an enthusiasm but to share it, to help others to make the connection...

'In 1969 a remarkable publication, *The Artist and the Book in France*, written by Walter Strachan was published in London. At that time I was a young librarian working in an art college library and the world of design and drawing unveiled within its pages was for me a revelation... The explosive originality of French book illustration was an unknown field — Walter Strachan opened the magical door to a whole new world.

'It was much later in 1986 when I was Keeper of the National Art Library that I got to know Walter personally and began to appreciate the importance of his close association with some of my predecessors as Keepers, in particular Arthur Wheen and John Harthan. Great collections in whatever field... are built up by the sympathy and excitement which develop between discerning curators and learned enthusiasts. The collaboration which can flourish, as it has in the case of Walter Strachan and five generations of Keepers of the National Art Library, creates untold riches and diversity...

'Even in his eighties, Walter was still supporting the National Art Library and lecturing in the V&A on Mario Prassinos, Abram Krol and

Albert Flocon. His love affair with the French livre d'artiste has resulted not only in the major scholarly work on the subject but also the enrichment of the nation's collection'.

13 'As soon as I have received one letter I immediately want another': letters to Pierre Lecuire, Wendy Taylor and Albert Flocon

All the letters that follow, save one, were sent from 10 Pleasant Road, Bishop's Stortford, to Pierre Lecuire and Albert Flocon in Paris and to Wendy Taylor in London.

To Pierre Lecuire

20 February 1962

Cher Monsieur,

The two items you sent me* have arrived safely and I thank you for them. Although time is needed to digest new things when they are so — literally — dazzling, let me tell you *at once* that I am very impressed, especially by the *estampilles.* It is a magnificent invention and I congratulate you and your gifted and original collaborator... I have written this very day to the Victoria and Albert Museum, proposing to come and show them these *belles pages...*

I very much hope we may meet in Paris, where I shall be from April 18th...

March 8 1962

Cher Monsieur,

Yesterday I took the opportunity, as promised, to show the Victoria and Albert Museum, in the person of the chief librarian, the proof pages from your two books, *Règnes* and *Dédale.* He was very impressed by them — really and truly, for he is an extremely sensitive man. The problem — fantastic as this may seem for such a great museum — is one of finance...

* Proof pages from *Règnes* by Pierre Lecuire, with 13 uninked *estampilles* by Etienne Hadju and *Dédale* by Pierre Lecuire with 22 etchings by André Lanskoy.

May 6 1962

Cher Monsieur

Thank you for your warm welcome and hospitality... It gave me an unforgettable pleasure to see your texts in those magnificent books, each, so it seemed to me, presented in a manner marvellously suited to their respective contents. We have a shared interest and I found our exchange of views enthralling. I have just shown your pages to Henry Moore and his wife Irina. They were very impressed, particularly by *Règnes* (typography, text, everything.) Moore knows Hadju's sculptures so he was all the more interested in the *estampilles.* He was thrilled by the double page of text — a dazzling design ('Why don't we have books like this?')...

December 30 1962

Cher Monsieur Lecuire

...Good news! I have had the idea of arranging an exhibition of *livres d'artiste* at the Ashmolean Museum in Oxford... The Ruskin Master of Drawing has spoken about it to the Director of the Museum... [and] is to visit me in a week's time, to see my things — books, proof pages etc. — and I will show him the fine pages from *Règnes*, which will certainly be included in the exhibition. They have also asked me to give a lecture in Oxford on books by the *peintres-graveurs* of the Ecole de Paris... I believe this project, backed up by a catalogue, will be yet another step towards the *magnum opus...*

The other day I bought a fine drawing by Beaudin (1934) from the well known collector, A. Zwemmer. It is an airy delight, full of joy and vitality, very modern, yet very classical...

July 22 1976

Cher Pierre

The owls* have landed, after a flight held up neither by the postal service (no postmarks) nor customs.

Under cover of night!

* Lecuire had sent him a comprehensive illustrated ornithological work on the subject of owls.

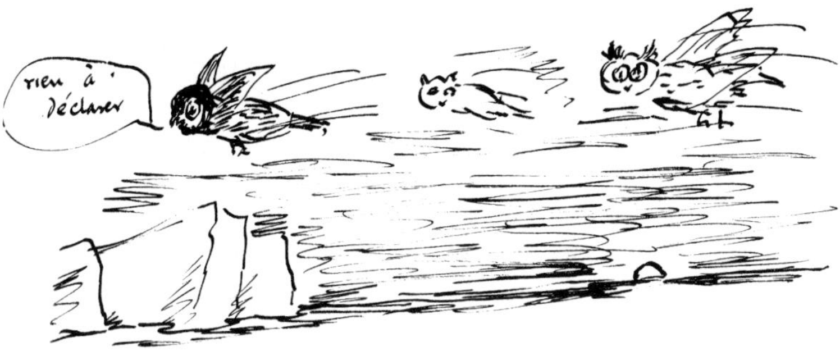

It is a very handsome book — well produced and full of information... Many thanks, from Margaret too, of course. It was an inspired idea on your part...

I've ordered the book by Georges Limbour on Beaudin, for whom I have a particular fondness, as draughtsman, painter and sculptor...

Yesterday I led a group of young people on an 'architectural trail' around B. Stortford — sons and daughters of the people I give my lectures to... Together we examined, drew and discussed the 'curiosities' of the town. Three hours. I came home exhausted. Some of them were enlightened and intelligent. I watched one of them make an excellent drawing of an owl carved in wood in the parish church. That's how time flows under the bridges of Bishop's Stortford. I cherish this correspondence with you. Not a scrap of it is thrown away...

I have just at this moment received a request from Beaudin to write a preface to his exhibition at the Musée Rodin...

To Wendy Taylor

November 1st 1981

Dear Wendy, (may I?)

The pleasure was mutual. We so enjoyed your visit and having such a memorable reminder in the shape of the fine 'Octo' maquette* is marvellous. Margaret has given the wall a pale grey-blue backing for it, which shows it to great advantage. Yes, I'd love to come and see the 'Compass Bowl' at Bletchley when the moment comes — and your studio.

* Maquette for the sculpture sited at Milton Keynes, which would be shown on the back of the cover of *Open Air Sculpture in Britain.*

Meantime I plug on. The Blee brothers of Basil Spence partnership, with whom Lady Gibberd has put me in touch, are helping me to fill in gaps in my representation and I've just written to Dame Sylvia Crowe in case she has come across any 'environmental' sculpture...

Feb 14th 1982

Dear Wendy

Thank you for your good letter and enclosures. It's a lovely catalogue — I've rarely — in fact never — seen a better produced one with discreet backing of preliminaries and climax of colour photos. The final shot makes me eager to see 'Essence', sited somewhere not too far away. Good luck with it — a fascinating shape. One of my middle-aged audience to whom I was lecturing on modern sculpture — a society of novices — said to me afterwards, 'Now I understand: sculpture's about shape'. I didn't feel I'd wasted my time!...

'Sentinel' sends me reeling in its imaginative treatment of recalcitrant bricks...

What are the dimensions of 'Veer'? Would you put them on the verso of the photo when you find it?...

24th Feb 1982

Dear Wendy

After a lot of thought I've decided I can't do without the piece you brought at the same time as the 'Octo'! It must be the one you brought into the house... I don't recall its title but assume from your last (welcome as usual) letter it must be 'Veer'? If so, it may be the one sketched below of which you either sent or left a photo?...

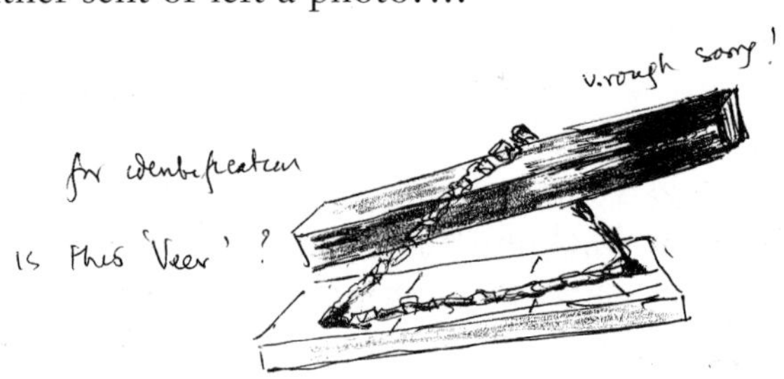

28th June 1982

Dear Wendy

Not that man again, you will be saying! The special reason is that having corrected the site of your 'Compass Bowl' to its rightful Basildon, Essex, I failed to ask you to pinpoint its location for the caption I put in the Guide. An underpass in the town — number or name of roads leading to it?...

We simply love 'Veer', as do all our friends. One associates chains with being shackled but here one is escaping!...

18th October 1982(?)

Dear Wendy

A very grateful Thank you for the new photographic material and the slides (timely all, as I shall show the latter at Harrogate Wednesday morning — I go tomorrow — and then at Kenwood — lecture to Highgate folk)... I am mounting (with Blu-tack) a sheet of your material for these two lectures — I always have a supplement of such sheets for people to gather round and ask questions before or after the talk — more direct...

We are amazed how you get through all your commissions. I have my work cut out... We've just got back — yesterday — from the Lakes. We were taken round the latest Grizedale sculpture and also saw the Hepworth, the Hoskins at Kendall. Lady G[ibberd] has done her foreword. That might push the business on. Liliane Lijn's new piece unveiled while we were away but photos en route. I don't mind missing ceremonies!

It's a lovely batch you've sent. How you've livened townscape, landscape — you should glow with pride, if you've time!...

January 26th 1983

My dear Wendy

You apologize for going graphic instead of finding words! Actually you couldn't have contributed anything to that portfolio* that could have pleased me more. It's

* Wendy Taylor had contributed an etching to a portfolio of rhyme sheets offered to Strachan to mark his eightieth birthday

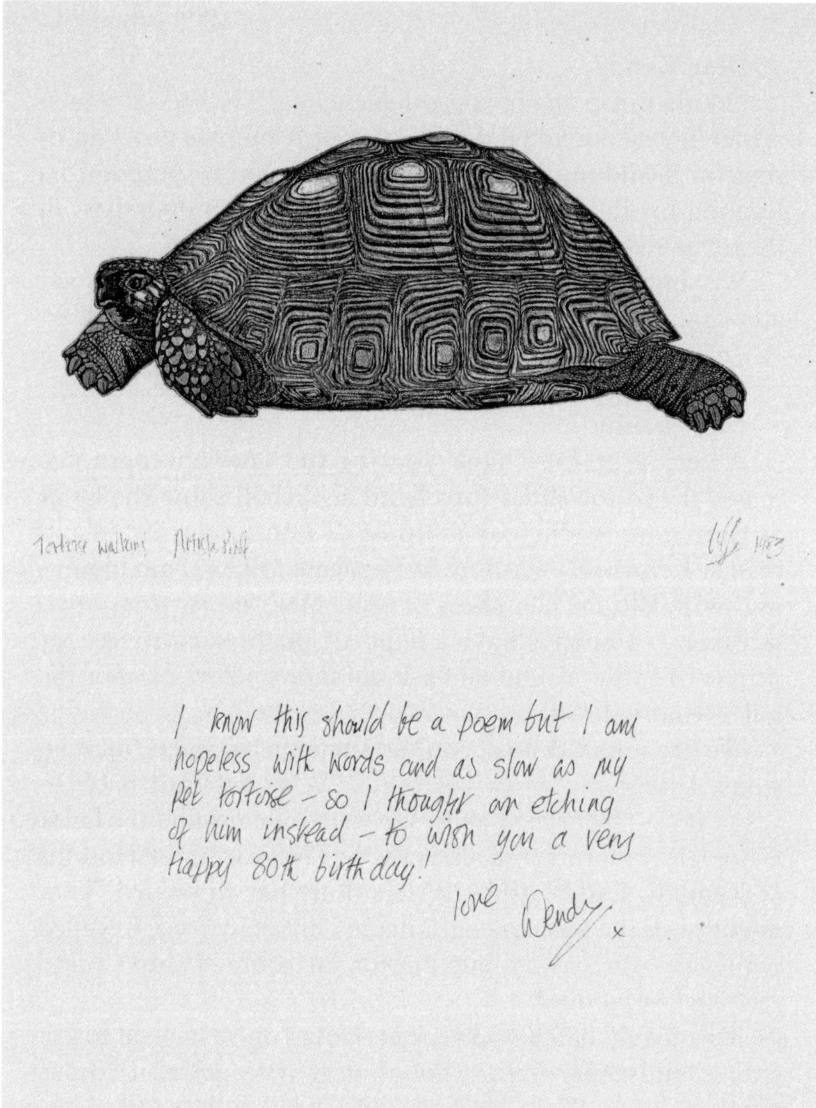

absolutely lovely, the very armour-plated essence of the tortoise — your personal tortoise — a superb etching.

Yesterday was good, ending with Margaret cooking Dover sole and crême brûlée — and champagne from one of those nice ex-pupils of mine…

To Pierre Lecuire

January 2 1984

Cher Pierre

If the news of Christopher's death was a shock to you both, you can imagine the effect on Margaret and myself who knew him for a quarter of a century and regarded him as a member of the family... We were not unaware of the highs and lows of his life. He was always either on the crest or in the trough of a wave, in the words of Day Lewis's sonnet sequence, 'all's dark or dazzle'...

March 20 1984

Cher Pierre

... I remain immersed in my work, the fruits of which will see the light of day in June. A guide, but more than that, a study, tables, technical information — with a total of 552 sculptures by 195 sculptors, all illustrated. The last stages have left me exhausted. Originally the plan was 250 sculptures, 100 sculptors. I have tramped through all the sculpture parks in different regions of this fair land of ours, with my photographers (all of them former pupils). What good fortune!... Perhaps this book will introduce sculpture to a section of the public who have been unaware of it until now...

You are right, I must follow my chosen path. Spring proclaims its presence — our blackbirds in their churchwardens' attire walk about on the lawn but an icy wind continues to blow — unaccustomed here — as if to tell us a certain warmth is still lacking.

Margaret adds her cordial greetings to mine, wishing you and Mila, despite everything, much activity, much success...

To Wendy Taylor

May 29 1984

My dear Wendy

Before I go off for another proof discussion at Zwemmer's I must *write* you our congratulations on Matthew Tom. It was *'che bella sorpresa!'* indeed... You must take it easy, really easy, for a bit and surrender to your new, fascinating role!...

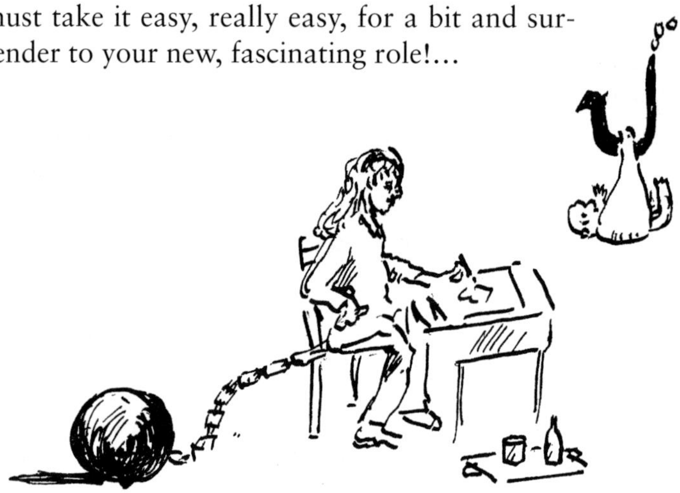

To Pierre Lecuire

August 2 1984

Cher Pierre

... My current solace is still Proust. This time round I am struck (towards the end of *A l'ombre des jeunes filles en fleurs*) by his humour and the aptness of his observations on all kinds of things... I like his style and allusive language — the quotations, the love of the letters of Madame de Sévigné expressed by Madame de Villeparisis (I'm thinking of going back to them!). And how these words of Madame de Sévigné touch a chord in me! 'As soon as I have received one letter I immediately want another. Receiving one is all I live and breathe for. Few people can understand how I feel'. (A quotation that ought to have appeared in the preliminary pages of *The Living Curve!*) Allusions to La Fontaine too. How many times, after the first thrill at the publication of a new book of mine do I feel myself *'Gros Jean comme devant'*.

December 1st 1984

Cher Pierre

... I am eager to convey to you the delight... that Madeleine Pont takes in your little masterpiece, *Déserts...** I have just (yesterday) given my lecture, with annual exhibition, in Cambridge (the eleventh) where, of course, with little groups I turned the revelatory pages of *Déserts*, alongside those of the Lanskoy!...

May 12 1985

Cher Pierre

It was extremely kind of you to have taken the trouble to decipher, type out and photocopy the text of that important letter from Jacqueline Guillaume Apollinaire...

It seems I am incapable of refusing any service asked of me. Last Thursday it was the turn of the Bank of Switzerland (head office in London). They asked my advice on their plan to commission sculpture for their piazza and a bas-relief for the interior of a vast building which is in process of being transformed. It took up a whole day — meeting and lunch with the Swiss committee, tour of the outside of the buildings and the surrounding area. At the end we drew up a list of the names I had recommended. (They put forward several Swiss candidates of course — but quite mediocre.) It goes without saying that Wendy Taylor is one of them. (She has fifteen open air sculptures represented in my guide and has already completed another two.) I shall await the result with impatience...

On Friday retrospective exhibition of Reg Butler at Royston, ... for which I wrote the introduction at his widow's request. Then a three-day visit to Edinburgh, where I've been invited to give a lecture on sculpture parks. But before that a lecture at the Solent on Moore and Hepworth and another one in Cambridge...

I seem to be showing off! In fact if I had foreseen the situation with Margaret here — she is better, but still far from well — I should not have succumbed to all these temptations...

* *Déserts:* five sonnets by Pierre Lecuire to the memory of Christopher Hewett, published in 1984 with dry point etchings by Brigitte Simon.

Nevertheless I'm finding time to read Gracq's *La Forme d'une Ville* (excellent). I greatly admire his mastery of your language and borrowings from ours! It is tremendous. I am fascinated by his descriptions of Nantes and Saint-Nazaire, his countless literary allusions, international as well as French. No dull passages where in theory there ought to be, given the absence of any precise core to the book and of any incidents. It is the world of the mind.

Cambiamo discorso. I am thrilled that the issue of *Private Library* pleases you. It is an elegant production, all the more because it is a very special number, over which Christopher's spirit presides. Happy that my remarks about *Déserts* do not displease you...

I will not close without wishing you good luck for your entry into the animals' cage, real — or mythological! No doubt you will tame them all...*

To Wendy Taylor

June 5 1985

My dear Wendy

What a seesaw of ups and downs — 'ups' in your work, which is a cause for rejoicing. Dockland — *vive les Docks!* — and the piece is impressive.** I see it towering up, equally effective vertically, horizontally, and form so ingeniously integrated...

Somehow we've... managed to plant dahlias, stocks, asters, nemesias (having first to dig a space!)...

August 9th 1985

Dear Wendy

Very nice to hear from you and to hear things are going — well — never 'smoothly' — it's the wrong word, but in full steam ahead! — Docklands presentation completed. Basildon with the 'go ahead', only the wretched Swiss a 'no go' area of the City!... What a farce it all was and a

* Lecuire was working on his *Bestiaire*, with etchings by Tal Coat, published in 1985.

** A reference to the 'Spirit of Enterprise' maquette.

complete waste of time for me and disappointment to you and Peter Thursby (interior suggestion)...

I'm revising my whole translation of Alain-Fournier's letters, done for Christopher Hewett... but held up by his death... Carcanet will publish it... I can do that in quiet(?) intervals, probably during rain in the Lakes (a week in September) or here when Jacko is not demanding my attention (Margaret walks him twice a day) — playing and racing (him not me) round the garden like a young colt. So the Fournier revise and retyping is the main programme.

Luckily we had a superb twelve days in Cornwall, on eleven of which I could practise my famous back crawl in a cool (and how!) refreshing sea...

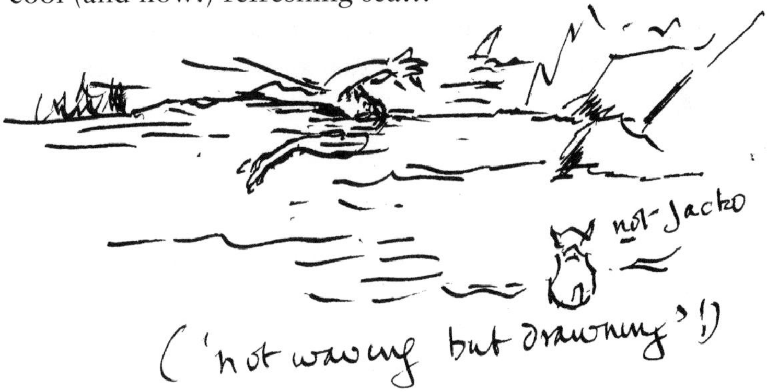

To Pierre Lecuire

November 1985

Cher Pierre

... Here is a piece of news that will interest you. Following the second visit here made by the Director of Western Art at the Ashmolean Museum with the Librarian of the Taylor Institution, the decision, taken with enthusiasm, is to accept my gift of a number of the *livres d'artiste* that I possess... and more or less my complete collection of *bonnes feuilles*. The Institution has an enormous collection of *un*illustrated French books and the librarian is enthusiastic about giving students and other Francophiles access to the pages of these classical and modern texts in illustrated editions. This will not prevent the Ashmolean Museum mounting partial exhibitions from the collection at intervals, beginning with a substantial one at the start of 1987...

Naturally this depends on the *assentiment* (assent) of the committee at a *meeting* (meeting)... I think I may be using invented vocabulary — but you must blame it on the blow to the head I received when I fell flat on my face on the con-

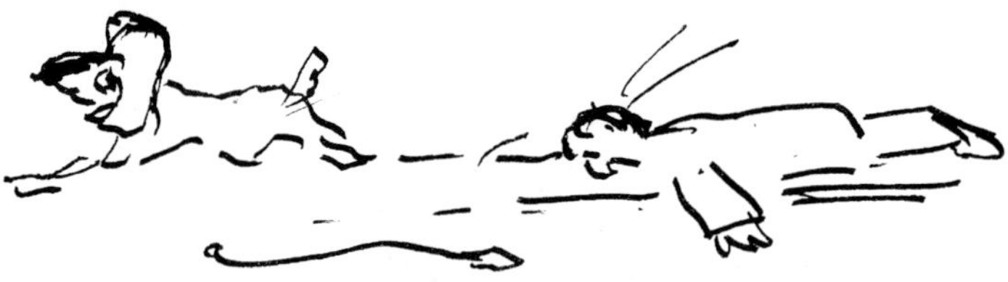

crete path in the garden running after Jacko. I hope I shall not look too much like a boxer at my next lecture in Birmingham!

April 3 1986

Mon Cher Pierre

Now that I have had time and enjoyed the treat of leafing through the splendid pages of your *Bestiaire* and studying each etching closely, I can add a more considered appreciation of this masterpiece to my first thanks by telephone. It will occupy a historic place in this originally mediaeval genre, revived by Buffon, which awaited a Toulouse-Lautrec, as the *Cortège d'Orpheé* awaited a Dufy. And now, as I have said, comes your *Bestiaire*, which for me completes the circle. I visited Chastel as long ago as 1950. Then there was the Krol, the Lorjou... But yours is the pinnacle and will rank alongside the Picasso/Buffon... *Le Bestiaire* is... an apotheosis for you as poet-typographer. It seems to me that you have never gone into a theme in more depth, captured its essence better in your evocative, mysterious lines of verse; never composed the page better, with areas of incomparable whiteness (offered by the Moulins de Larroque paper). The title page makes its announcement like the discreet note of a horn (not a trumpet), as if 'from the depths of the forest'. Discreet, like the traditional Garamond typeface, laid out with all your skill as the book's architect, impeccably printed by François de Ros.

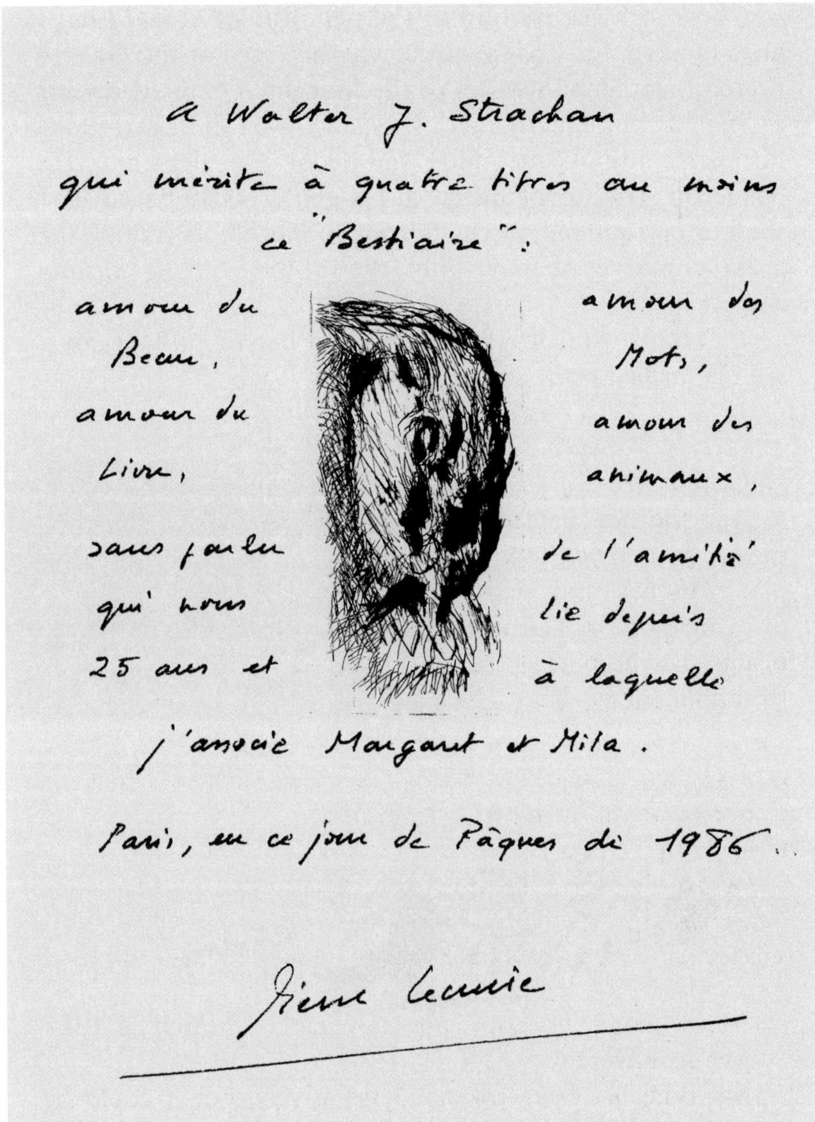

à Walter J. Strachan
qui mérite à quatre titres au moins
ce "Bestiaire":

amour du Beau, amour des Mots,
amour du Livre, amour des animaux,
sans parler de l'amitié
qui nous lie depuis
25 ans et à laquelle
j'associe Margaret et Mila.

Paris, en ce jour de Pâques de 1986.

Pierre Lecuire

The etchings impress me, I linger, of course, over the birds of the night... the cats, the cat immersed in its own gravity... the dog scratching itself. No hint of sentimentality nor anthropomorphism, which is why I find the spirit of these etchings so attractive, as I do the palpable rapport between poet and artist. How sad that the latter died before the book could be published. I am glad of the fact that he saw his work realized up to the penultimate stage. I have always liked Tal Coat's work, whether seen at the Galerie Breton (near Saint Sulpice) or the Maeght... Now he reveals a different but equally revelatory side; even the inscriptions in reverse add an intriguing and decorative element... He has left a striking memorial to his genius as an engraver. I shall often contemplate the falcon (solitary in its frame), the geese (a marvel of spare line), the rabbit — *'petit masque d'agate'*.

... Thank you, in all sincerity, on behalf of Margaret, who is thrilled by it, and myself...

April 27/28

Cher Pierre

... Another piece of news. My article (with pen sketches and wash drawings) on old Cornish bridges has been accepted for publication...*

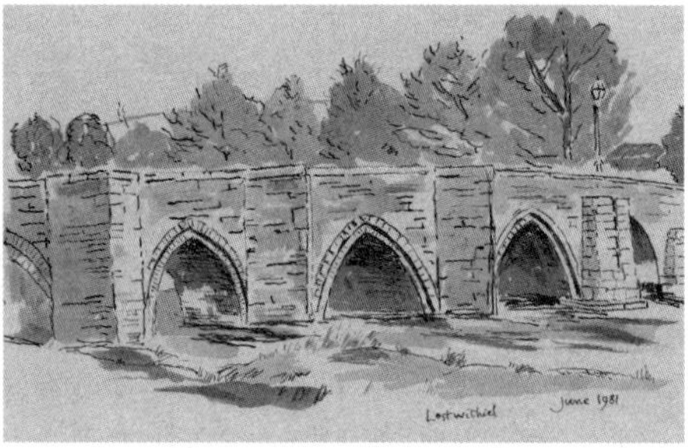

To Wendy Taylor

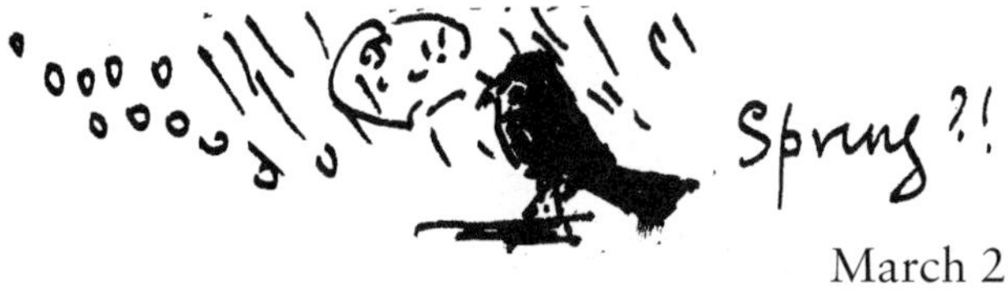

March 26 1987

My dear Wendy

My time has been taken up negatively, but it could be argued gratifyingly, seeing my collection of *livres d'artiste* and *bonnes feuilles* (artists' proofs etc) into the Taylor Institution Library, Oxford. There was an exhibition of about a fifth of the total material for five weeks in the Ashmolean Museum with a preview and dinner in Balliol for the guests (hordes!) but happily twenty of my friends, including Geoff and Jean (ex St Hilda's) and Simon, presently 'up' at Oxford. It

* By *The Countryman.*

involved another visit to see where the collection will be kept and can be consulted. Pat Gibberd took me over on the first occasion... She also took me out to give my tapestry (Lurçat/Moore) lecture at St John's Wood... I fitted in two hours at the British Art exhibition, fortified only with a Welsh rabbit — *but* Fortnum and Mason's version. I also called in at Liliane Lijn's 'show' (is the word) at Fischer's!... The result is a blister on my big toe... Nevertheless [I'll be going to] a two-day Modern Language Conference at Cambridge. I *can* hold my head high — my *Towards the Lost Domain* got twenty-one good notices (and a *Kaleidoscope* and *Critics' Forum)* and special congratulations from the author's nephew Alain Rivière...

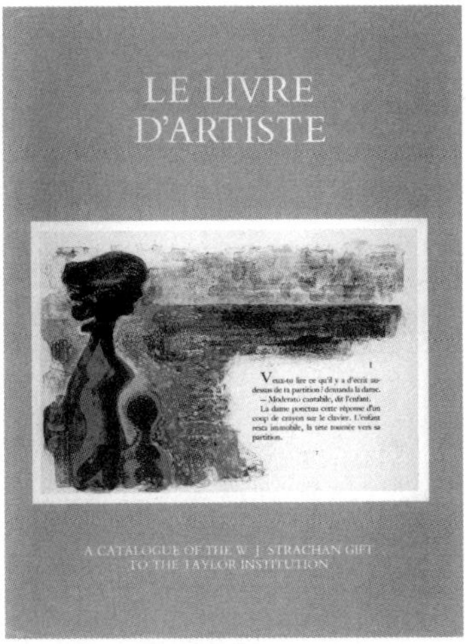

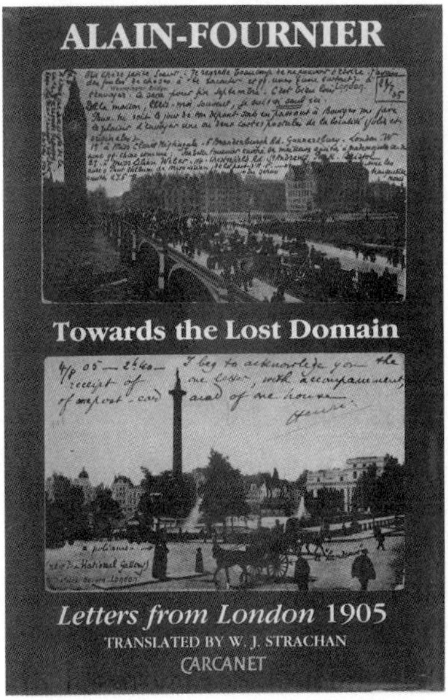

I'm working slowly on a new edition of Albert Camus's *La Peste*. Camus is my hero, philosophically. Life is ridiculous, *la condition humaine*, but let's work together and make the best of it...

May 26 1987

My dear Wendy

I'm in full spate on the reprint of *Open Air Sculpture*! I've already got round to nine new items in London and have just heard how much I missed in the Leicestershire (school and college) catchment... I'll get [Chris] Elliott himself to ferry me round. He remains supportive, has bought at least fifty copies of *Open Air Sculpture* and may publish my booklet on Moore... There is too much new material for photos of every new piece — forty-six in Grizedale, for example — so some will just be listed...

To Pierre Lecuire

September 7 1987

Cher Pierre

... I have just offered the Scottish National Gallery of Modern Art seven sculptors' drawings and three lithographs, which the director is happy to accept, either during my lifetime or after my death. These things will lend greater reality to the documents and transparencies from my archives, will animate them...

October 1987

Cher Pierre

Please excuse the ballpoint pen. I'm in the car with Jacko beside me, waiting for Margaret to return from the shops. I don't like *far niente.* I plan to slip several photos of the Ashmolean exhibition into the envelope which awaits them...

The other news is that here in the East we have had a storm — nay a veritable hurricane. The train I intended to take to Cambridge was derailed by a fallen tree and a colleague (we were going to a twenty-four hour conference) had hardly stepped out of his car when a wall collapsed onto it and totally flattened it (it, not him). Similar stories from all over on the part of my fellow members of this society of modern language teachers...

But in fact, all went well. An excellent talk about the *raisonneurs** in Molière's plays. I suggested that in *Le Misanthrope* this role is more or less shared between Alceste and Philinte... Good talk about the poetry of Hoffmanstha l... I am the only surviving founder member of this society, started in 1926 when the professor of French invited his most promising students to join...

* The arguers.

To Wendy Taylor

February 3 1989

My dear Wendy

... We put a metal table with four Geoffrey Clarke maquettes in the Library case yesterday. I got the Head at gunpoint before he went to Australia — ! 'That's the way to do it!'

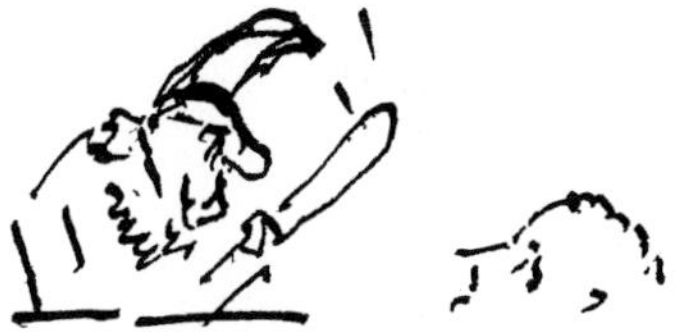

Actually a lovely group — another acquisition for B.S.C., which gives me vicarious pleasure...

... I had to wait two hours in the clinic before the surgeon saw me.

Clinic
They wait to be weighed on scales like so much meat
To be assessed. Some come on staggering feet
Or in wheelchairs or hobble on two sticks.
Young pregnant wives give contrast to the mix.
Each with a hope, though fifty years apart,
One to survive, one for a life to start.

(So I passed the time composing this!)...

Feb 28 1989

'The first blossom was the best blossom'

My dear Wendy

It's always cheering to receive your lively letters, even when they report — fortunately [only] *temporary* — disasters, such as the loss of documents! I speak as a fellow spirit!

Today — sun so bright on our crocuses, opening daffodils, start of the weeping cherry. I feel I can face the 'op' on March 9 (hernia through digging)... *Meantime* I lecture at Newmarket on the seventh on Rodin and Bourdelle...

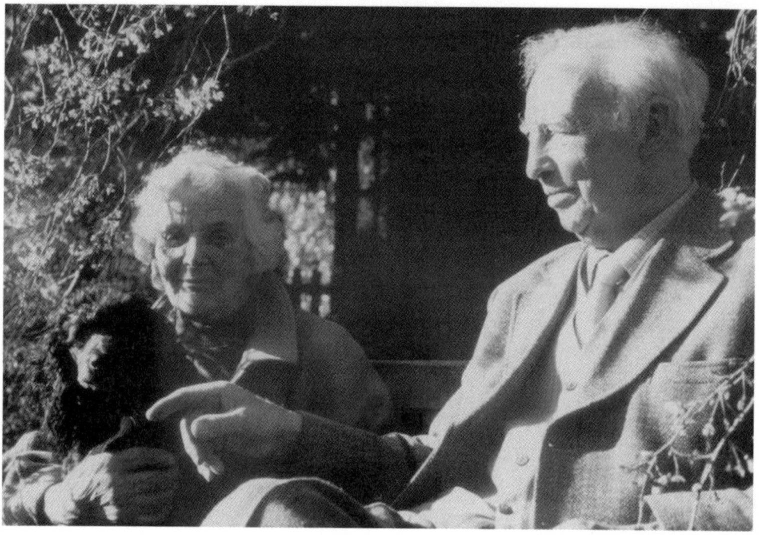

I've an article, which *may* be taken, on first and last [issues of] literary and art reviews 1923-1984, in which I was involved... So much research into my store of these periodicals — many revelations. I have vintage *Horizons* etc. I am 'the man who never throws anything (any letters) away', according to Cecily Mackworth in her latest book...

To Pierre Lecuire

May 23 1989

Cher Pierre

... I've been satisfying my gluttonous appetite by writing two articles on literary and art reviews for *Contemporary Review* ... and one on Bourdelle for *Modern Painters* (with the blessing of Rhodia Dufet-Bourdelle) to coincide with the big Bourdelle exhibition at the Yorkshire Sculpture Park. Preview tomorrow (French ambassador etc) but, alas, I'm giving a lecture that day in Sussex!

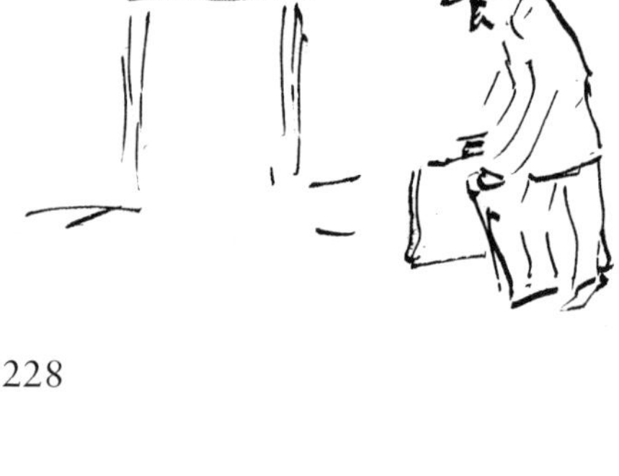

Train journeys pose problems... but I'm often given a helping hand by total strangers. England, though uncultivated and philistine, is at bottom kind-hearted...

To Wendy Taylor

June 11 1989

Dear Wendy,

How goes it? Molto rapido, I expect... This last Wednesday, thanks to a former pupil, I had a day at the Yorkshire Sculpture Park... for the Bourdelle. I'm partial only to the less 'heroic' (men lunging swords etc) work. But I like the Gothic-inspired pieces — reminiscent of twelfth-century Chartres etc pillar statues...

April 21 1990

My dear Wendy

... Apology for the delay since your cornucopia awaited me at the GPO on our return from Beccles in Suffolk, where we shared a house backing onto the river Waveney. A charming small town with an excellent second-hand book-shop, where I picked up a Max Beerbohm: cartoons — *The Nineties*, a first edition of poems by Ted Hughes and a book by an old friend... Percy Muir, *Children's Illustrated Books* (a minor love of mine). I managed, despite a cold wind, to do two thumbnail sketches...

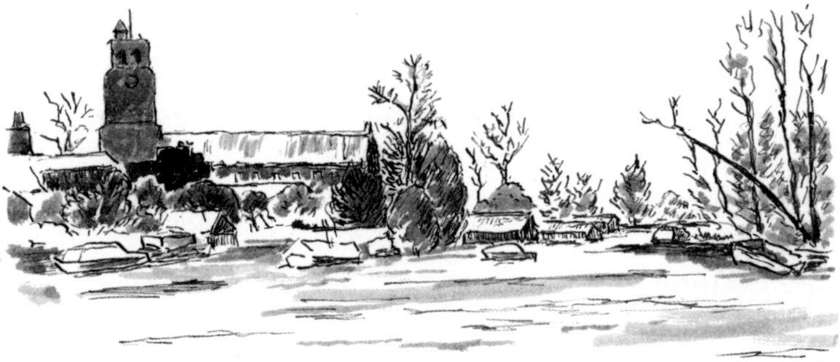

Despite your back and thumb you have achieved wonders... The photos (good to have several viewing angles) are splendid... They've given the 'Globe Sundial' the full treatment! Mostly one searches in vain for the sculptor's name. Mind you, your work has now such a personal identity it hardly needs naming...

Contemporary Review is interested to consider my piece 'Around William Morris'... He has often been on the periphery of my life, partly through his secretary, Sir Sydney Cockerell, at the Fitzwilliam Museum, then later at his home in Kew... It all began when we read *Jason* in my junior school, then *The Earthly Paradise*, *News from Nowhere* etc... All Golden Age stuff but also the craft movement — I have two little books by W.R. Lethaby. Not all adulation. I take Cobden Sanderson's view of Morris as a printer... First, though, a D.H. Lawrence poem* and my piece on my great grandfather...

Then there's the garden, but how glad I am of it. Former pupils have given us such a finely carpentered seat (worthy of Morris) for outside.

I must stop. I am determined to catch the Saturday midday post. It is 11.57...

D.H. LAWRENCE AT ZENNOR

When you exchanged your villino, near Lerici,
for Cornwall,
the Ligurian sea for cold Atlantic waves,
the certain sequence of near-tropical sun,
the 'shining grey' olive-trees, lively with lizards,
for Padstow in winter,
the great winds, the sea 'smoking white above the cliffs',
the pre-Arthurian Celtic flicker of Cornwall,
did some residual puritan guilt
reconcile you to leaving lemon and fig-tree,
wild rosemary and oleander of Fiascherino?

Then, Zennor, the Tinner's Arms,
What were your thoughts as you beheld the great boulder
from which John Wesley preached Salvation
to grim-faced miners, grey as granite?
You with your memories of pink Briassa rock,

* Published in *Contemporary Review*, August 1990.

the silhouette of Portovenere
against unforgettable sunsets,
you, author of *The Rainbow*
whose spreading radiance
no magistrate could quench.

June 9 1990

My dear Wendy

... Thanks to Timothy Rogers, ex-principal of Desford Community College in Leicestershire I gave a lecture at the Courtauld in their new HQ, Somerset House. A great success and more enjoyable inasmuch as a nephew not seen for years, farming in Zimbabwe turned up! A one-time art student at the Ruskin and not having lost his interest in the work of the engravers of Atelier 17 (S.W. Hayter etc.) My host, a permanent lecturer there on modern art, Sarah Wilson, is a very good propagator, too, of French artists. So I've left them with some 130 slides, all made from my collection of *livres d'artiste*, when I've delivered my last lecture(?) to an amateur society in Saffron Waldon and a lecture at Aldeburgh (this month) and one at Old Sarum — again thanks to my devoted ferryman!...

I've been asked whether I will consent to the B.S. College collection being named 'The Walter Strachan Gallery'... I've got a Robert Macbryde at the framers and the collection is really progressing...

July 28 1990

My dear Wendy

... I ... got to the Tate 'On Classic Ground', which I very much enjoyed... I don't feel I can justifiably ask to be ferried to the Hayward show, judging by the catalogue. I wouldn't swop anything of mine for *any* item there. Strange vagaries of sculpture when the aim seems to [be to] produce the impermanent and works on the grand (but they are *not* grand) scale.

I think I approve rather of more modest works sited in the open air on the Dorset cliffs and *some* of the sculptures sited in the Peterborough catchment.

August 5 1990

Dear Wendy

... It was lovely to have your seaside card... What childhood is complete and fulfilled without sand, seaweed, shrimps, rock pools!...

I've managed my two lectures, Courtauld and Aldeburgh and now I'm invited to lecture at the V and A on Jean Lurçat, whom I knew and whose tapestry (in particular) I greatly admire. As a man, his simplicity and unpretentiousness remind me of Henry Moore.

I've plenty to do. Poems, articles and the memoirs... Time is the problem. I give too much of it to the business of the College Gallery — just got a small bronze by Christine Fox, who is now well represented in East Anglia (Peterborough, Rufford Park etc). She ran the sculpture school at the C[ambridge] C[ollege] of A[rt] and T[echnology], where I was a part-time lecturer...

To Pierre Lecuire

November 30 1990

Cher Pierre

Well, to judge from the article on you in *L'Oeil*, Homer's apotheosis was as nothing beside yours! Quite seriously I salute your work, your pertinacity, your gifts as a poet, typographer and orator...

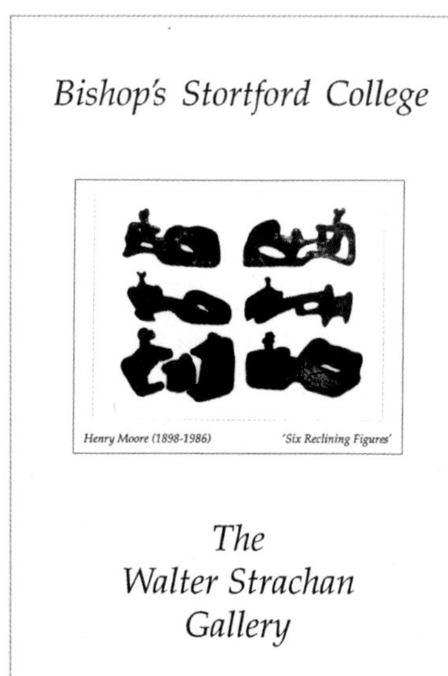

On this theme* I jokingly quoted Fouquet and the motto on the gate at Vaux-le-Vicomte: *'Quo non ascendam'*** (my Gallery is on the first floor up a staircase) and mentioned the fate that awaited him after the visit of an envious Louis XIV... After two

* At the opening of the Walter Strachan Gallery

** To what heights may I not rise?

speeches full of praise my response was perforce for the most part self-deprecatory… I quoted W.B. Yeats:

> An aged man is but a paltry thing.
> A tattered coat upon a stick, unless
> Soul clap its hands and sing, and louder sing
> For every tatter in its mortal dress…

I return now to the daily routine as chief cook and bottle-washer, reflecting on the good moments and encouraged by many letters that bring me consolation, like yours received today…

To Wendy Taylor

February 1 1991

Dear Wendy

… I had two marvellous surprises — one the swell Pléiade edition of the *Journal* of André Gide… His neo-pagan (North Africa) philosophy, like Camus's, appeals to one side of my character. Not the puritan genes of my great-grandfather, James Strachan…

The other surprise was the arrival of a very good bronze from Peter Thursby… It can stand next to my Robert Adams and opposite 'Octo'. It, too, has a loop theme I feel sure you'd like…

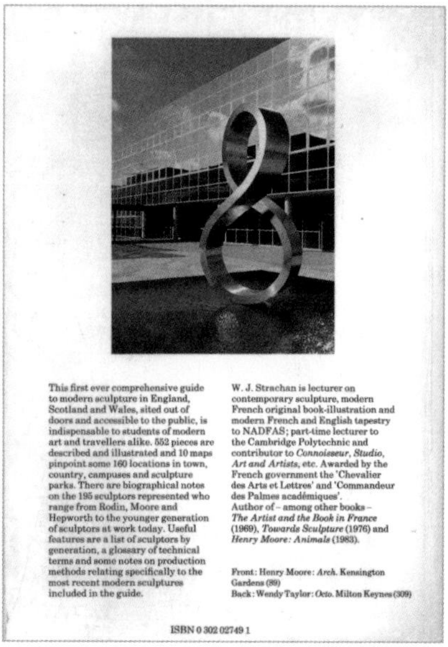

My great moment has been [to be] asked to do the Preface to Vol VI of Avati's *catalogue raisonné*. So I was delighted to receive a lovely mezzotint (a rose) with *'votre magnifique préface … absolument parfait'*. I had done it in French…

March 17 1991

Dear Wendy

In connection with the exhibition of twenty-three of my French *'hiboux'* and *'chouettes'*, I have to write notes on the artists...

Legs prohibited my attending the celebratory dinner [for Avati] in Lausanne but I shall get Number 1 of the *'éditions de tête'* in due course, so I'm still considered as a kind of *'eminence grise'* in that field, which consoles me for my period of masterly inactivity.

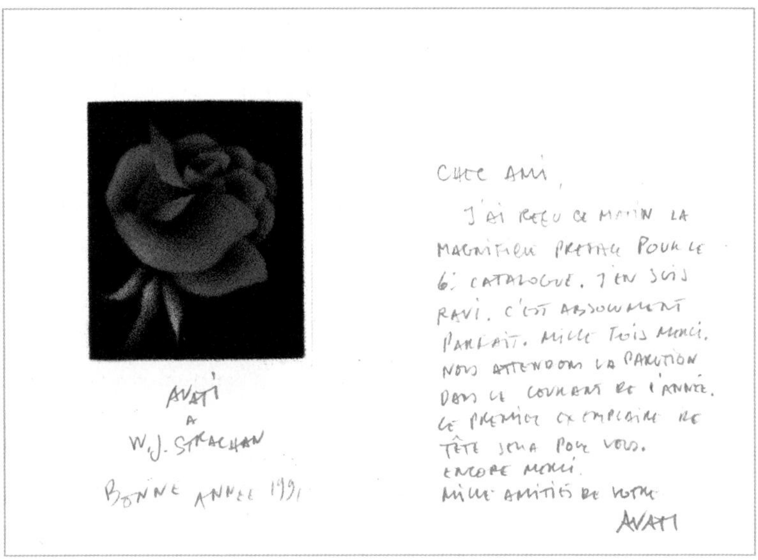

It extended to the article I have on 'Maillol and the Nymph' in the current (spring) issue of the *Art Quarterly* — organ of the National Art Fund... Anyhow it puts Lucille Passavant, Maillol's *first* model and *only* pupil on the map and will delight her heart. She was the model for the centre figure of 'The Three Nymphs' by Maillol in the Tate, which the National Art Fund, in fact, presented. So a happy story for an ageing sculptor and gifted wood engraver of Virgil's *Bucoliques*, of which I have the suite of sixty...

Do come and ... see new framed pictures and drawings etc. This house has to be my gallery and library — the garden my landscape...

May 5 1991

My dear Wendy

It's always an excitement among all the mass of the everyday postal delivery to catch sight of your characteristically vigorous hand... Life is at present characterized by 'peripeties', to use a Hardy word. The struggle against physical problems... Diversified by such incidents as catching my hair on fire while frying chops...

... My article in *Art Quarterly* has served to put ... Lucille Passavant ... on the art map in Paris. She reports a visit from someone at the French Academy wanting to convert her house-studio and vast grounds into a national museum!...

... I have disobeyed Lewis Carroll's rules for young letter-writers: first deal with the subjects raised by your correspondent etc... I love to think of Matthew indifferent to a sea water wetting. How I loved my own seaside days at Bridlington — never discovered the sea could be warm till, with the children, we went to Dorset, then Cornwall...

August 12 1991

My dear Wendy

Owls: I saw them yesterday at the V. and A. smashingly exposed — couldn't be better.

Then on to Mr Tate's Gallery and Constable. Such *rich* paint and such vigour and strength, then suddenly the exquisite 'rain shower', almost de Staël as a simple state-

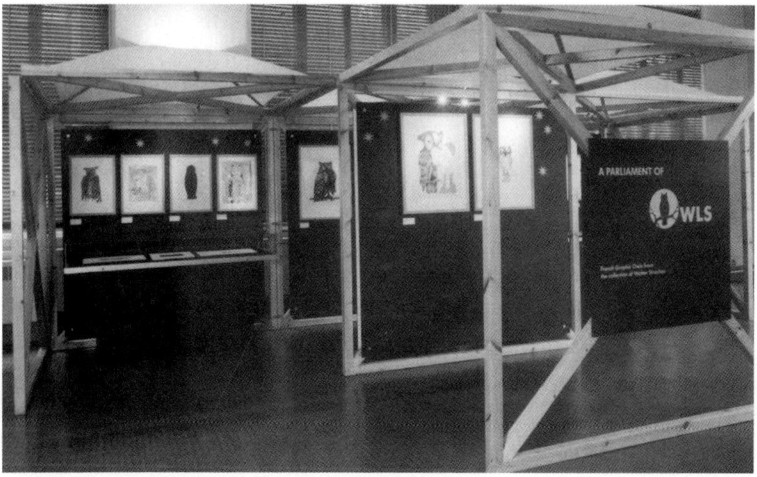

ment. The V and A sketch versions, which one never gets to see, now so well lit and grand and a Lake [District] waterfall (though he wasn't happy up there) stylized à la Francis Towne. Never happy away from the Stour Valley — his 'Mont Saint Victoire'.

So, a good day seeing art from a wheelchair...

July 8 1992

Dear Wendy

... I have an article for *Private Library* on French Bibliophile Society Banquet Menus (illustrated, of course, includes a Picasso). Publication timed for Jan '93, my ninetieth year to heaven! Further, another article to write on the making of a *livre d'artiste*, *Le Lézard* by Signovert... So I hope to go out with all barrels firing. Perfectly fit except for 'me leg!'

Book progresses — [I've] got to Lewis Carroll and the Hatch sisters...

To Pierre Lecuire

July 21 1992

Cher Pierre

I have no words to express my thanks to you for having sent me the Moore catalogue. One of the best (and I have a great many), if not *the best* that I possess...

Other news: bad. Margaret — of necessity — will move into a private home on Saturday. Here she was no longer eating and needing help all the time. Geoffrey, Jean and I have visited this small establishment where she will be well looked after.

August[?] 21 1992

Cher Pierre

I have been picturing you at Varengeville or some seaside resort. The little book by José Corti* — MANY THANKS — is welcome in this gracquian house. (I think I have all his [Gracq's] books.) I remember Corti so well — the shining,

* Publisher of Julien Gracq's novels.

sparkling eyes, the Voltairian smile, the mocking tones that greeted me on each visit to the rue de Médicis. And *Provisoirement définitif* is both moving and fascinating. What a saint — his wife... All told in this somewhat archaic and personal style — unique? Many thanks. I shall mention it when I next write to Gracq, who rather like me, now has to limit his travels to outings on the banks of the Loire...

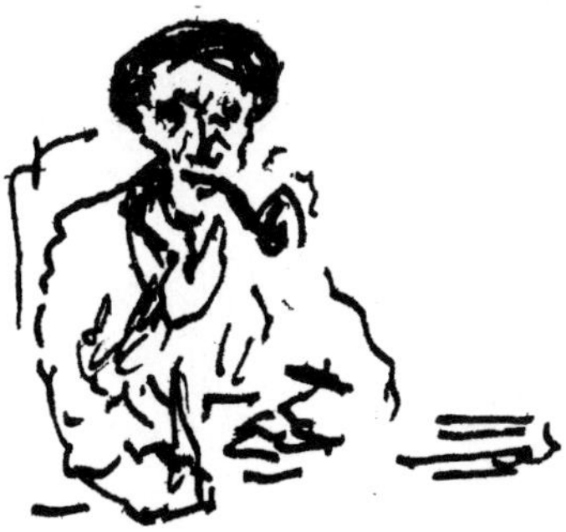

October 5 1992

Cher Pierre

... If I neglect you it is because there are many problems... I miss Margaret greatly... Happily she seems at peace but — 'O what a noble mind is here o'erthrown'. At least she has a memory for the music she recognizes... She has a room that looks out over open fields, very green, with rabbits browsing...

My article on menus is in proof and eventually there's one commissioned for *Private Library*, 'The Making of a *Livre d'Artiste*', based on *Le Lézard* by Francis Ponge, with etchings by Jean Signovert, whom I met, I think in 1953 (is he still alive?). I possess all the elements in the form of artist's proofs. These will go to my collection in Oxford — where there is going to be an exhibition (at the Ashmolean) of Roger Vieillard (one of whose admirable engravings I have just had framed (*Discours de la Méthode: 'Comme un homme qui marche seul et dans les ténèbres'*))...

January 12 1993

Cher Pierre

... This is a difficult time for me. A kind of family banquet (not bibliophilic) is being arranged for me and the old boys of the College want to honour me in a similar way. I also have to visit the dentist... I have ten days left to get myself into shape... I'm impatient to get on with my work — the stages in the development of a *livre d'artiste* — this

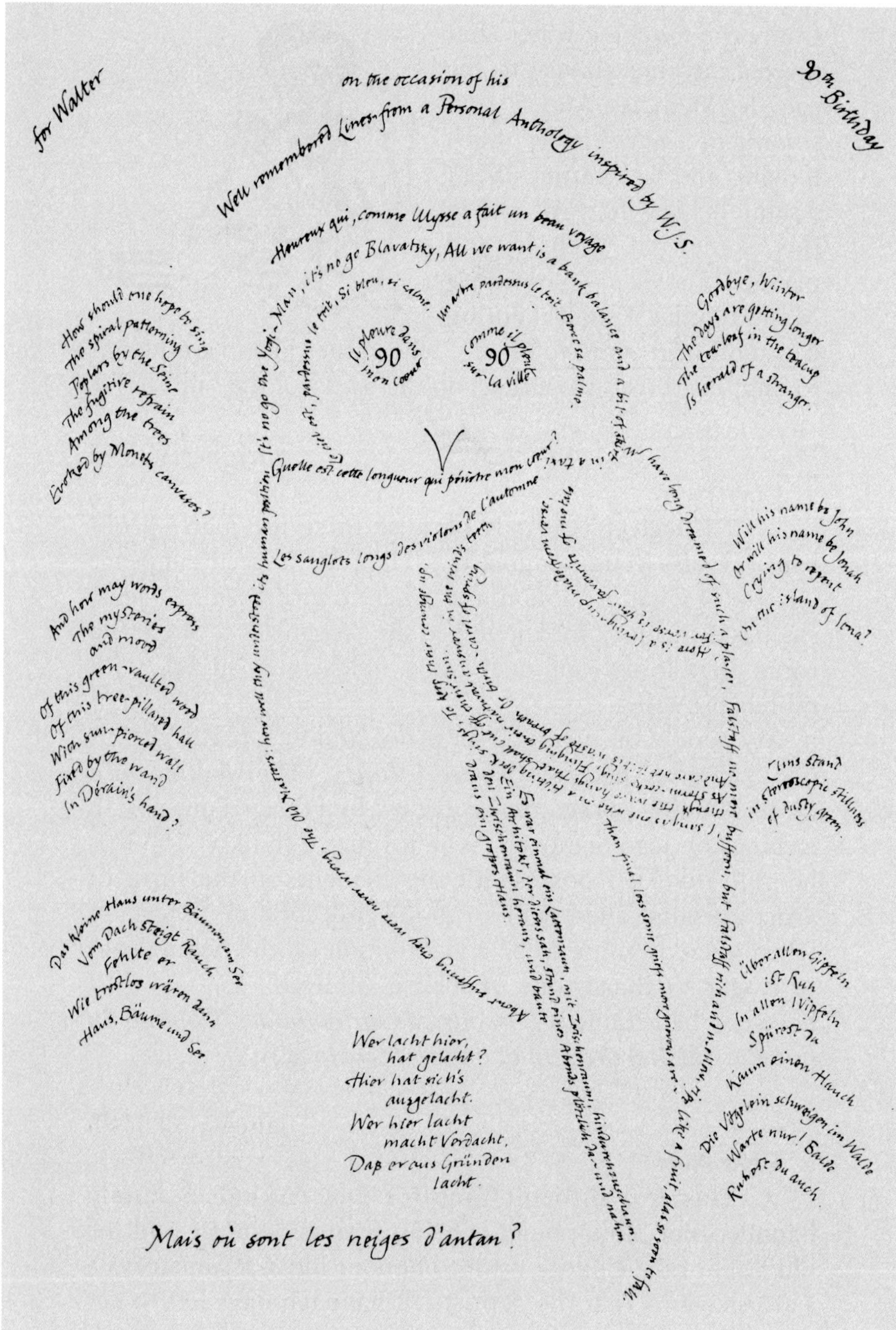
for Walter
on the occasion of his
90th Birthday
Well remembered Lines from a Personal Anthology inspired by W.S.
Heureux qui, comme Ulysse a fait un beau voyage
Man, it's no go Blavatsky, All we want is a bank balance
Le ciel est, par-dessus le toit, Si bleu, si calme.
Un arbre par-dessus le toit, Berce sa palme.
Il pleure dans mon coeur 90
comme il pleut sur la ville 90
Quelle est cette langueur qui pénètre mon coeur?
Les sanglots longs des violons de l'automne
How should one hope to sing
The spiral patterning
Poplars by the Seine
The fugitive refrain
Among the trees
Evoked by Monet's canvases?
And how may words express
The mysteries and mood
Of this green-vaulted wood
Of this tree-pillared hall
With sun-pierced wall
Fired by the wand
In Derain's hand?
Das kleine Haus unter Bäumen am See
Vom Dach steigt Rauch
Fehlte er
Wie trostlos wären dann
Haus, Bäume und See
Goodbye, Winter
The days are getting longer
The tea-leaf in the teacup
Is herald of a stranger.
Will his name be John
Or will his name be Jonah
Crying to repent
On the island of Iona?
Elms stand
in stereoscopic stillness
of dusty green
Über allen Gipfeln
Ist Ruh
In allen Wipfeln
Spürest du
Kaum einen Hauch
Die Vögelein schweigen im Walde
Warte nur! Balde
Ruhest du auch
Wer lacht hier,
hat gelacht?
Hier hat sich's
ausgelacht.
Wer hier lacht
macht Verdacht,
Daß er aus Gründen
lacht.
Mais où sont les neiges d'antan?

time the personalities as much as the techniques.

I have just reread *King Lear*. Perhaps it wasn't the moment for this! But what understanding both of human cruelty and tenderness...

To Wendy Taylor

January 23 1993

My dear Wendy

What a wonderful book and what a wonderful, if undeserved, dedication!* ... I don't know of any book on a sculptor as completely representative as yours. How well you kept pace with your colour photos. You really handed it all over on a plate to Edward L-S and he has done his stuff very thoroughly.

I do miss any acknowledgment of the lyrical spirit that informs many of your pieces — but I may have missed references in my first hurried reading... He does justice to your wit and paradox. Are you the Magritte of Sculpture? To me that would be a great compliment but these analogies are misleading...

A nice thing about Margaret (small consolation). She can remember *music*. I send tapes of Beethoven, Brahms, Schumann and she listens and says: 'We know this'. She even sang words of *The Mikado* to the record... I wish I could get over more often...

Celebration lunch: family 24 Jan — school etc Feb 13.

To Pierre Lecuire

April 3 1993

Cher Pierre, Chère Mila

I have sad news to report. Margaret died on March 30, a sudden heart attack. She did not suffer... It was unexpected. The week before she was listening to tapes — Schubert, Bach (adagio — Brandenburg concerto), Prokofiev 'Classical Symphony', poems by Wordsworth, Robert Frost, remembering her childhood, memories of Jean and Geoffrey's youth, of the 'Lakes'...

* She had sent him a copy of *Wendy Taylor* by Edward Lucie-Smith (just published in 1992).

Her symbol was the rose — fresh, traditional, *'rosa alba'*, famous for its scent, it grows beside the front door. The arch of climbing roses. Her creation. As were two gardens (from 1927 to 1936, from 1947 [to]...). All in all, a happy life, a blessing to others...

May 22 1993

Cher Pierre

I have been thinking of you as I leafed through an excellent book on Braque... (Editions Le Point)... I have eight in the series... rediscovered at a good moment for my research. Dates? Important, because they mark my steps towards various projects. 1970 meeting with Couturier: decision to write about drawings and maquettes for sculpture... But I am neglecting my purpose — to thank you for your necrological research.*

I admire your pertinacity... With heroic obstinacy, accompanied by the indefatigable and patient Mila, you have confronted the directors and librarians of the great museums and libraries of the world one by one. You have a great advantage. You are the indisputable genius of the *livre d'artiste* (by whatever name), the *accoucheur* of great editions. Furthermore you have all the charms of Orpheus in taming great artists, from de Staël onwards...

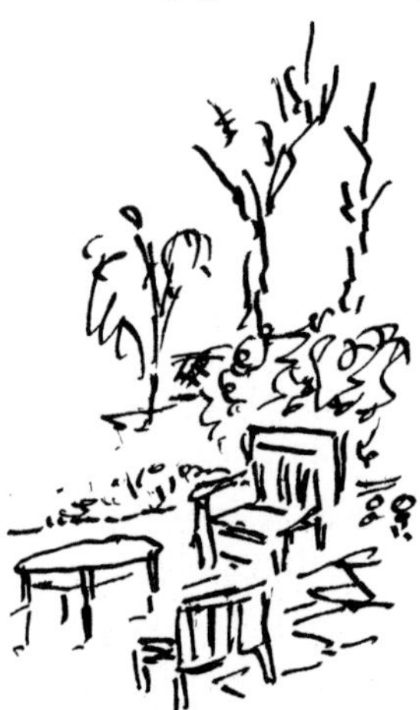

One consolation, in the formidable task that faces me is reading the vast collection... of occasional messages, especially after the appearance of *The Artist and the Book*, including *your own* and... that of J.J.J. Rigal: 'The future will judge but I believe your efforts made over more than thirty years will be one of the rare testimonies to the epoch of the illustrated book...'.

The garden is splendid, thanks to the family's efforts: rose arch (created by Margaret) now repaired. Petunias,

* Probably to assist him in writing the article on the *livre d'artiste* for the Macmillan *Dictionary of Art* (published in 1996).

pansies, antirrhinums, planted by whoever arrives on the terrace — the centre of operations...

Geoffrey has four good titles for Christmas. Alison's husband is making 'pop' videos and in his absence she weaves like Penelope. (There is also the little Dexter). Jean, as Labour candidate [for the Council] in Norwich (very Conservative) has reduced their majority! Simon makes innumerable friends in France, Germany, Switzerland... Susan has qualified as a medical herbalist.

That is my report. Madeleine Pont, my friend of forty years, continues to spoil me — with a big volume of variations on the alphabet. I have just had a Krol framed (dedicated to Margaret)...

June 26 1993

Cher Pierre

... I have been thinking of you and Mila as I looked at some excellent photos of the chalky beach with Braque strolling in the middle distance (in the Le Point *Braque*) — at Varengeville, your earthly paradise — as Cornwall is mine. (Etretat too)...

The V and A will put on a little exhibition in 1994 of engravings from books they hold in the library by Vieillard, Flocon and Krol, together with additional material I possess, as a homage to those engravers...

July 8 1993

Cher Pierre

... By coincidence (*'et comme c'est curieux'*) Giles Barber of the Taylor Institution was in Dijon on the opening day of the retrospective exhibition of engravings by Krol... So I received a postcard with a joint message from both of them...

A young woman, a research student at Wolfson College, Oxford, Deborah Fenn, inspired, it seems by the proof pages in the Walter Strachan Gift, is pursuing her studies in Paris on the subject of the making of a *livre d'artiste* and plans to create one after serving an apprenticeship at the *atelier* of an intaglio printer. Very intelligent. She *greatly* admired your Aix-en-Provence catalogue and other things of yours. She arrived at 3.30 and didn't leave until 10.30pm! I was exhausted — in a good cause, I hope...

My fond wishes,

Walter

P.S. Signovert died in 1982: a friend sent me the information.

To Wendy Taylor

August 24 1993

My dear Wendy

It must be my turn to write! Not that I have much news... My two great-grandsons, Thomas (5), Dexter (1), are tremendous — bright, active, loving Jacko... I miss trips but hope to attend unveiling at the College of a bronze by John Farnham... My collection at Oxford much visited. I've bequeathed my ... owls to a grateful V and A...

To Albert Flocon

September 17 1993

Bien Cher Ami

I have been rereading your letters from the beginning of 1993. I hope all goes well with regard to your exhibitions in Metz and Germany and that you are in good health...

I have proposed to the V and A Museum that they should exhibit in a series of display cases (separate ones for each artist) the books which their library possesses by yourself, Krol and Vieillard, 'Three Engravers'. I would add to these some artists' proofs which you have all kindly given me. The Director has happily agreed to this proposal... It was I who introduced these books to the librarian. It is not much but it is a gesture all the same. My very best wishes to you and Alice...

To Pierre Lecuire

October 13 1993

Cher Pierre

... They have proposed the title 'Walter Strachan and the Cult of the Livre d'Artiste', but I opposed this. I don't like the comme W.J. Strachan.. There's a shortage of papper in Paris. Amitiés. Abram

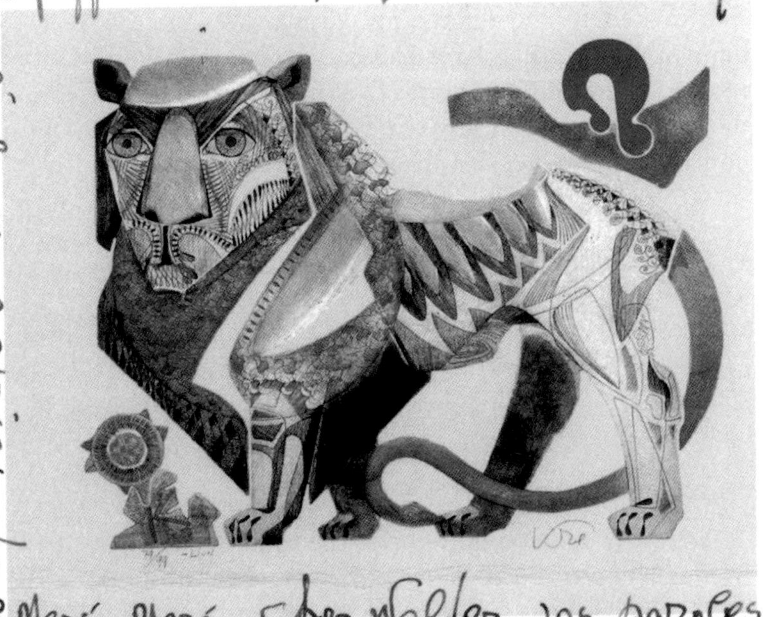

Merci, Merci cher Walter. Vos paroles d'encouragement me touchent beaucoup. Vous ne les faites pas depuis hier ainsi elles ont d'autant plus de prix pour moi. — D'après votre lettre je crois comprendre que votre idée de nous présenter au Musée, W + A est en bonne voie. J'ai demandé à Dijon de leurs envoyer le materiel de l'annonce de l'exposition. Ce que vous me dites de la galerie W.J.S. au College Bishop's Stortford, est a mon avis un témoignage de reconnaissance que toute une generation d'élèves vous doit, à qui vous avez dispensé ce supplément d'âme que l'on ne trouve dans aucun manuel scolaire

Imaginez ma surprise ; retrouver Gilles Barbier a mon vernissage à Dijon, nous pouvions évoquer ensemble notre cher ami word 'cult' in this context (it smacks too much of esoteric religions). I suggested *your* phrase: 'defender of the *livre d'artiste* in England'. True and less precious?...

Vieillard has already been honoured at the Ashmolean (I was invited to the dinner for his widow... in Oxford — impossible [to go]!). Krol has had a retrospective in Dijon; Flocon several in Germany. It's a good moment to celebrate them, however modestly, in London. I think it's partly a homage to myself...

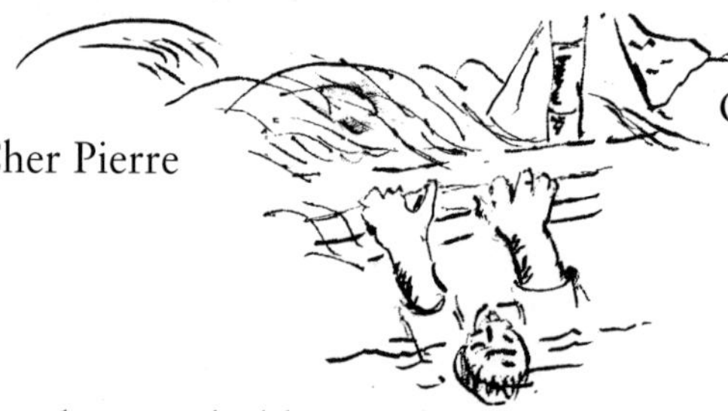

October 15 1993

Cher Pierre

You have to hold on tight to the rail, as one of my artist friends has written to me. Your own: 'Everything is in the head when the legs give way' reassures me...

This morning Madeleine Pont sent me a press cutting with her letter, a review of Philippe Soller's biography of Bossuet... I have so much enjoyed my third reading of *A la Recherche*... I've also been reading the Victorian novelist George Eliot's masterpiece *Middlemarch*, which has a Tolstoyan breadth. For me a revelation.

Bossuet. How grateful I am to my French master at school for introducing me to the classics of the seventeenth century — Pascal, Bossuet, La Bruyère, Sévigné... Passages from Pascal and Descartes are still in my memory...

November 18 1993

Cher Ami Flocon

I'm writing in haste. I cannot find the proof pages you kindly gave me long ago (for my book and articles) for *Châteaux en Espagne*... which I want to show in the cases at the V and A exhibition... It is possible that I have given them as additions to the Walter Strachan Gift at Oxford — but they are not in the original catalogue (and the Director of the Taylor Institution is away). The V and A representatives insist that they must have all my materials and my introduction before the end of December!

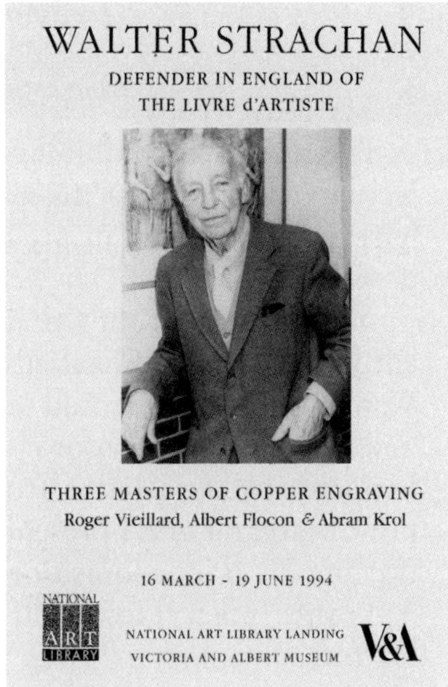

Could you possibly find several proof pages... especially for *Les Châteaux*, to add to what I have... The Museum are going to display their copies, with open pages, of *Traité du Burin*, *Perspectives*, *L'Univers des Livres*, *L'Alphabète de Victor Hugo*. So you see I need illustrations from true *livres d'artiste*, to balance what I have of Krol... and Vieillard... The display will be modest but well mounted. There will be a catalogue with my introduction... There it is. I hope I'm not pleading in vain for (ironically) Castles in Spain!

With my good wishes and apologies...

Alexandra Hospital, Harlow, Essex
December 7 1993

Joyeux Noël
à Albert Flocon (Mentzel)
de la part de W.J. Strachan

(All is well. I have retrieved two pages from *Châteaux en Espagne*, which I had presented to the Walter Strachan Gift at Oxford — for the duration [of the exhibition] at the Museum. Fortunately I had completed my introductory article before being incarcerated in a clinic for observation. How impressive *L'Oeil du Graveur* and *Une Poétique de la Vision* are!)

To Wendy Taylor

January 10 1994

My dear Wendy

I've just been combining cheering myself up… with collecting a little data from your wonderfully exuberant letters… I am back in my own home, guarded by a lying down rhino*…

You ask me about the display I've set in motion (with enthusiasm from Elizabeth Esteve-Coll and Jan van der Wateren)… I wish I could see it and Elizabeth offers me a V and A car but it's agony even in an ambulance… As it happens, today a letter from the Tate — the Alan Davie print Margaret and I presented is on show among an exhibition of new print acquisitions…

I recite [poetry] to myself in the long nights and am grateful for a memory… Your letters — disaster, triumph — always cheer…

Jan 28 1994

My dear Wendy

What a wonderful surprise! And the excitement here as I unrolled the sheet to disclose OWL and delight was succeeded by admiration. A lovely, subtle drawing… A cause for celebration in my sitting room (at present like a nursery with flowers, from carnations to daffodils). The V and A legacy has been ratified… it departs only with me. So yours, framed, will be among them here and I feel inclined to treat it as a family heirloom — one owl in memory of the Collection at the V and A of fifty-five!…

I have come to the conclusion that you are not just a great talent but a genius! Especially on the *sine qua non*: invention, originality…

The sundial theme which you rightly pursue (and I love the sea-urchin-like 'Globe Sundial')… It seems, the sundial theme, to be your 'Reclining Figure', 'Mont Saint Victoire'… Lovely… Tied up with history, like the wayside sculptures on the Dorset coast beyond Portland to Lulworth… Like ancient shrines — milestones… nautical…

* A print Taylor had given him, that hung in his bedroom.

IN CLEAR-CUT PLANES

In clear-cut planes the eye finds satisfaction,
The rock hardness of the edgy stones
That weight the shore, the contours of these bones
Scoured clean and whitened by the waves' action;

Comfort in the roundness of a pebble
Centuries have gone to form, this fossil shell
Ribbed and resistant to the constant swell,
So old that time is imperceptible;

Solace in the softness of the idle
Weed that lifts and sways to the tides' surges.
Renewing life in rock-pools it submerges
And in ourselves as we stand by the earth's cradle.

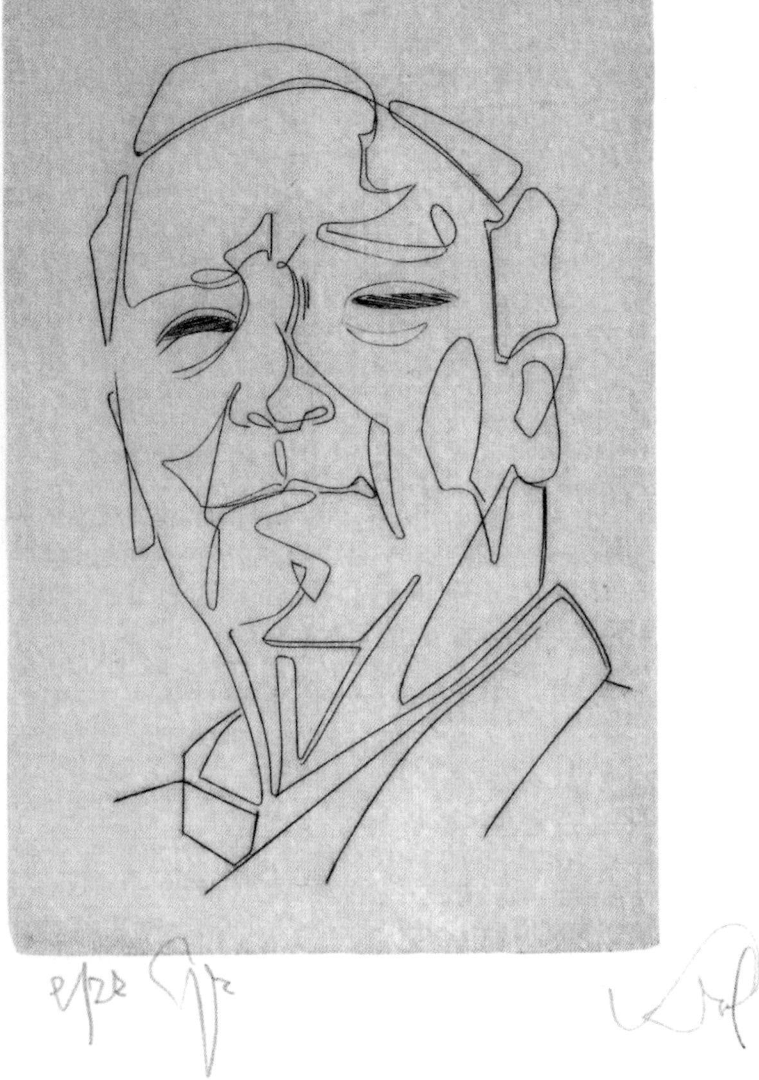

APPENDICES

Appendix A
Bibliography

Books written, translated and edited by Walter Strachan

POEMS

Strachan, W.J. (1947). *Moments of Time: Poems by W.J. Strachan.* London, Sylvan Press.

Strachan, W.J. (1948). *Apollinaire to Aragon: Thirty Modern French Poets; Translated with Introductory Essay*, London, Methuen & Co. Ltd

Strachan, W.J. (1950). *The Season's Pause: Poems by W.J. Strachan.* London, Secker & Warburg.

Strachan, W.J. (1976). *Poems by Walter Strachan.* London, Christopher Hewett.

THE LIVRE D'ARTISTE

Strachan, W.J. (1969). *The Artist and the Book in France: The 20th Century Livre d'artiste.* London, Peter Owen.

Strachan, W.J. (1987). *Le Livre d'Artiste: A Catalogue of the W.J.Strachan Gift to the Taylor Institution.* Oxford, Ashmolean Museum and the Taylor Institution.

SCULPTURE

Strachan, W.J. (1976). *Towards Sculpture: Maquettes and Sketches from Rodin to Oldenburg.* London, Thames and Hudson.

Strachan, W.J. (1983). *Henry Moore: Animals.* London, Aurum Press.

Strachan, W.J. (1984). *Open Air Sculpture in Britain: A comprehensive guide; with a foreword by Lady Gibberd.* London, A. Zwemmer Ltd in association with Tate Gallery Publications.

MEMOIRS

Strachan, W.J. (1988). *A Relationship with Henry Moore 1942-1986.* Bishop's Stortford, Elliott Group.

PUBLISHED POSTHUMOUSLY

Strachan, W.J. (2000). *Masks and other poems, Images by Abram Krol, Vincent Guiro, Peter Thursby, Peter Rhoades, Jacques Houplain, Ivor Livi, Louttre B., Jean Peschard, Robert Blanchet, Wendy Taylor, Mario Avati, Natalie d'Arbeloff, Geoffrey Clarke, with an afterword by Geoffrey Strachan.* Llandogo. The Old Stile Press in collaboration with the Walter Strachan Archive.

FRENCH FICTION IN TRANSLATION

Bazin, H. (1950). *Grasping the Viper.* London, Secker and Warburg.
Gracq, J. (1951). *A Dark Stranger.* London, Peter Owen Ltd.
Bazin, H. (1952). *Head against the Wall.* London, Secker and Warburg.
Bernanos, G. (1953). *Night is Darkest.* London, The Bodley Head.
Chardonne, J. (1955). *The Wife of Jean Barnery.* London, Peter Owen Ltd.
Chardonne, J. (1961). *Pauline.* London, Peter Owen Ltd.

ITALIAN FICTION IN TRANSLATION

Pavese, C. (1955). *The Political Prisoner.* London, Peter Owen Ltd.
Strachan, W.J., Ed. (1955). *Modern Italian Stories edited and translated by W.J. Strachan.* London, Eyre & Spottiswoode.
Pavese, C. (1956). *The House on the Hill.* London, Peter Owen Ltd.
Cacciatore, V. (1959). *The Swing and Two Other Stories.* London, Eyre & Spottiswoode.
Emanuelli, E. (1959). *The Man from New York.* London, Macdonald.
Pavese, C. (1959). *The Comrade.* London, Peter Owen Ltd.
Fogazzaro, A. (1962). *The Little World of the Past.* London, Oxford University Press.
Pavese, C. (1963). *The Beach and A Great Fire.* London, Peter Owen.

GERMAN FICTION IN TRANSLATION

Hesse, H. (1957). *The Prodigy.* London, Peter Owen & Vision Press.
Hesse, H. (1958). *Demian.* London, Peter Owen & Vision Press.
Hesse, H. (1961). *Peter Camenzind.* London. Peter Owen & Vision Press.

AUTOBIOGRAPHY AND LETTERS IN TRANSLATION

Crosland, M., Ed. (1965). *The Marquis de Sade: Selected Letters.* London, Peter Owen Ltd.
Strachan, W.J., Ed. (1986). *Henri Alain-Fournier: Towards the Lost Domain; Letters from London, 1905, translated by W.J. Strachan.* Manchester, Carcanet Press.

FRENCH ART BOOKS IN TRANSLATION

Lhote, A. (1950). *Treatise on Landscape Painting.* London, A.Zwemmer.
Lhote, A. (1953). *Figure Painting.* London, A.Zwemmer.
Francastel, G. (1956). *Italian Painting: Byzantine to Renaissance.* London, A.Zwemmer Ltd
Dorival, B. (1957?). *Twentieth Century Painters; Nabis — Fauves — Cubistes.* Paris, Editions. Pierre Tisné.
Brion, M. (1959). *German Painting.* Paris, Editions Pierre Tisné
de la Souchere, D. (1960). *Picasso in Antibes.* London, Lund Humphries.
Marx, C.R. (1960). *Rembrandt.* New York, Universe Books, Inc.
Serullaz, M. (1960). *French Painting: The Impressionist Painters.* Paris, Pierre Tisné Editeur.
Gindertael, R.-V. (1961). *Hans Hartung.* Paris and New York, Pierre Tisné Editeur. Universe Books, Inc.

Llobera, J. (1972). *Alive to Art: Introducing Subjects and Skills.* London, Frederick Warne & Co. Ltd.
Llobera, J. (1972). *Alive to Art: Portraying People and Places.* London, Frederick Warne & Co. Ltd.
Pierre, J. (1974). *A Dictionary of Surrealism.* London, Eyre Methuen.
Baltrusaitis, J. (1977). *Anamorphic Art.* Cambridge, Chadwyck-Healey Ltd.
Pierre, J. (1977). *Pop Art; An Illustrated Dictionary.* London, Methuen.

EDUCATIONAL EDITIONS OF FRENCH TEXTS

Strachan, W.J., Ed. (1952). *Ici Paris.* Oxford University Press.
Strachan, W.J., Ed. (1956). *Ici les provinces.* Oxford, Oxford University Press.
Camus, A. (1959). *La Peste; edited by W.J. Strachan.* London, Methuen Educational Ltd.
Duras, M. (1968). *Moderato Cantabile; edited by W.J. Strachan.* London, Methuen Education.

***

VOLUME CONTAINING LETTERS TO HIM TRANSLATED BY WALTER STRACHAN

Hewett, Christopher, Ed. (1984). *The Living Curve: Letters to W.J. Strachan 1929-1979; with a foreword by William Anderson.* London and Manchester, Taranman Ltd in association with Carcanet Press Ltd.

Appendix B

Poems by Walter Strachan referred to in the text.

Enclosed with the letter to Percy Horton dated February 4/5 1942

AUTUMN MOOD

Willow leaves droop,
accents of sadness,
after the Autumn frost;
elms and silver-birches
shed on the sodden earth
their golden coinage.

On rose-tinted wings the maple seeds
flutter hesitantly down;
and the last leaves of the poplar
signal farewell.

Foreigners and coldly aloof
in their perpetual and metallic green,
the pines look on, unmoved;
but the softer larch
sweeps graceful arms,
scornfully,
over the tawny carpet of her needles.

Only the new buds of the chestnut
glinting through the ever-diminishing foliage
proclaim their faith in the renewal.

TRIBUTE TO VIRGINIA WOOLF

Your silenced voice speaks in the written word
Each word weighed out and placed with craftsman's care
A swan's down pillow, uncompromising sword,
A misty horn, or flute-note ringing clear;
Bravely you voyaged on your unknown road
That none but errant soul like yours would dare;
While they at safer distance, wondering, trod,
You caught each spirit-whisper in the air
From past or present wherein you easily moved
And turned your searching wit on those you loved,
Lighting the elusive beauty of the spray
That topped the waves, to us so samely grey
In ebb and flow; for your experienced mind
Both knew and feared the sadness it must find.

TRIBUTE TO ST PAULS

Rising from the embers of the other fire,
The calculated beauty of your dome
Replaced the gothic aspirations of the spire,
Made London rival to Bramante's Rome.

War — and your beauty now a carapace;
Vulnerable what we would most protect;
Anxious, we turned our eyes upon this mass,
This monument to its own architect.

Still, we recall how on those fearful nights
Lit, as triumphant for a victory,
Among the gaunt and gutted satellites
Your radiant outline stood against the sky.

CHARTRES

On the anniversary of its liberation, August 1944

How peaceful life flowed there in other days
Between the Wars, half-hidden that malaise
Which stalked the land of France under the gaze

Of carrion-neighbours, hovering in wait,
Till those despaired who saw, alas, too late
Relentless claws descending at your gate.

Four dragging years when to the mind distraught
Your jewelled windows bled — an anguished thought —
Frowned your grave statues, exquisitely wrought,

And cloud-backed spires, beloved of Corot's brush
Gave hope to those below where waters splash
The ledges and the busy housewives wash…

Years while you kept alive the sacred flame
To leap when winds of Liberation came —
And men of Chartres died for your fair name.

KITE-BAN LIFTED 1945

Quivering kite
Caught in the train
Of turbulent wind
Before Summer rain

A coloured note
In a grey sky
Child's challenge to
Monotony.

Child's eye below
Watching it sail —
Crimson question-mark
The darting tail.

Mounting, mounting,
A link between
Torn clouds above
And solid green.

A new-found toy
In a tugging fist
Clinging to joy
It had all but missed.

NATIONAL GALLERY REVISITED

Patterned complexity again
Of the indigo umbrellas in the rain;
Renoir's demoiselles in waisted jackets
Smile to themselves their happy secrets.

Rubens arrests with renewed force;
The vast landscape, the taut, muscular horse,
The less obvious care lavished on
The distant magpie, the incidental swan.

El Greco's *Agony in the Garden*
To us who have learned how men's hearts harden
Has a new message and we marvel
At the strange, strident miracle.

PERFECTION'S IMAGE

Admire but envy not perfection's image,
the white swan,
swimming along our lives' perimeter,
on and on.

The dazzling arabesque,
the inscrutable mien,

the black mask
that bounds the narrow brain,
make us forget,
as she forgets
last season's cygnets —
lost as we are in wonder at this grace
that decorates the visible world —
the possessiveness
of a jealous race.

A strong wing unfurled
divides our ways...
Watch from the fringe
her strange
mysteries.

WINTER WALK

A prisoner of mood,
I walked down to a wood
Through a mist; so alone
In each frost-aching bone,
Till the first spectral tree
Came and beckoned to me;
And beyond the dim meadows
Overhung by faint shadows,
A strange, ghostly sun,
Like the disc of the moon,
With a sudden freakish beam
Set the tree-tops agleam;
An island of trees
Washed by lavender seas,
Remote in the grace
Of their white, crystal lace,
So dignified there
In the mist-laden air;
And the fetters were gone,
As I walked back alone.

Appendix C

Gifts and bequests by Walter Strachan to public institutions

1 The W.J. Strachan Gift to the Taylor Institution

This is Walter Strachan's collection of complete *livres d'artiste* and original proof pages from such books, gathered over some thirty-five years, as described in Chapter 8, and presented to the Taylor Institution Library in 1987, representing over 250 books, from the Bonnard/Verlaine *Parallèlement* of 1900 to the Tal Coat/Lecuire *Bestiaire* of 1985.

The Taylor Institution Library is open, free of charge, to all matriculated members of the University of Oxford, and to others engaged on the advanced study of European literature, on application.

Taylor Institution Library, University of Oxford, St Giles', Oxford OX1 3NA. Book enquiries: 01865 278 158 Fax: 01865 278 165 enquiries@taylib.ox.ac.uk

2 W.J. Strachan Bequest to the Scottish National Gallery of Modern Art.

The bequest consists of sculptors' drawings and graphics by F.E.McWilliam, Bernard Meadows, Oliffe Richmond, Ralph Brown, David Nash, Gio Pomodoro, Reg Butler and Lynn Chadwick, together with the photographs of over 550 public sculptures used to illustrate the first edition of *Open Air Sculpture in Britain* as well as a large number of further photographs of sculpture not included and the substantial collection of Walter Strachan's research materials for that book, referring to the work and careers of almost 200 sculptors, and for his other writings on post-war British and European sculpture. Also a wide range of catalogues for sculpture exhibitions in Britain and Europe from the 1950s to the 1980s. These are held in the Dean Gallery, Edinburgh.

Enquiries to: The Curator, Archive and Library, Scottish National Gallery of Modern Art, Belford Road, Edinburgh EH4 3DR. Telephone: 0131 624 6200: Fax: 0131 343 2802

3 Walter Strachan's Bequest of Owls to the Victoria and Albert Museum.

The bequest was agreed in the summer of 1993 and embraces 58 prints, drawings and paintings of owls, some fifty of them by artists of the twentieth-century *livre d'artiste*. These were the framed pictures that proliferated up the staircase, and eventually along the top landing as well, at 10 Pleasant Road, most of them given by the artists themselves or by French artist friends who knew of Walter Strachan's passion.

They include images by: Aïzpiri, Avati, Beaudin, Bertini, Buffet, Chastel, Ciry, Dali, Flocon, Gantner, Gischia, Goerg, Guiramand, Guiro, Haas, Krol, Le Corbusier, Lorjou, Lurçat, Minaux, Mumprecht, Oudry, Passavant,

Peschard, Picard-le-doux, Plisson, Prassinos, Ramondot, Riopelle, Spitzer, Ubac, Vieillard, as well as a *'Calligramme poétique'* by Pierre Lecuire and Patrick Cullen's original calligraphic owl.

The Walter Strachan Collection of Owls is held in the Department of Prints, Drawings and Paintings at the Victoria and Albert Museum. The following is a summary of the museum numbers of the prints and drawings which form the collection. Beside the numbers are appended the 'pressmarks', location references which will enable the works to be quickly accessed by anyone going to the Print Room to see them. (Most of them are housed in pressmarks WD226 (drawings and paintings) and MP55A (prints).)

Museum numbers and locations of prints and drawings (F.218-274-1994) in the Walter Strachan Collection at the Victoria and Albert Museum

Museum Numbers	*Pressmarks*
E.218, 219, 224-226, 231-236, 238, 250, 255, 261, 264, 265, 273, 1994	WD 226
E.220-223, 227, 228, 230, 237, 239-248, 251-254, 256-260, 262, 263, 267-270-1994	MP 55A
E.245-1994	1126B
E.249, 271, 272, 274-1994	CC 127/1 (Office 608)
E.266-1994	MA1 (Paintings Office)

Victoria and Albert Museum, South Kensington, London SW7 2RL
Telephone: 020 7942 2000: Fax: 020 7942 2266
www.vam.ac.uk

INDEX
of names and titles of works